THE EMPIRE

Constance

0  50  100  150  200
MILES

The
•Milan
VISCONTI

Cividale

Venice

Bologna

Savona
Finale
Genoa
Porto
Venere
Florence
Livorno
Pisa
Siena

Rimini

Adriatic Sea

PAPAL
STATES

e St
orat

Corsica

Montefiascone
Viterbo
Corneto
ROME
Anagni
Fondi

KINGDOM
OF NAPLES

NAPLES
Nocera

dinia

A N E A N   S E A

Sicily

# THE ANTIPOPE

PETER IN 1408
From a contemporary sketch in the Livre Vert Mineur de Perpignan
(*By courtesy of the Director, Archives des Pyrénées-Orientales*)

# ALEC GLASFURD

# The Antipope

(PETER DE LUNA, 1342-1423)

A study in obstinacy

ROY PUBLISHERS, INC.
NEW YORK

*Library of Congress Cat. No.: 66-21800*

*Printed in Great Britain*

CETERIS ANTICARDINALIBUS

# Contents

|  | Encounter in Peñíscola | 9 |
| 1. | Avignon | 15 |
| 2. | Rome | 39 |
| 3. | The Schism | 65 |
| 4. | Spain | 86 |
| 5. | France | 111 |
| 6. | The Way of Cession | 127 |
| 7. | The Siege | 158 |
| 8. | The Way of a Conference | 188 |
| 9. | The Way of a Council | 228 |
| 10. | Peñíscola | 256 |
|  | Notes | 269 |
|  | Bibliography | 273 |
|  | Chronological Table | 276 |
|  | Index | 279 |

# Illustrations

| *Peter in 1408* | *frontispiece* |
| *Avigon today* | *96* |
| *St. Catherine of Siena* | *97* |
| *St. Peter's and the Vatican* | *112* |
| *A Pope by the Castel Sant'Angelo* | *113* |
| *Aragon* | *192* |
| *The Duke of Berry* | *193* |
| *Louis of Orleans* | *208* |
| *Peñíscola today* | *209* |

'Or siatemi virile, e colonna che mai non manchiate!'

ST. CATHERINE OF SIENA (1378)

'Voluit alios piscare, sed ipse, proh dolor, piscatus est.'

ALFONSO OF JAËN (1378)

'Il est du pays dez bonnes mulles. Quant elles ont prins un chemin, l'en lez escorcheroit plus tost que l'en lez feroit retourner.'

AMEILH DU BREUIL, Archbishop of Tours (1406)

'Mais Dieu mercy, je croy que Benedic a bien extirpé a court de Romme ceste symonie.'

GUILLAUME FILLASTRE, Dean of Reims (1406)

'Son exits ab gran dolor e molts plants e plors, vehent a tal persona fer tan gran errada.'

PEDRO DE ÇAGARRIGA, Archbishop of Tarragona (1418)

# Encounter in Peñíscola

PEÑÍSCOLA, on the luminous Spanish coast, eighty miles north of Valencia, is everything that a Mediterranean fishing village should be. The houses, some of them white and others colour-washed a pale, faded blue, climb up in tiers above the harbour, clinging like barnacles to the sunny side of a great rock that was once an island but is now hooked on to the mainland by a sandspit. Down on the quay the fishermen mend nets stretched between their big toes or tinker resignedly with ancient Spanish diesel engines. At the back of the quay is a line of brown ramparts; you pass through a wide archway, noticing, if you are heraldically minded, an unusual coat of arms (a crescent moon, points downwards) and walk slowly up in the morning heat through successive levels of cobbled, blue-shadowed alleys, alive with donkeys, barefoot children and strings of threadbare, stone-bashed washing.

Right at the top you reach the entrance to the medieval castle, a huge polygonal bulk of masonry, featureless and formidable. Once inside these second gates, the cheerful confusion below gives place to cavernous vaults, a wide deserted courtyard and terrace, austere ruined halls with high windows and vast empty fireplaces. Every-thing has been swept bare by the sun and the wind. These ruins are not mellow like northern ruins; there is something odd about them; for a fleeting moment, as the sun beats down relentlessly on the terrace, they seem to jump and flicker as if they, or you, had been displaced in time like the Ghosts of Versailles. The impression passes, these walls are solid enough. Yet they are singularly unphotogenic. You turn for consolation to the view, which stretches far along the coast and out to sea.

Here among this gaunt, bleached masonry you meet Papa Luna.

This was his castle, the gate-keeper tells you, where as pope (or some say as antipope, anyway as Benedict XIII) he held out for the last eight years of his life, a very old man who would not yield to his enemies, no longer recognised as pope by half the countries of Europe, from Scotland to Sicily, but only by the Count of Armagnac, and evasively even by him. That is about as far as you can get, what with the gate-keeper's history and your own Spanish, of rather Valencian; in fact the last bit is not clear to either of you. Perhaps, you reflect, it was not all that clear to the Count or Armagnac himself.

You take leave of the gate-keeper ceremoniously, and he points to the turret at the seaward corner, a small cube of windswept stone in which the old pope lived and died, and you go up the little flight of steps and through the narrow door with a half-defaced papal escutcheon above it (that crescent moon reversed, again) and stand in the small bare room. And there you stare through the window-slit at the hard blue sea, and think of the old man doing the same 500 years ago, and over that horizon lie the countries which rejected him and all the spider-webs of power. Spider-webs making dusty planes in the shaft of sunlight that comes through the window, personal webs and political webs and ecclesiastical webs, these last the densest and most dust-laden of all, and at their centre lies Rome where, if Benedict XIII had his rights, his legitimate rights, he ought to be now. Only he is not recognised. . . .

Now who was this Papa Luna you ask yourself, this Benedict XIII? What was a pope doing here on this rock on the lonely Spanish coast? Medieval popes spent a lot of their time out of Rome, of course, in places like Anagni and Viterbo and Orvieto, driven out by the climate or German emperors or the volatile population of the Trastevere. But surely Peniscola was rather far to go to? Well, the gate-keeper mentioned a date about 1400, and that was the time of the Great Schism, with popes at Avignon as well as in Rome. In that case, why was not Papa Luna at Avignon if he could not be in Rome? Would they not recognise him even there? With a great effort you recall that there was another Benedict XIII who lived much later, in the eighteenth century; the Old Pretender had dealings with him. He was an Italian as they all were by then; you cannot remember anything else about him, but he was Number

XIII. Presumably that must mean that the Roman Church of today does not recognise the earlier Benedict XIII either. So he, this Papa Luna of Peniscola, was an antipope. The Middle Ages were full of antipopes, they continued off and on up to the Renaissance. After that no one thought it worth while to be one. You look at the spider-webs again, and through the narrow window-slit at the sea and the sharp horizon, and you feel you know a little of what it felt like to be a medieval antipope.

Across the courtyard again, through the empty cleansing sun-light, and into a ruined hall on the other side which has an apse and must have been the chapel. And there you find something to surprise you: a large modern commemorative tablet to Papa Luna, erected and inscribed by some official body in this painfully orthodox country. The text is sympathetic; in lapidary Castilian it speaks of his virtues and declares that he held out here from a conviction of right and duty. Not till the Day of Judgment shall we know the whole truth. So this man can have been no ordinary medieval anti-pope, no accommodating puppet of some clerical faction or anti-clerical emperor, to be set up and deposed again at need. Evidently, as something has already told one, he had a stronger personality and there were larger issues at stake. Who was he, and how did he come to end his days on this rock, still defiantly asserting his tremendous claim to be the head of Christendom and St. Peter's lawful successor?

To stand on his rights as he saw them, when all the rest of the world (except, doubtfully, the Count of Armagnac) no longer saw things that way—how very Spanish! Does that, perhaps, explain the marble tablet? Did the people who put it up, in spite of their conventional disapproval of antipopes, recognise in him something almost as symbolic of their national character as Don Quixote, something so tremendously Spanish that they had to commemorate it, however much their good bishop might shake his head?

And if the official view rejects his claim and reckons him an antipope, is that necessarily the last word? Law is not the same as history. No institution can be a completely reliable guide to its own past. It may declare authoritatively its beliefs and purposes at any given moment, but it is too much to ask it to do so with a time-factor thrown in. The *Official History of the Russian Communist*

*Party*, running into so many mutually contradictory editions that only a specialist (or an ambitious Soviet citizen!) can be expected to keep up with them, is an extreme case in point. But perhaps a revealing one. Was this Antipope Luna the Trotsky or the Bukharin of his day?

Spanish obstinacy or dialectical subtlety? Or both, and more? What were the schemes and memories that streamed through that brain in that stone cell? If only one could recapture those pounding thoughts that have ebbed away into the stillness of great libraries. One would walk into a queer corner of European history, follow fascinating debates within a logic far removed from one's own, and meet a most remarkable character.

*

The facts about the life and times of Peter de Luna can be disentangled from the books listed in the Bibliography, among many others. To interpret his character, on the other hand, calls for a fresh approach. On this a word of explanation is due.

By well before the end of his career, Peter de Luna's opinions and existence had become equally inconvenient to all the main parties in Church and State throughout Europe. As historians have usually sympathised with one or other of these currents, it is hard to find a general history of the period which treats him either convincingly or fairly.

So we must start with the opinions of those who know him best. And on one basic point at least they are virtually unanimous. His contemporaries Clemanges and Alpartil, St. Catherine of Siena and St. Vincent Ferrer, and now modern specialists such as Cardinal Ehrle, Fr. Doizé and M. Noël Valois—these and many others, all with their various axes to grind, unite in respecting his personal integrity. He may have been wrong from the start, they say, or he may have taken this or that wrong turning, but his motives were always sincere. If he stone-walled, prevaricated or even cheated, it was to serve something larger than himself. He was not, as superficial reading might suggest, a careerist or a crook.

For the rest, his learning, charm and force of character were clearly outstanding. For two decades he played all his competitors off the stage. Naturally the achievement did him no good. Yet he could rise above mere vanity. His real trouble was intellectual. Obstinacy on his heroic scale is rooted in reason. We see him the prisoner of his own strict canonist logic, struggling in good faith with his chain of difficult decisions, each heavy link leaving a weal on his hands.

So colourful a life calls for something less austere than a treatise. He was a man, not a mere factor in an historical process, and no account of him can begin to be adequate unless it tries to look into his mind and heart and even to give some glimpses of the world as he saw it through his own eyes. This is not always easy; the material is unexpectedly full at one moment and scanty at the next, and to interpret even the best of sources calls for some guess-work. The writer can only claim that his reconstruction of Peter's life is less imaginative than it might seem at first sight, that the dialogue is taken from written records, and that even the smallest detail is derived from some piece of evidence, probability or hint.

What a garrulous age he lived in! Its memoirs, legal depositions and diplomatic reports contain innumerable fragments of direct speech and sometimes whole conversations, so that Glandève's preciousness, for example, minces even through the dusty barrier of medieval Latin. The men of the time wore their hearts on their sleeves and observed each other closely, maliciously, recording such small things as Alys de Turenne's needle and John XXIII's owl. If their vision lacks charity and breadth, that is because they saw the Middle Ages falling to bits all around them. Self-protection made rebels or cynics of them, for the most part; but what is the true conservative, one by nature and education and position, to do at such a time? The unexpected, the fascinating thing about Peter's problems is how modern they seem.

As regards the Schism, no one was better placed or better qualified to discover the truth. His reaction suggests that the Urbanist case is a good deal less watertight than the more committed Church historians seem to assume. As a matter of fact, the Roman Church, wiser than some of her followers, has never made a dogmatic pronouncement. We are left, then, with a free choice. To the writer Peter appears as a conservative, as the last of the great autocratic popes of the medieval tradition, while those who find his story too disquieting may take refuge in the belief, supported by many prim authorities, that he was only an antipope.

In any case his story is a warning. We are still searching for Unity of various kinds, and none of them will come easily. Peter's search led him into a cul-de-sac. It was a tragedy, for he had greatness in him. But the lives of his lesser contemporaries often cross the border into comedy or even farce. The Great Schism was an utterly fantastic episode, a *reductio ad absurdum* as complete as any in history. The absurdity is an essential element. The story would be incomplete without it. And to smile at the politics of religion need not always be a sign of impiety.

# CHAPTER 1

# *Avignon*

O N a blustery January morning in the year 1376, while flurries of almost horizontal rain slashed down from Mont Ventoux and scoured soot and old bird's-nests from the haphazard roofs and chimneys across the street, the Cardinal Deacon of Santa Maria in Cosmedin stared through one of his unfashionable round-headed windows and thought hard about what he was supposed to be doing in Avignon.

Peter de Luna had only just moved in. His *livrée*—the local name for a cardinal's residence—was one of the least distinguished in the town, an old roughstone building in a side-street nowadays called the Rue Grivolas, situated in an unambitious quarter and rather far from the Palace. These circumstances, however, did not worry him unduly. It was all he could afford at present, and his previous dwelling at Montpellier had been still simpler. The room, a large one, was furnished starkly but with dignity. One good tapestry on the walls, also a sober wooden crucifix and, hanging from a peg, the red hat in all its splendour, new last month. The furniture, solid and sparse, revealed a disregard for comfort that was most uncommon in Avignon *livrées*, whose occupants were wont to look after themselves extremely well. But Peter de Luna was a Spaniard, the only one in the Sacred College at that moment. His ideas of how a great gentleman should live were more austere. Not fanatically so; perhaps the discomfort, whose existence he registered at the back of his mind, would be mitigated in time. Meanwhile, it did not matter, it was nothing.

The least uncomfortable chair in the room was occupied by the Cardinal's cat, an inseparable companion for whom we have documentary evidence, and one who, in the opinion of both cat and Cardinal, fully earned his status in the partnership by eliminating mice from such ancient buildings as Their Eminences were called on to inhabit.

In one respect the room was generously furnished; there were a great many books. They lay on their shelves in apparent disorder, their bindings simple for the most part, sometimes worn. Clearly they too were not for ornament but for use. Books of any sort were disproportionately expensive; this, it seemed, was how the Cardinal spent some of his money. Only a few were devotional. The core of his library consisted of works on jurisprudence, but there were also classical authors, several versions of Seneca in particular, and an assortment of curious and interesting subjects. For Peter de Luna was one of a select species that has flourished in every civilised age, the university don who has turned from teaching and research to politics.

Until now he had been a professor of both laws—canon and civil —at Montpellier, a small but forward-looking university in the Midi much frequented by Spaniards. As such he was in minor orders and the holder of one or two benefices, deriving from them a very modest addition to his income, for a certain degree of clerisy was inseparable from academic life. But he was not a priest, not even now as a cardinal. Indeed one brief episode, nine years back, had been most unclerical. His family connections had involved him with the fortunes of Henry of Trastámara, who claimed the throne of Castile from Pedro the Cruel. He took part in the battle of Nájera or Navarete, when Henry and his French allies were worsted by an equally cosmopolitan army under the English Black Prince. After the defeat, young Peter de Luna guided his Pretender across a wide stretch of doubtfully friendly country and over the French frontier. Then he went back to his books at Montpellier. For whatever reason, he did not leave them again to join in the next round, by which Henry finally won his throne.

Peter was a younger son. His family, the Counts of Luna, had their seat in the farthermost up-country corner of the Kingdom of Aragon. He was born in 1342 in the castle of Illueca, whose long narrow ruin still strews its broken tiles down a plunging hillside into the olive-groves and the dark red furrows below. His boyhood can only be imagined, though we can be sure that horses, falcons, books and strong family loyalties filled much of it. But the details are unknown. There is even a common mistake, which has got into the history-books, concerning the date of his birth.[1]* The Lunas were a powerful clan, distantly connected with the royal house of Aragon, and more exotically with the last Muslim king of Majorca. In so class-conscious a society as the Sacred College of Avignon, blue blood was one of the things that mattered. Combined with his high reputation as a jurist, it had done much to secure him his present appointment.

For his own part it had not been conventional ambition that had brought Peter to Avignon, nor even, though he was a religious man, an overwhelming desire to serve the Church. The impulse came from his own subject, law and government. From his professorial chair at Montpellier he had watched and applauded the growth of centralised administration. It was in the air; all the more advanced kingdoms were attempting something of the sort; and the Church, as was fitting in so intellectual an organisation, was well ahead of the secular powers in developing the new techniques. The Curia, then, was where he belonged, the place where his abilities could unfold to their fullest extent. Part of him, too, was a man of action. He could not stay in the study and the lecture-room for ever.

The great organism he had joined had its nerve-centre in the Palace. Day after day Peter had mounted his well-groomed mule, turned to the right outside his simple round-arched gate, and made his way thither through the maze of crowded streets, escorted by one or two familiars and preceded, as was only proper, by a servant with a bell. At its stroke the crowds would part quickly and do him reverence, the halberdiers would turn out smartly at the Palace gate and the officials would bustle up to receive him in the great court-yard. All this deference he found deeply gratifying, for he was not yet thirty-four, a Spaniard, and only human. And each morning, in spite of so auspicious a beginning, the questions and doubts would cast their shadow as he spent the hours being conducted from room to room in this great ant-hill of pale ochre stone and debatable activity which successive popes had raised and added to. For the Palace, for all its apparent solidity, was a make-shift.

It was a confused building, complicated and vast, towering symbolically above the glum little cathedral, several centuries older,

* See Notes on page 269.

B

which stood between it and the river. From the outside the seven huge towers and the tall crenellated walls, though pierced by graceful windows, were those of a fortress. That was a necessity in this unsettled age. Inside, much of the space was taken up with housing the administrative offices and legal tribunals of the Curia. Here was a sober world of its own, stone passages and solid square chambers, well built but curiously cheerless. Cardinal de Luna had already visited the Treasury or *Camera Apostolica*, an ambitious department which tried to control all the others, and there they had impressed on the newcomer how important it was for him to go at once to the *Camera of the Sacred College*, which administered the cardinals' collective finances and their cut of certain lucrative taxes in particular. After that he had spent some days being introduced to the Apostolic Penitentiary and the judicial departments spreading downwards from the Rota. Tomorrow he was due to visit the Chancery which, with its seven sub-divisions, coped with papal correspondence in all its protean forms.

The south-eastern and more recent part of these buildings was a palace in the strict sense, reputed the most magnificent in Christendom, with fine lofty halls and luxuriously furnished apartments, their walls hung with splendid Flemish tapestries or aglow with frescoes by the best artists from Italy. Simone Martini's work in particular was a joy, just the right blend of the spiritual with the elegant. But Simone Martini had died here thirty years ago, leaving his paintings unfinished. How was it, Cardinal de Luna wondered, that no other artist who had worked here since then had achieved that line like a fisherman's cast or caught that clear, singing harmony of forms and colours? Perhaps it linked up somehow with what they were all doing in this building. For he found their activities unexpectedly disquieting.

The Curia's achievements and problems were part of the logic of its recent history. It had all started some eighty years ago, when the energetic and high-handed Pope Boniface VIII had quarrelled with everybody in sight, and with the Colonna family and the King of France in particular. His enemies, French and Italian, joined forces and kidnapped him; and though he was rescued next day, the famous outrage at Angani broke the fiery old man's spirit and he died. This defeat proved that the papacy could not stand alone, and a few years later the Holy See was transferred from Rome to Avignon, where there was an enclave of papal territory on the French border. And there the popes had since remained, better protected from violence but more responsive to political pressure from Paris.

To compensate for their failure to veto the policies of kings, the popes had set methodically to work to control the clergy. In the course of nearly seventy years' residence at Avignon these seven French popes had enlarged the central organs of Church government almost out of recognition. A thousand little matters that had once been dealt with locally, by bishops and abbots and chapters and the like, now came to Avignon for settlement or approval, where a small army of sharp-faced canon lawyers sat ready to consider them. The Church gained in uniformity, if that is a gain, but these services were not to be had for nothing. Avignon demanded legal fees, taxes and *ex-gratia* contributions, *servitia*, tithes and annates, all on a greatly increased scale and supplemented by still more dubious exactions.

In theory there was something to be said for all this. Hitherto Peter de Luna had remained unimpressed by those who denounced Avignon; they were most of them disappointed Italians, he thought, who wanted the pickings for themselves. He had lectured brilliantly and approvingly on the growth of centralised papal government. But now, for the first time, he was seeing the centralised governors at really close quarters, seeing them not as an abstract process but as men, and he found the sight rather different from what it had looked in the lecture-room.

His disillusionment started with the Sacred College. Their personal animosities went deeper than he had realised, and he had never seen wealth on such a scale. Princes of the Church should live in some style, but not in all this luxury. They were too comfortable. Peter had a Spanish contempt for mere comfort, and their soft way of life offended his sense of decency. A whole town had grown up across the river, on French soil, to provide space for their villas and palaces, their stables and retinues and establishments. Villeneuve-lès-Avignon, they called it. The Church's money could be put to better use.

How had they all got here? Not as theologians or as shepherds of souls, but as younger sons of the nobility and as canon lawyers. These were the people who got to the top at Avignon. Peter could not quarrel with the qualifications, which were precisely his own. Yet he felt they should not be the only ones. He would have liked selection to be wider.

And now, below the cardinals, there was emerging a new profession unlike any other, clerics and jurists but with a difference, a new type of man, it almost seemed to him, intelligent but curiously unenterprising, competent but uninspired. The type, he reflected, was sure to spread, albeit slowly. It was not confined to the Curia alone; secular rulers were using these people too; and as power grew ever more centralised and complicated, the more of them there would be and the more mechanically they would do their indispensable work. Would they even, in time, take over every decisive function and mould society in their own likeness? The prospect was a very distant one, but meanwhile they were people to have on one's own side. Already they were beginning to make the cardinals look like an expensive anachronism.

Meanwhile every conversation turned sooner or later to the one immediate problem: should not the Pope and his court return to Rome? The Pope himself was known to be contemplating the move. It was inevitable, it seemed, and yet almost universally unpopular, save among Italians and the very devout. Opposition took the form of unhappy reminiscences of how the last attempt had fared. Peter, as a newcomer, was an obvious target for these stories.

About nine years before the late Pope Urban V, whose piety was deeper than his roots in Avignon, had insisted on taking himself and the Curia to Rome, defying the horrified objections of his French cardinals and considerable diplomatic pressure from the royal government. His way back was smoothed by the military genius of Cardinal Albornoz, who, after fourteen years of warfare, had restored some semblance of order in the Papal States, and who was able to greet Urban on his arrival with a truckload of town and castle keys. (Peter was related to Albornoz, perhaps a point of some significance.) But as ill luck would have it, this martial prelate died just after Urban re-entered his Italian dominions. The pious experiment had accordingly failed. An overwhelmingly French Curia found Rome an impossible place. The demagogue Rienzi and his insolent republic were a recent memory. Local factions, as in other Italian towns, defied each other from their innumerable peel-towers and private fortresses. Churches and papal buildings were in a ruinous state, food was scarce, the local wine deplorable. The Lateran had been burnt down twice that century. There were bread-riots in the Campo de' Fiori and hired cut-throats down every side-street. Very soon the Romans, who had welcomed the Holy Father with tears of joy, drove him out to take refuge in Viterbo, where the English soldier of fortune Sir John Hawkwood besieged him, while the rest of the Papal States relapsed into their habitual anarchy, and the venerable governor of Perugia had to let himself down from his walls by a rope in the dark.

After three years of this not even the diatribes and fell warnings of the Swedish prophetess, Bridget, could avail to keep Pope Urban V in Italy. He returned to Avignon and died there almost at once, which was exactly what Bridget had prophesied would happen if he dared to abandon his rightful place. She was undoubtedly inspired; the only question, and one long debated in clerical circles, was, inspired by Whom?

On this subject the Vice-Chancellor had no doubts whatever. Pierre de Montirac, Cardinal of Pamplona, had resolutely refused to accompany Urban V to Rome, and events had proved him right. How, he asked, could the Church be governed efficiently and decently from a nest of bandits like that? He was a large, elderly, able man who did not suffer fools gladly, hot-tempered and rather high-handed, a French aristocrat from the south-west. Most of the cardinals came from that part of the country; they were the 'Limousins' and he was their senior. His views on Bridget were clear-cut and uncharitable. The Devil had sent her. In opposing what she stood for, his notions of public and private interest coincided perfectly, as they so often do in ultra-conservative minds like his.

Bridget soon followed Urban, no doubt intending to see to it that his prosecution was properly conducted. She left an extraordinary volume of her *Revelations* behind her. From Rome her daughter Karin was moving heaven and earth to have her canonised. One of the first commissions to which Peter found himself appointed was the one charged with examining Bridget's works with this cause in mind. It was a difficult cause, heavy with implications. But in the meantime, to the old Vice-Chancellor's disgust, his department was being required to file a fresh series of letters from yet another holy woman in Italy, one who had, so it seemed, stepped straight into Bridget's shoes.

And so, when Peter called on the Vice-Chancellor, it is not unreasonable to suppose that he was shown a copy of the latest letter from Catherine of Siena. If so, he may have skipped the first part, containing firm advice to the Pope on how to conduct his diplomacy with Pisa, but his eye must surely have rested on the following passage:

> I have heard that you have created some more cardinals. I believe that it would be more to the glory of God and would serve you better if you took care to choose virtuous men. When the contrary is done it is a great disgrace before God and does much harm to Holy Church. And after that we need not wonder if He sends His judgments upon us, for it is but just. I implore you to be more manly and God-fearing in doing your duty.

It was a disquieting thought that if Pope Gregory XI had been more manly and had done his duty, Peter would still have been lecturing at Montpellier.

The Dominican tertiary, for such was Catherine's formal station in the Church, went on to demand a better General for her Order. She gave His Holiness the names of two people he could consult about the appointment. She would write to them too. Presently came some personal guidance for His Holiness himself.

> This is what I would see you do. If, hitherto, you have not been very firm, I beseech you now to use what time is left to you like a brave man. . . . And fear not, Father, all the storms that will gather overhead. . . . Take more care to appoint good shepherds and good governors in your cities, for the rebellion has come about because of the bad shepherds and the bad governors. Go forward and perform the two things that you have begun in holy intention, which are your coming to Rome and the holy, sweet crusade. Arise, Holy Father, no more slackness! Courage, courage! And come, come and comfort your children the servants of God. We await you with love and longing.

The letter was typical of her approach. It was a portent, as Peter may have recognised. But there was much else in the Chancery to claim his attention that morning—most of all the formidable Vice-Chancellor himself and his right-hand man Prignano, and the curious contrast between them. It is hard to imagine two more dissimilar beings.

Bartolommeo Prignano, who plays no small part in Peter's story, was a short, stout man in his late fifties, with a heavy face full of knobs and folds and yellowish in complexion, out of which a pair of large, dark eyes protruded sadly. His manner was self-effacing and his voice, a thick one, was slightly coloured with the odd, nasal accent of his native Naples. Born of humble parents, and brought up in the most densely populated and underprivileged quarter of that teeming slum, he had risen by sheer hard work to his present position. He was the model civil servant, diligent, quiet, methodical, unimaginative and long-suffering. His only foible lay in a rather dismal sort of honesty, which made him reluctant to accept the smallest favour or even the customary perquisites of his office, such as his share of the *servitia minuta*, a gratuity which every newly appointed prelate expected to pay. In return for his long service in the Curia they had made him a bishop—not, of course, that he was given a real, solid bishopric, worth anything much in terms of prestige or cash; it was only one of those countless little cathedrals down in the foot of Italy with a resounding name and, as likely as not, the west door off its hinges. Acerenza. No one has ever heard of it. Not even Bishop Prignano himself was expected to go there, so long as he remained a permanent official of the Curia.

In fact the appointment made little difference. He went on living like a mere canon, had no house of his own, and possessed no more than one mule and a nag for his attendant on the rare occasions when he went out.

In the Vice-Chancellor's eyes Prignano was a dim little man but a useful one. He treated him with scant ceremony and piled work upon his shoulders. What else was he there for? Behind his back they all called him the *episcopellus*, using the diminutive.

Peter was less inclined to make the mistake of despising Prignano. Unlike these lordly Frenchmen, he respected hard work. And he was a Southerner too himself, though of a very different sort; on the short side, it is true, but neat and distinguished-looking where the other was plebeian. Peter was rather proud of his well-knit, wiry physique and dressed a shade too carefully, as short men and Southerners often do. Perhaps his long oval face, aquiline nose and strongly arched eyebrows were a throw-back to the Arab side of his ancestry. His somewhat oriental features made him look older than he was.

There was another bond between Peter and Prignano. For different reasons they both held a rather exaggerated idea of the institution they served.

In all ages it has been possible for an intelligent man to be a devout Catholic and yet highly critical of the Curia's role in politics, and by the end of the Avignon period it was hard to find anyone who thought otherwise. If the Avignon Curia was no worse than the age in general, it was not noticeably better, and a year or two of work there tended to breed a certain cynicism. But Peter, a new arrival, was intellectually starry-eyed about centralised rule and canon law, of which the papacy was the exponent and the fount, while in Prignano's case the papacy filled a wide emotional gap. This colourless, over-conscientious official, who knew little of the pleasures and rewards of life and was exploited and bullied by everyone, must needs be a romantic at heart with an unduly glamorised concept of the power he served. That was what gave him the will to pace steadily down these long grey corridors lined with pigeon-holes and precedents.

Prignano, therefore, was one of the very few senior members of the Curia who had swallowed the most extreme papalist propaganda without reservation. The over-zealous outpourings of the monk Augustinus Triumphus, holding up the pope as an unlimited monarch, sovereign in every field and sharing power with no one, ran contrary to the facts of life and the spirit of the age, but the book was at the little bishop's bedside.

He too, in turn, had his faithful subordinate, an owlish, anxious young German named Dietrich von Nieheim (or Niem). No doubt Peter met him also, and recalled that Dietrich had attended some lectures of his at Montpellier a few years back. It is to be feared that young Dietrich was what his modern fellow-countrymen call a 'cyclist', one who bows his head low and at the same time treads down hard with his feet, and that this was what drew him and Prignano together.

And the Pope, His Holiness Gregory XI? There is no indication of Peter's relations with him. We have nothing to go on save the admonition, a half-jesting, half-serious pun on Peter's surname, which Gregory added when he gave him the red hat.

'Beware lest your moon should suffer an eclipse!'

Peter may well have thought that the advice was not in the best of taste. However, the sequel shows that he took it to heart.

★

While Peter was finding his way through the corridors of the Curia, Gregory's crisis was coming to a head. Should he make a fresh attempt to return to Rome? We have seen the long-term difficulties, as provided by the Romans themselves. There were also two immediate obstacles, the violent opposition of the Avignon establishment and the state of war with Florence.

No great ideological issue stood behind this war; it was merely that the Pope, as a temporal ruler, was territorially involved in the crude power-politics of central Italy. His legates there behaved like Gauleiters. Florence complained of 'encirclement'. The war, once thunderously declared, proceeded on Italian lines without decisive engagements. Gregory was preparing to send a fresh army of Breton mercenaries to the Romagna, and it was hoped that the energetic Cardinal of Geneva would prove himself a second Albornoz. Still more was hoped from the effect of the ban of the Church on Florentine trade. For their part the Florentines were conducting a vigorous and not unsuccessful propaganda among the many small townships in the Papal States, urging them to declare themselves independent republics.

At this point Catherine of Siena stepped in. Somehow she managed to persuade the government of Florence, the splendidly named Eight of War, to appoint her as their ambassadress to Avignon. She was coming to make peace. Meanwhile her latest letter to Gregory pleaded for some understanding of the Florentine case.

. . . for it seemed to them that they had suffered so many
wrongs at the hands of the bad shepherds and governors that
they could do nothing else. For when they smelled the stench
of the way of life of many of your governors—and you know
they are incarnate demons—then that and their fear drove them
to attack you. . . . Father, I beg mercy for them. Forget their
presumption and pride. . . . I tell you, sweet Christ on earth,
from Christ in heaven, that when you act thus, without anger,
they will all come and bow down their heads before you in
repentance. Then you will rejoice and we too. . . .

Oh, sweet Daddy, make haste to raise up the banner of the
most holy cross, and you shall see the wolves become lambs.
Peace, peace, peace, so that the war may not delay the coming
of this sweet time! And if you still wish for vengeance, then
revenge yourself upon me, miserable creature that I am, and
punish me with torments and even with death. For I truly
believe that my sins are the cause of much evil, and of much
disorder and strife. . . .

Woe, Father, I die and yet I cannot die. Come, come, and
resist no longer . . .!

To the Vice-Chancellor and other pessimists Catherine's words
had an ominous ring. One could foresee that she was likely to have
her way. She would put the whole business on a highly emotional
level, and that was something almost invariably fatal to any successful diplomacy by the Holy See. It was its weak spot. Once the
turtle-doves started cooing about love and forgiveness and peace
and goodwill, Gregory would be morally bound to lose his head,
while the Florentine bankers would not. A few more such letters,
or worse still a visit, and she would persuade him to start off for
Rome without any proper political guarantees. And history would
repeat itself, only this time it was sure to be worse.

Peter, like everyone else, spent much time pondering the problem.
He was always slow at making up his mind. He disapproved already
of many things at Avignon, of the arrogance, luxury and display,
the benefice-mongering, the obsession with money and social
rank—things, he considered, all of them directly traceable to the
French influence which dominated the papal court. On the other
hand, the Avignon machine was technically a most efficient one,
and was still doing a great deal of extremely useful work—universities and learning promoted, canon law strengthened, some of the

Orders reformed, uniformity of practice encouraged throughout Christendom. A move to Italy might undo the good and the bad alike. Was it worth while?

He postponed his decision. He had not enough facts to go on.

Meanwhile, when his other duties allowed, he sat in his *livrée* with his cat, reading steadily through the *Revelations* of the saintly Lady Bridget. It had struck him that it would be as well if at least one member of the investigating commission were to do so, and he was the most junior of the three cardinals who had been appointed to sit on it. Besides, it was Lent.

He approached the task with a characteristic mixture of scepticism and reverence. The scepticism was induced by that old cynic the Vice-Chancellor and by the text itself; indeed, in our own time, so unchallengeable an authority as Mgr. Debognie has not hesitated to declare that St. Bridget 'intermixed with the gifts she received from heaven a great part of her own burning imagination'. But reverence was present as well. Peter had not had the calling, training or ordination of a priest; he was a cardinal deacon at a time when the title meant literally what it said and the job went to a well-connected jurist. Nor had he ever tried to travel along the high, lonely paths of mysticism. Yet he practised the religion of the valleys more sincerely than did many leading churchmen of his day, and he held those few who dared to climb higher in genuine though not un-critical respect. The mountains, he thought, are dangerous; some of the paths up there lead to heresy or absurdity or religious mania; no traveller has ever been able to bring back a serviceable map of that wild terrain, though many have tried. Instead, they return with miscellaneous fragments of strange crystalline rock. Much of it crumbles to pieces when one handles it, but occasionally there are jewels too, hard and bright and durable.

But it would seem that the pious Bridget had only brought back some more conglomerate. He turned again to one of the more coherent passages.

> Behold, the clergy break all the Church's laws. Their cassocks are short, and under the cassocks they have swords and coats of mail. Shamelessly they embrace their mistresses and their children. They have turned convents into brothels. Countless numbers die without the sacraments. The world is filled with

serpents, and the fish of St. Peter dare not raise their heads for
fear of their venom. Oh Rome, Rome, I must cry for thee now
and mourn thee, as the prophet mourned for Jerusalem. The
roses and lilies in thy garden are choked by weeds, thy walls are
broken, thy gates unguarded, thy altars overturned, thy chalices
sold, thy fires of sacrifice quenched. The sacred vessels have been
carried off to Babylon, the sword of the fear of God has been
cast away, and in its place is a bottomless sack of money. The
ten commandments have been refashioned into one, and that
is: Bring hither the money!

Peter could only shake his head over these lamentations. There
was a grain of truth in what Bridget said, and yet her picture of the
Church as a whole was as distorted as her zoology. And if these
clergymen she complained of had managed things so badly as to
have children, what were they supposed to do to them? Beat them?
Bridget was a Swede; it was an example of the sexual prejudice that
Northerners have against Latins. Considered more seriously, it was
the old, irreconcilable conflict between the prophet and institutional
religion. Peter had cast in his lot with the latter. He was beginning
to feel less censorious towards those other members of the commission who had flatly refused to read any more of Bridget for the
present.

He had only to look out of the window, and Bridget's strange
world was gone in a flash, and life took its place. For Avignon
claimed all a man's attention. The Curia and its workings were a
fascinating study, and on its fringe one could meet distinguished
colleagues in jurisprudence, diplomats, foreign bankers and confidential agents, artists, scholars, experts on Tartary or the realms
of Prester John. One could hear sound views and scandal, learn one's
way through a vast network of policies and personal relationships,
seek to disentangle the valuable intelligence from the worthless.
There were reformers with useful ideas, charlatans by the score, and
a horde of benefice-hunters to be dodged or satisfied.

Then there were the court ladies, relatives of the Holy Father and
of the Limousin cardinals, who enjoyed many privileges and could
in no way be dodged, with their feline intrigues that could make or
mar a career, their discreet liaisons, their gossip and their ostentatious
pieties.

And there were the diversions. The hawking parties, for instance, which met on bright spring mornings when the mistral had slackened. The space in front of the castle at Villeneuve was an incomparable setting, the great bulging towers and the proud view of the city of the popes across the river. Peter knew all there was to know about hawking. He recalled splendid days on the hard, bare uplands of Aragon, which had been better country for the sport than these small hills covered with pine-scrub and this closely cultivated plain with its rows of poplars and cane wind-brakes that interrupted vision. In fact hawking at Avignon, like everything else there, was mainly a social occasion, conducted with gaiety and grace but not quite serious. Yet even on these lines, it was a good disinfectant. If money had to be splashed about, this was a pleasant and harmless way to do it. Some hours in the fresh air, with hawks and horses, at least gave these people's minds a rest from benefice-mongering, angling for each other's jobs and wondering how they could go to bed with each other's ladies. It was better than those over-lavish banquets, which cost a ransom, and where there were too many things like quails' tongues, too much to drink, too much jewellery worn and too much empty talk.

His martial-minded colleague the Cardinal of Geneva never missed a meet. It blew the cobwebs out of his head and kept him fit for his coming campaign in Italy. Besides, once on a horse he need not worry about that limp of his, which he took so much trouble to hide. He was a powerfully built man, with a square head on a neck like the trunk of an oak, and wide-set eyes that looked very straight at you. Behind them was a mind trained to take quick decisions. Anyone less ecclesiastical, in the usual sense, it would be hard to imagine. Yet he fitted into Avignon. Robert of Geneva was clearly the sort of man who would rise high in any profession, and nobody could doubt that he was excellently qualified to be a cardinal, and better still to be a cardinal legate, charged with restoring order in the rebellious Papal States.

Such was Avignon, a way of life whose time might be running out, to be lived the more fully for that very reason. On the surface Peter found it agreeable enough, but there were moments when he wondered whether he could ever really fit in. When one came to think of it, it was very strange that the Church, or rather its head-quarters, should be in the hands of these people. Not that they were wicked; they were intelligent and capable, occasionally worked quite hard if they had to, and usually managed to enjoy themselves without outrageous scandal. But one seldom met a naturally Christian soul among them.

★

Catherine, to the Vice-Chancellor's disgust, had arrived. Her boat had come toiling up the Rhône, the blunt bows butting forward at an ox's pace against the stiff current. From some way off her disciples (she never travelled with less than twenty) had eagerly pointed out the Palace of the Popes, rising on its ridge above the willows and poplars on a slow curve of the river bank. Then the whole town had come in sight, lit from the left by the soft sunlight of a June evening, St. Benezet's famous bridge with the chapel standing on it, the stalwart bastions behind the delicate spars of the shipping, the many church towers that befitted the administrative capital of Western Christendom. It was altogether delightful, a page from the *Très Riches Heures du Duc de Berry*.

But Catherine, through her half-closed visionary eye-slits, saw nothing of this late-Gothic beauty. For her the view held only Gothic gloom. As afterwards when she looked out over Florence, a still more famous view, the city seemed overshadowed by swarms of devils. Their black bats' wings flapped balefully over the gay pastel-coloured towers, as they do in Giotto's fresco at Assisi. For Catherine, papal Avignon was Babylon, the sinful city where the Vicar of Christ had most foolishly allowed himself to be entrapped. Led by Petrarch (whom she had not read) all right-thinking people in Italy had long been protesting in vain against this captivity. Now at last she, Catherine of Siena, had come all this way to get him out. And she was accustomed to obtaining what she wanted.

To lead the Pope back to Rome was her ultimate aim, but few knew more than that she had come to reconcile him with Florence. The government of that city, the anti-clerical Eight of War, had perforce agreed to her going as their ambassadress; like everyone else they found Catherine an extremely forceful character. Their war aims, for that matter, were not altogether unreasonable, as even she had to admit, for the policy adopted by Gregory and his legates towards Florence had not even the most tenuous connection with Christianity, and was being furthered by raids into Florentine territory and embargoes on the export of food from a rich province into a famine-struck one. But such considerations made no appeal to Catherine; her mind was made up on this as on all similar subjects. It was sacrilege to resist the papal legates, even if they behaved like 'incarnate demons', and that was an end of it. She had spent the last few months doing her best to dissuade Lucca, Pisa and other cities from joining forces with Florence. In appointing her their envoy-extraordinary, therefore, the Florentines can hardly have expected her to act with discretion or even with loyalty. And in fact they gave her no very definite instructions or powers, and were careful to send a more orthodox mission with a less conciliatory brief a month or two after she had left. Yet for the moment, however improbably, she was the Ambassadress from Florence, and this fact doubtless made her journey easier. Catherine was well aware that even a saint must have a ticket to travel on.

Peter took care to be present when His Holiness granted her an audience.

This first occasion was formal, or at least was meant to be. Catherine spoke for long stretches at a time. She spoke emphatically in her Tuscan dialect, the hard 'c's whipped into vehement 'h's. Her confessor Fra Raimondo summarised from time to time in Latin, with more discretion than accuracy. 'Dearest sweet Daddy' became 'Holy Father', and something about smelling the stench of the sins committed in this place was toned down too. Gregory leaned forward in his throne to listen at first, but after a time it would seem that he gave up like everyone else and let his attention wander, because when she finished at last he told her very briefly that he would leave the whole thing in her hands, always saving the dignity of the Church, which of course was no answer at all to what she had been saying about the war with Florence. She looked puzzled and quite human for a moment, and the master of ceremonies hurried her out before she could infringe protocol by speaking again or going into an ecstasy. Fra Raimondo was most co-operative in this final manœuvre.

The Vice-Chancellor and his friends breathed again, and began to believe that Avignon would survive her visit after all. They laid various traps, but her selfless sanctity was proof against them. During her stay she and all her disciples were lodged, as befitted an ambassadress, in a vacant *livrée* not very far from Peter's.

Naturally the ladies of this medieval Barchester were anxious to meet her. The Countess of Valentinois, their doyenne, expected a great enrichment of her own spiritual life from the encounter. The others were bursting with ordinary human curiosity. They discussed her appearance interminably—the slight, sloping-shouldered figure in black-and-white Dominican robes that we see in Vanni's portrait, the long wasted face and the eyes the shape of thin almonds, which see things we do not see. They were Sienese eyes; it was plain to them all why her fellow-townsman Simone Martini had painted the eyes of his saints in that strange manner.

At the first opportunity they fell upon her, their tall horned head-dresses bobbing foolishly up and down as they chattered. There was a linguistic impasse, only partially resolved by Fra Raimondo. Catherine, a magpie mobbed by whooper swans, looked less and less amiable, if that adjective could ever be applied to her, and finally she turned her back on a particularly gushing lady who was the close friend of a cardinal. Seeing Fra Raimondo's face as she did so, she remarked loudly and defiantly, in simple Romance words which passed the barrier of language easily enough,

'And if you could feel the stench of her sins as I do, you would do just the same!'

After this incident there were two schools of thought about Catherine. The Countess, who led the favourable one, was allowed to attend mass in Catherine's private chapel and watch her go into an ecstasy. Alys de Turenne, a straightforward girl who thought she was a fraud, went with her.

When Catherine had received the sacrament, she remained there before the altar with her arms crossed and her hands spread flat. She was motionless, pale, sightless, rigid. The mass came to an end, the priest left the chapel, and still she did not move. The Countess, all a-twitter, approached and knelt down behind her to kiss her feet, from which the sandals dangled loosely. Alys followed her and presently took her place. Producing a long darning-needle, she gave the sole of one foot a sharp prick. Nothing happened. Alys was an experimental young woman. She jabbed quite hard. Then she put the needle some way in and waggled it about. Still no reaction. The ecstasy was real.

Alys looked at the slight, rigid figure in front of her, first in amazement, and then with horror. It was a kind of temporary death. Convinced that this was no white magic, she stood up quickly and ran out of the musty chapel into the hot Provençal sunlight.

\*

Peter, when he heard of this incident, reacted in the opposite way. Peter was a Spanish intellectual, with a mind that was both extremely practical and weighed down with a brooding sense of destiny. As we have seen, he had something of an unfulfilled mystic in his make-up. He did not even share young Alys' healthy reaction against hysteria. Being a man of the world, he was glad that she had put Catherine's ecstasy to the test, for there were plenty of religious charlatans about, especially in Avignon, and it would be stupid to be caught by one. Now that point had been settled. Catherine was genuinely in touch with the unseen. And, as her phenomena were so closely associated with the mass, her unseen could not be other than the highest.

Her coming was no accident. She was a holy woman with a message. She was their destiny. Even the Vice-Chancellor, who was an old misogynist and opposed to her politically, had been impressed by the power behind her letters. She had come to change all their lives, and they needed changing. The Church at Avignon had run into a dead end. There were too many clever politicians, too many mole-like bureaucrats, too many corrupt prelates, too many sporting cardinals, too many silly women.

He tried to recall everything he had heard about Catherine. How her heavenly visions had begun when she was six. How, in spite of all that her shocked lower-middle-class parents could do, she had utterly refused to grow up like the other little girls in the street. How she had never willingly given a moment to anything but religion; how she had turned her bedroom into a cell, undergone weeks of penance after her elder sister had made her have a hair-do, jumped into scalding water to anticipate the pains of purgatory. How she had fallen into trances and been levitated upstairs. How in one significant vision she had been married to Christ Himself with a ring and heavenly witnesses. How she had become a Dominican tertiary and nursed the sick with selfless devotion. How, to punish her own squeamishness as a nurse, she once deliberately drank a cup of pus which she had just pressed out from a patient's suppurating sore. How she had a particular devotion to the sacred Blood, and how in fact the sight of any blood at all transported her into a prolonged ecstasy, as had happened when she accompanied a young man to his execution and caught his head as it fell from the block; on returning to consciousness she could not bear to wash off the bloodstains from her clothes. How the shrewd Dominicans had examined her, found her free from heresy, and appointed that safe man Fra Raimondo to be her confessor. How she gathered a band of disciples and set forth on holy missions. How these activities led her into politics. How she had preached submission to proud and worldly cities, and the crusade to the English captain, Sir John Hawkwood. How she had written all those letters.

To us, equipped as we are with welfare officers, hygiene, psychiatry and common sense, medieval sainthood in its extreme form appears not only remote from our own experience but downright wrong-headed. Even if we try to ignore the fantastic details as mere period quaintness, Catherine's life as a whole is vitiated for us by its utter disregard of moderation. Moderation is what the modern Anglo-Saxon world lives by. Life without it would be unbalanced and totalitarian, or at least violent and thoroughly uncomfortable, as it was in the Middle Ages. Peter, however, was the most medieval of men and a Spaniard to boot. Moderation is still at a discount in his country. So his reaction to these stories was very different from ours.

It is certain that he was one of the very few cardinals who took the trouble to see her and to try to get to know her. He also had some conversation with Fra Raimondo. The rest of her disciples, of course, were pathetic grown-up children, one shy and melancholy, another too talkative, all much too dependent. He got rid of them all and concentrated on Catherine.

It seems they discussed the justification for cardinals. As they talked, it became clear that Catherine's scheme of Church government did not allow much place for them. Gregory was her *dolce*

*Babbo*, the Holy Father with absolute power. Only, rather illogically, he was much in need of Catherine's guidance. Those immediately below him were all too often 'incarnate demons', a wide category in which she assembled almost all the prominent figures of fourteenth-century public life. Among the more recent entrants were the governors of the Papal States. She had made this abundantly clear to their master, Gregory, in Letter 196. As for cardinals at Avignon, was it likely that they were any better?

Peter tried to explain to her what a cardinal's functions were. There had to be devolution. The cardinals were given many essential tasks to perform. They were, he said, or at least they ought to be, pillars of the Church. This made some impression on her mind and she added the word to her stock of images, to be used later on when required. He felt that she was beginning to consider him as a somewhat inadequate but architecturally justified pillar.

Having found in Peter a potential ally, she lost no time in bombarding him with her imperatives. The Holy Father must go to Rome. He must fulfil the good resolution he had made secretly before his election. It was the will of God that he should go. Any hesitation would be a wickedness which God would punish. What reasons for hesitating could there be? Fear of the political difficulties? He must be a man and put aside all fear. If he failed in his duty, then he might have cause to fear. The Florentines would not submit? She would write to them and they would be as submissive as lambs. The King of France did not wish the Pope to leave Avignon? She would write to him too; he must also make peace with England and take the cross against the infidels. In this way he would be doing God's will and hers. The Duke of Anjou was coming to raise objections? She would go to stay with him in his castle and make him raise troops for the holy crusade instead. A Franciscan saint had warned Gregory that he would be poisoned if he went to Rome? Fra Raimondo, her Dominican confessor, would tell anyone what to think of so-called Franciscan saints, and poison could be obtained anywhere. The cardinals doubted the wisdom of the move? Then they were incarnate demons after all. But she would overcome them.

She began to recite a prayer which she had specially composed. She recited it on all such occasions. On a subsequent one Gregory's notary had the presence of mind to take it down, and it has been preserved.

'Woe is me!' she began, bewailing her own sins, but soon passing on to other people's. 'Open the eyes of Thy Vicar, so that he shall no longer love Thee for his own sake, or himself either. . . . Or else we must all perish, for upon him depends our life and our death. . . . I offer my body as a sacrifice. I offer my flesh and my blood. Let the blood be drained away, let the flesh be hacked in pieces, let the bones be cloven. Let Thy Vicar tread my bones asunder and the marrow in my bones, if only he will obey Thy will. . . .'

She went into a trance, Fra Raimondo looked worried, and the disciples let Peter out.

★

In any conversion personal impact counts for more than arguments. This is particularly true when the active agent is someone like St. Catherine. Peter, however, was a trained jurist holding a responsible position, and back in his own room he tried hard to rationalise the experience. He went over the arguments in favour of a return to Rome at that moment. Modern liberal historians, shocked at the idea that Catherine could have been more than a minor factor in the move, have done the same, though only with limited success.

The Italians demanded that the Pope should return—but were they only thinking of the patronage and prestige which would come their way again? And they would do nothing to smooth his path.

England, Germany and some other countries distrusted the papacy while it stayed at Avignon—but would they be any more amenable to a papal court at Rome?

The French did not benefit so greatly from Avignon that they would go to any lengths to prevent the Pope from leaving—but they would be unco-operative once he had gone.

Avignon was unsafe, as a raid by a company of freebooters had proved not many years ago—but Rome was a great deal more unsafe, as Urban V had seen for himself.

The chaos in the Papal States made Gregory's presence there imperative—but there was much to be said for a safer base outside and for avoiding still deeper involvement in Italian power-politics.

The Romans were threatening to set up an antipope if Gregory did not come—but few would seriously support so blatant an impiety.

No, the case for making the move then, in 1376, was not over-whelmingly strong. What tipped the balance for Peter was definitely more emotional; the coolness he felt towards many of his colleagues, the conviction that so long as the French element predominated the Church would not be reformed, the feeling that some drastic step was overdue, the personality of Catherine.

The arguments became more public, until all Avignon throbbed with intrigue and talked of nothing else. From this period Peter acquired a lasting aversion to 'broadening the base of Church government', to collective rule by cardinals. A pope must be master in his own house.

How did Gregory himself make up his mind? Historians have argued. No one knows. Perhaps his thought-processes were not altogether unlike Peter's, though he wavered up to the end. In his case there was an added incentive; if the move were successful, he would go down in history as the pope who restored the Holy See to Rome. For that he might well be canonised. Peter and the Italian cardinals were in favour of the move, but their influence was slight. Catherine, needless to say, brought all her guns to bear on him, while from the other side his Beaufort relations implored him not to go. Catherine secured a last private audience.

'Do not be a frightened, little boy, but be a man! Open your mouth and swallow your medicine!'

It worked.

On the morning of 13 September the great courtyard of the Palace was a milling vortex of gorgeously caparisoned horses, regulation white mules and fancifully uniformed halberdiers. Pages and farriers, notaries and trumpeters, standard-bearers and theologians struggled to find their places in the column. The happy confusion which accompanies Latin outdoor ceremonial had long since given way to panic, for this was no pageant of a few hours' duration, it was an uprooting, probably for ever. None of the right people had been detailed, all the wrong things had been packed. The roll had been called seven times with varying results. It was too late. Gregory, supported by chanting clergy and acolytes, appeared at the Window of the Indulgence, while a long procession of dignitaries flowed slowly down the staircase and into the courtyard. A last frantic effort was made to stop him. His mother fainted, his four belligerent sisters scowled, several French cardinals burst into tears, and his aged father, Count Guillaume de Beaufort, threw himself down across the threshold to block his son's way. Gregory, taut and deathly pale, stepped over the grey head and went to mount his mule. The distracted master of ceremonies gave the signal to start, tuckets were sounded and the choir struck up an anthem, but the animal, as though stunned by the Pope's unfilial conduct or be-witched by the Beauforts, refused to move. Every possible aid was applied, but it would not budge. Another one had to be found. At last, long behind schedule, the procession left the Palace and clattered its way through undecorated streets lined by glum townsfolk who saw their livelihood departing for ever. Catherine and her disciples watched it go. So did the Vice-Chancellor and five other elderly or recalcitrant cardinals who stayed behind. Peter, who had an almost Roman feeling for omens, was disheartened. The journey had not begun auspiciously.

# CHAPTER 2

# Rome

N O one who has ever seen even the smallest organ of government on the move will doubt that to transport the papal Curia from the Rhône to the Tiber under fourteenth-century conditions was a desperate undertaking. A supreme pontiff and a saintly mystic might issue their commands, but it is worth while glancing briefly at the lesser folk who had to carry them out. How did the papal administrators face such a problem? One of them, a French bishop, has left us his impressions in very bad Latin verse, but if we want to know what was actually done, the account-books of the *Camera Apostolica* are a better source in every way.[2]

What they reveal is delightful. Once the decision had been taken in principle, the opening move was not in doubt. Of the whole vast papal bureaucracy, the first department to be mobilised was the cellar. Frascati is an acquired taste, and the senior members of the Curia were grimly determined that they should not be obliged to acquire it. Were they not accustomed to the delicate and generous vintages that slipped almost effortlessly downstream to their dinner-tables from Beaune and Châteauneuf-du-Pape?

The first relevant entry in the account-books therefore reads:

> *23 June.* Paid to Master Pierre Alamon, cellarer-priest to our lord the Pope, who is being sent to Rome with our lord the Pope's wine-casks, for his estimated expenses . . . 100 florins of the *Camera*.

Further entries reveal that he took with him, for a start, twenty-nine large casks and twenty-four of the smaller size made at Beaune.

Having seen the Reverend Pierre Alamon off with his precious cargo, the papal administrators set themselves to assemble a fleet to follow it. The Pope had only one galley of his own. When Urban V had gone to Rome, shipping had been provided free of charge by Queen Joanna of Naples, who owed much to the papacy, and whose ravishing beauty and unconventional freedom of manners were still the talk of Europe. But the nine intervening years had consolidated her political position and, by all accounts, left her morals much where they were. She now offered six galleys at 600 gulden a month apiece. Gregory's Treasury recorded the offer and its acceptance without enthusiasm, but shoals of gallant Italian historians have rushed to her defence. Why should not the poor little Queen be businesslike? The money would help to pay for some harmless frivolities in connection with her fourth marriage. And the French shipowners, who supplied five more galleys, were demanding 1,300 gulden a month each.

In view of the dangers there had to be a military escort, though one feels that 500 might have been more suitable than the 2,000 they took. 500 could have protected the papal court against rioters and bandits; 2,000 were too few to fight a war. The young Vicomte de Turenne, Gregory's nephew and Alys' husband, took the lead in recruiting whatever footloose soldiers of fortune the Cardinal of Geneva had not already taken to Italy. From now on an elastic sub-department called 'Candles and ects'. wrestled with the unfamiliar details of military pay and allowances. Raymond de Turenne himself received a generous 700 florins a month.

Vast quantities of biscuits, manufactured in the Palace bakery, provided victualling for the fleet as a whole. But for Gregory and his suite aboard the flagship things were done on a very different scale. Under the date, *31 August*, there appears in the accounts a truly Homeric shopping-list. The order in which the items are recorded suggests that this shopping-list, like many lesser ones, was composed by inspiration rather than by logic.

> 4 casks of vinegar, 6 carving-boards, 11 kegs for oil, 7 large choppers, 4 lengths of towelling and 3 of linen, 23 measures of white peas, 13 of beans and 3 quintals of broken beans, 6 calves, 24 sheep, 60 capons, 200 pullets, 50 partridges, 60 pigeons, 24 hens, 48 rabbits, 4,000 eggs, a mule-load of millet, 2 tins for holding sauces, and to mending one cask of peas which had burst . . .

There follows a formidable array of medieval ironmongery and

a quantity of spices which a modern chef would consider dispro-
portionate, but which may have helped to preserve the victuals at
first and to disguise their flavour later on.

> 42 lb. sugar, 56 lb. ginger, 50 lb. common spice, 26 lb. cinnamon,
> 12 lb. pepper, 9 lb. cloves, 4 lb. paradise seeds, 4 lb. saffron,
> 4 lb. Muscat nuts . . .

The list closes with relatively modest amounts of rice and flour,
two quintals of almonds and a little more ironmongery, doubtless
an afterthought.

We catch a glimpse of the papal treasurer on the road to Marseilles, keeping a wary eye on his mule-train of ready cash (62,000
French francs, 27,000 florins of Aragon and 4,000 silver caroli) and
perhaps equally on the escort of seven 'brigands' who were detailed
to accompany him. And, in a happier mood, there is the Reverend
Pierre Alamon, cellarer to His Holiness, back again from Rome and
setting forth once more along the cypress-lined road in the golden
light of early September, earning reimbursement of 'his expenses
incurred in various places in Provence, preceding our lord the Pope
with pack-animals bearing barrels and flagons, including horse-hire
and the additional supplies of wine which he purchased on the way
to Marseilles. . . .'

*

The journey took nearly four months, and must have provided
Peter with material for nightmares for as many years. Everything
conspired against it, the weather, Italian politics and the inclinations
of the travellers themselves. They did not leave Marseilles until
2 October, when there was another emotional scene as the Grand
Master of the Knights of St. John gave the order to cast off, and
Gregory himself broke down in tears at the sight of the fair land of
France receding for ever. Any optimism there may have been concerning the Mediterranean in October was instantly dispelled.
Gales blew intermittently, and always in the wrong direction, for a
fortnight, driving them into shelter at a dozen little places along the
Riviera. The voyage nearly ended altogether off Monaco, when the
ropes parted, the sails were blown away, the anchors dragged and
the rocks and breakers came unpleasantly near.

For the first ten days of this, it is likely that Peter's mind registered only one fact concerning these resorts; they were where the ship's motion stopped. But at last the gale blew itself out, and he found his sea-legs. By the time they put in at Savona he was more receptive. Pre-industrial Savona, a well-appointed little town cut neatly in half by a small river and with a castle on the heights on either side, made an excellent impression and was fresh in his memory thirty years later.

At Genoa the news was bad. The Cardinal of Geneva, who had taken the field with his ten thousand Bretons some months ago, was learning that an Italian campaign is not so easy as it looks from outside. At Rome too the situation was what nowadays Foreign Office spokesmen describe as fluid. The Italians were not going to be helpful. Gregory held a consistory. It voted emphatically for returning to Avignon, by land. For over a week everything hung in the balance once again. But Catherine was watching them.

The Florentines had long since disowned their ambassadress, leaving her dependent on her own resources. But part of Catherine's technique (though never, of course, used for unworthy ends) was to mix on nothing less than the highest social level, wherever she might be. It is therefore no surprise to find her and her platoon of disciples comfortably installed in one of the best mansions on the fashionable Via Canneto. She had very sensibly taken them there by road, arriving fresh for action a few days before Gregory.

Nothing so clearly indicates the influence which Catherine exercised at the height of her powers than the fact that she made no attempt to come to see what was happening. Poor Gregory had to go to her. He went along late one evening, as inconspicuously as he could, feeling exactly like a schoolboy in a scrape. Would she let him off? Please, might they go home now? Good gracious, no! They had only just started. So that was that. The Grand Master and his seamen were mobilised, the Sacred College was admonished, and on 29 October the papal fleet put out guiltily to sea once more.

Again contrary winds held them up. Days passed at Portofino and Portovenere. They reached Livorno and stayed there a week. Off Elba they ran into the worst storm of all. The ships were scattered, two of them sank, and a venerable prelate, less agile than his companion Cardinal Lagrange, was drowned. The rest reassembled in the little round harbour of Port Ercole, whence they limped on down the Tuscan coast and at last came to Corneto, the modern Tarquinia. Here at last they were within the borders of the Papal State. They landed thankfully. It was already well into December.

Even then they could not be in Rome for Christmas. Relations between the popes and the civic authorities on the Capitol have almost always been strained, right down to the time when a town-planning committee of freemasons carefully designed a whole district so that the dome of St. Peter's should not be visible at the end of each street. The medieval Romans were more forthright. If they tired of a pope he was well advised to leave. They had driven out Urban V. So there had to be exploratory talks, negotiations, agreements, guarantees. The process took five weeks. For the Romans it involved breaking off relations with Florence despite powerfully worded appeals from that quarter, appeals composed by one of the early Renaissance humanists in such elegant Latin that in Rome they had the greatest difficulty in reading it. Meanwhile Gregory's party celebrated Christmas on the many-towered hilltop of Tarquinia, while in the tombs outside, beneath the rolling cornlands, smiling Etruscans feasted subterraneously and poured out more ambiguous libations.

By this time there was not a single member of the expedition who did not long to finish the journey as quickly as possible, and Catherine's Christmas letter (No. 252) was felt to be merely tiresome.

> . . . Be a Vicar worthy of the name! As for the contrary winds, which you describe as dangerous, there are far more important things to attend to. A pope should expect a few contrary winds, anyway. Be a man, and go forward to meet these dangerous winds! . . . Keep moving, and you will come to enjoy the storms and the dangers.

The end of the journey was in sight at last, and on a January evening the treasury officials sat huddled in a draughty corner of the old palace at Corneto and struggled to balance their accounts. Never before, they thought resentfully, had the august records of the *Camera Apostolica* contained so many strange and unsuitable entries. How awkward everything was that came under their homespun

Latin heading, *Pro domini nostri pape guerra et recessu*. All these payments to mercenaries amounted, in their opinion, to a war, even if not a strictly classical one, and was not this whole unfortunate voyage a 'recession' from the decencies of Avignon?

Look at these entries! A trail of small undignified claims for compensation all along the Riviera. A heap of salt on the quay had been trampled and spoilt at their first port of call. At Portofino the sailors had somehow set fire to a wood, and various inhabitants of unreliable appearance but great rhetorical gifts had to be indemnified, as well as one particularly importunate fellow for 'twelve cockerels and one cock which were stolen from him in the said port, as he affirmed on oath'. Then a long entry covered all that trouble at Livorno. The cavalry had disembarked their horses to exercise them, whereupon the skippers had flatly refused to take them on board again, and the dispute was only settled by an additional payment made on the authority of our lord the Pope himself. 500 florins for Cardinal Lagrange to cover his personal losses when his galley struck the rocks. Doubtless he would be asking for more. At least the other prelate had been drowned, and his property (if any) would escheat to the treasury.

And latterly the Grand Master, as admiral of the fleet, had taken to ordering incomprehensible equipment. Was it really necessary so late in the voyage? 'Six instruments of iron called grappling-hooks, and two iron chains, and two other instruments, also of iron, called capstan-ratchets (?) which the said lord admiral gave orders to be made. . . .' A rather niggardly sum of 32 florins, 2 shillings had been distributed to the convents of Corneto for Christmas. 25 florins for the pilot who had brought them from Marseilles, and 100 (in very small change) to be scattered to the crowds as they entered Rome. And last of all a small payment 'to Galeazzo, trumpeter of Corneto, and his assistant, for services rendered in our lord the Pope's palace there on account of the absence of a bell, which did not exist in that palace'.

Altogether, it had been a trying period.

★

At last they were able to set sail again. A day brought them to Ostia. The low, unhealthy coastline and the sluggish river depressed them, and the French looked incredulously at the entertainment on the river bank, the best that Ostia could provide at short notice. They saw elderly gentlemen dancing staidly up and down, we are informed, blowing wheezy trumpets and holding up flickering torches above their bald heads.

Next day the galleys rowed upstream and berthed opposite San Paolo fuori le mura. The great basilica still lay in ruins, thirty years after the earthquake which had shattered it. They all disembarked and the triumphal entry began. It was an historic day, 17 January 1377, and one's first sight of Rome is always an experience.[3]

Peter rode next to Cardinal Orsini, a bright young Roman patrician, who pointed out the sights of his native city. Here was the gate in the walls built by Aurelian, impressive in its brown bulk and already eleven centuries old. The pyramid to the left, Orsini said, was the tomb of Remus. Likely enough. A choir sang and Gregory received the keys on a cushion.

Peter was unprepared for what met his eyes inside the gate. There was no city, only a wilderness which stretched for miles. Poisoned by economic decline and endless civil wars, Rome had shrunk inside its shell like a dying crab, leaving space for blighted wastelands, straggling allotments and vineyards yielding an atrocious wine that tasted like the lead seals on long-forgotten papal bulls. A scattering of refugees' hovels, decayed convents, grubby little churches and frightened clusters of tall thin fortified towers, built of fragments of ancient masonry and many of them burnt out in recent strife. And everywhere the nameless, nondescript, weed-grown ruins, a crumbling brown if antique or blackened if modern, all of them casual latrines and the haunt of snakes and footpads.

To the left, across an empty space, they saw Monte Testaccio, the hill of potsherds, a huge spoil-heap of broken jars left there by classical wine and oil importers. This, Peter learned, was where nowadays the Senate and People of Rome celebrated their latter-day carnival by rolling little red carts down the steep slope, loaded with live pigs which the unwilling Jews were forced to pay for. At the bottom the People finished off the pigs and fought for the free meat, while the Senate looked on benignly.

From here the procession skirted the Aventine, which the Savelli clan had turned into a private stronghold, and then the Palatine, whose huge ruins the Frangipani had fortified. Flags drooped for them over Constantine's arch, but the Colosseum, undecorated and undecoratable, treated the cortège with massive indifference. The building has always looked inwards, first at degrading martyrdoms, then in Peter's time at the misery of the slum-dwellers who camped in it, and nowadays at its own archaeologically pickled bones. Here the procession turned left, passing through the Arch of Titus and a melancholy, pastoral Forum, and thence up to the town hall on the Capitol, where there were glasses of strange wine and rhetorical addresses of welcome that nobody listened to. On through narrow streets decked with poor bunting, insanitary and full of latent violence, the district where most of the shrunken population of 20,000 had their homes.

In his progress through this extraordinary place Peter sometimes looked back to where Gregory, on a white palfrey and under a baldacchino held by the Senator and other notables, imparted his benedictions. But the mountebanks in front held most of his attention. There were a thousand of them, all in white, musicians and buffoons, clapping their hands in rhythm and capering obscenely past the desolation and the ruins, a surrealistic symbol of the rank life which clung to this unproductive site.

It was a pity, he must have thought, that Catherine was not here to see all this, though she would not have approved of the buffoons. Nor of the escort; Raymond de Turenne and his two thousand troopers followed close on the Pope's heels. She was always telling him not to come with armed men, but like a meek lamb.

All the same it was Catherine's triumph quite as much as Gregory's. For him it might turn out as short-lived as most Roman triumphs, but she would have her reward for all time. Even in this world too. When her Sienese fellow-countrymen came to paint the scene, the buffoons and most of the escort would vanish and she would be there, leading the Holy Father's palfrey.

They crossed a fine bridge with towers defending it. They passed under the walls of the Castel Sant'Angelo and through the crowded Borgo. Darkness was falling and there were massed torches in the square before St. Peter's. Wild applause. An unforgettable climax

to the day, to the past four months, to seventy years. Surely
Catherine should have been there? But travel was difficult and she
knew her duty; she would come to Rome when things went wrong.

\*

Was it really likely that they would go right? Hardly had the
festivities ended and Rome returned to normal, when news came
of the massacre of Cesena.

Cesena was a place as undistinguished as Guernica or Lidice or
Oradour-sur-Glane. It was merely one of the countless small towns
within the fluctuating boundaries of the Papal States that had some
modest dreams of wider liberty. The Cardinal of Geneva arrived
with Sir John Hawkwood, the town surrendered, and the Bretons
got out of hand and slaughtered nearly three thousand citizens.
Hawkwood deserted to the Florentines in the course of the year and
eventually earned his equestrian monument by Paolo Uccello, but
Italy never forgave the Cardinal.

He was less to blame than the policy he served. The Church was
conducting a war, a war against quite ordinary people to hold or
recapture territories from which it derived no real advantage. Some
fresh thinking on Church-and-State relations, together with a well-
policed Vatican City inviolate by sacred taboo, would have given
the popes a better prospect of independence. Even Catherine, a
theocrat if ever there was one, blamed Gregory for going on with
the war. 'Do not come with armed men. Seek souls rather than
cities.' It was the best piece of advice she ever gave him. But he had
had enough of her, and the contradictions of the Temporal Power
were beyond anyone's solving. His health broken by the strain,
Gregory lived for no more than fourteen months after his triumphal
entry. There is little doubt that if he had had the physical strength
he would have gone back to Avignon. The theologian Gerson, an
austere though not a first-hand witness, tells us that on his death-bed
he warned them all in the most solemn form 'to beware of all those
persons, whether men or women, who under the guise of religion
proclaimed their own infatuated visions, for he himself had been
led astray by such'.

For Peter it was different. Rome suited him better than Avignon, as is evident from his more varied activities. He found a decayed palazzo in the most populous quarter, close to the Tor Sanguigna, and began enthusiastically to restore it. He welcomed a social life that was less restricted. He got to know as many Roman laymen as he could and held open house for a group of reform-minded clergy. He explored the city indefatigably, fascinated by the Church's deep roots in buildings, names and customs. Hitherto he had looked on the Curia as no more than a juristic masterpiece, but now unquestionably he fell in love with the age-old organisation he served. This was where it belonged and where he belonged. He found a new happiness, and it dulled his critical sense. Under the influence of his reforming Italian friends, and helped by a Spanish streak of obstinacy, he kept on believing that the move to Rome had been justified, long after most responsible churchmen had come to see that it had not.

Naturally he visited his own titular church of Santa Maria in Cosmedin. At first he was sadly disappointed; he had imagined that his title as a prince of the Church must derive from some more grandiose building, something, say, on the scale of Santa Maria Maggiore. But that was before he got to know Rome. Then his small church's subtle, assymetrical, time-worn beauty began to appeal to him, and he realised how intensely Roman it was. Every period was represented, layer upon layer and the layers inextricably mixed up in the Roman way—even the pre-Christian, for those great dingy Corinthian columns half embedded in the walls of the nave must surely have stood there, free and splendid, long before the church was built. He admired the *schola cantorum*, a kind of Romanesque sheep-pen of low marble in the middle of the church, to hold the choristers, and to tell the truth was still more impressed by the Gothic canopy over the altar; in his day the Albert Memorial had not yet tried to copy it.

The clergy exposed St. Valentine's relics for their privileged visitor. St. Valentine, the patron of young love. For a moment his thoughts strayed wistfully along a half-forgotten path. He hastily brought them back to the patterned marble floor. It was perhaps the best thing in the church, and again something entirely Roman, for to make it the Cosmati craftsmen had simply sawn up classical pillars and marbles of different sections and colours into thin slices, and fitted the bits together in a charming geometrical patchwork.

There were circles and diamonds and wedges, yellows and blues and purples and serpentine greens, and a great round of maroon porphyry in the middle.

Outside, he saw an altogether admirable campanile, brown, foursquare, functional and enduring, and they smilingly showed him the Bocca di Verità, the half-obliterated river-god with his vacant, twisted stare and his toothless mouth which still had the strength to bite off a perjurer's finger. Just by the door a former holder of Peter's title, dead these two centuries, had placed his monument. 'Alfanus, an upright man, seeing that all things pass away, built this tomb for himself lest his memory should perish altogether.' Rome would become his home, thought Peter, he would live richly and usefully here, making his contribution to Church government and the canon law, repairing this titular church of his and his old palazzo too, making many friendships, and in time to come his own tomb would look well on the other side of the doorway.

★

Meanwhile, they would have to elect a successor to Gregory. It was obviously going to be a most tiresome business.

The first hint of the coming storm was given when the Cardinal of Glandève, a priggish character, allowed himself to be drawn into an argument with 300 excited Trasteverini in the courtyard outside Santa Cecilia, his titular church in that aboriginal quarter of the city. They pushed forward a spokesman, who asked politely enough whether the cardinals intended to elect a Roman or an Italian pope, one who would be sure to stay with them and not go off to foreign parts. Glandève—his actual words have been preserved[4]—delivered one of his pedantic little lectures. They did not do at all well to ask for a fellow-countryman as pope; instead, they should ask God to inspire Their Eminences to choose a person who would best serve Him and the Church, whether he was a Frenchman, or a Spaniard, or wherever he might come from.

Instead of being abashed by this little homily, as a good peasant from the Alpes Maritimes would certainly have been, the man waved his arms and raised his voice by an octave.

D

'All right then! If you won't choose a Roman or an Italian, you didn't ought to call yourselves the Roman Curia. The Avignon Curia, it ought to be by rights, or wherever it is your lordships are pleased to go to!'

'The Roman pope belongs to the whole world,' argued Glandève truly but unwisely in his old-maidish voice. 'Don't you understand that the whole world is his diocese? He can live wherever he likes, wherever he likes. And wherever he may happen to be, he does not cease for a moment to be Bishop of Rome. In the same way I am Bishop of Glandève, and I have to live far away from the town in my diocese. My town isn't called Glandève actually, but you wouldn't understand. But I don't stop calling myself Bishop and Cardinal of Glandève because of a little thing like that. In fact most of my colleagues in the Curia are in the same position. Do you see now, my sons?'

'I'll tell you how it is, Your Eminence. Ever since Pope Boniface VIII died, and that is longer ago than any of us here can remember, France has been sucking Rome and Italy dry. And now we want to suck France dry for a bit!'

The argument being reduced to this vulgar economic level, Glandève felt there was nothing more to be said and withdrew in dignity up the steps and into his chambers. He left the crowd in no doubt that, from their point of view, the worst was going to happen. From the Trastevere the news spread quickly over the rest of Rome and grew in the telling, until the ripples reached Peter's house in the Via Tor Sanguigna.

Here, as for several months past, Don Alfonso was doing most of the talking. Peter's local adviser bumbled in daily to unload his cargo of inaccurate news and gossip. Inspired by the Vice-Chancellor's example, Peter had been trying for some time to find a reliable subordinate. But in the general upheaval it had not been easy, and this elderly Spanish clergyman of transparent goodness represented, so far, the best he had been able to achieve. Alfonso, once Bishop of Jaën, had resigned his see ten years ago in order to lead a life of holy simplicity in Rome. He had been Bridget's adviser and still watched over her almost equally saintly daughter Karin, who, since her mother's death, had spent these years in Rome too, engaged in conspicuous pieties and in urging Bridget's canonisation.

When Peter arrived Don Alfonso had made himself useful, introducing his Roman friends and clerics of the reforming party. But hitherto it had not been possible to put him to regular work; perhaps indeed, thought Peter in his pessimistic moments, it never would be.

In fact Peter's local expert had only succeeded in persuading his chief on a single issue, though he talked continuously on many. He had insisted that the Cardinal ought to be buried in a smarter church than Santa Maria in Cosmedin. For the sake of peace, and because modesty somehow seemed out of place in Rome, Peter had agreed, and his architect was now devising a highly ornamental resting-place to be erected in the basilica of San Lorenzo.

But now Rome held more immediate problems for them both. As Don Alfonso commented on Glandève's lecture and its reception, he had to admit that the Romans, those dear, good-hearted fellows among whom he had spent so many happy years, had been overdoing it. There had been a painful scene after Gregory's funeral, when the city councillors began to argue with the cardinals, pressing them to declare publicly, before the conclave, that they would elect a Roman or at least an Italian pope. Since then they had never stopped passing resolutions and pestering everybody in the Curia. And now the common people were joining in. Every day brought another disquieting incident. A great hulking man stopped the Cardinal of Limoges in the street and said to him, 'Remember if you don't give us a Roman or an Italian pope, all you cardinals from across the Alps are going to be knifed!' Those were his very words. Anything could happen. It was a good thing Cardinal de Luna had just made his will.

Peter discounted the rumours of impending violence. He liked the Romans. Naturally they would be very excited, but that was probably all. It was more important to consider who should be elected pope. He discussed this at some length with Don Alfonso.

The French had a majority in the College of Cardinals, but they were divided among themselves. The Limousin group, hitherto dominant, wanted the Cardinal of Poitiers, but the others felt it was time that the Limousin monopoly was broken. There were five out-and-out Limousins, plus perhaps two or three hangers-on, but that only made eight at the most, and eight was exactly half the number present in Rome, who would be voting. The Limousins, therefore, could not secure their two-thirds majority, or even, possibly, a majority at all. The Cardinals of Geneva, Brittany and Glandève were strongly anti-Limousin, and so were the four Italians in the College.

Of these last, none was very suitable. The Cardinals of Florence and Milan were territorially tied up with the Church's enemies, old Tebaldeschi had one foot in the grave, and the other Roman, Orsini, was too young and too generally distrusted.

Only Peter was left. He was an unknown quantity and a very recent entrant to the College. It would not be him.

For his own part he had no strong preference. He did not much like the Limousins. Very probably he thought that, provided the Roman populace did not scare them out of their wits, the French cardinals would find a compromise candidate, that is, one of their own number other than Poitiers. It might well be Viviers, who was a Limousin by origin but who had not identified himself so closely with the dominant clique. If the French could agree on Viviers, they would be able to elect him. In that case Peter, who was on good terms with Viviers, would almost certainly vote for him too.

Meanwhile the Romans were getting out of hand. They posted guards on the city gates, ostensibly to ensure the conclave's safety but actually to prevent the cardinals from leaving the city. They immobilised every boat on the Tiber for the same reason. All members of the local nobility were ordered to leave, including those whose official duty it was to protect the conclave; the Counts of Fondi and Nola held office in the Curia expressly for that purpose. At the same time a large number of hillmen from the wild Sabine country began to pour into Rome. They were easily recognised in the streets by their rough clothes, their smoke-blackened jerkins of chain mail and their crude weapons. They joined with particular vehemence in the clamour for an Italian pope. Such folk do not normally take an interest in ecclesiastical affairs unless it has been made worth their while.

The cardinals protested in vain. The two Counts would not be allowed to stay in Rome and protect them. Instead, the city ward-captains or bannerets would undertake to keep the crowd away from the Vatican. Someone suggested holding the conclave in the Castel Sant'Angelo, but the bannerets would not hear of it. And the castle, though a small French garrison held it, had not been provisioned for a long siege. The 2,000 troops which had escorted Gregory from Avignon had disappeared.

The cardinals had been strangely complacent. The exception was their self-appointed military expert. The Cardinal of Geneva's zeal in this role had been in no way dampened by his inconclusive fortunes in the field. He was back in Rome now and he took matters in hand. He had made an appreciation of the situation. His campaign in the Romagna had taught him something about hillmen, and he therefore put no trust in the bannerets' guard of city apprentices. The conclave would be held under duress, and only Prignano could save them. Prignano, more indispensable than ever, had become acting Vice-Chancellor and had been given a step up in rank by being made Archbishop of Bari. And now, said Geneva, he would save them all. The Cardinal spent his time going round Rome, calling on his colleagues and explaining his plan. Why Prignano? He was the only suitable Italian they had, the only one they could be sure of, the only one who had always done what was wanted of him. They would stage a bogus election, and afterwards, once they were all in safety again, it would be easy to make him stand down.

He called on Peter in his house by the Tor Sanguigna. The more cautious and non-committal Peter was, the more animated Geneva grew. At the end of the interview he raised his breviary and flourished it in the air. He carried one, his critics always felt, not so much from piety or for use as because without it people might say he was improperly dressed, like a captain-general without his baton or a modern regimental officer without his cane.

'By this holy book,' he declared in ringing tones, 'we shall have no other pope but the Archbishop of Bari!'

The words were audible far beyond Peter's door. They were remembered.[5]

*

Peter and Alfonso discussed the little Archbishop as a possible candidate. Only if they were forced to choose an Italian, said Peter. Why not in any case? said Alfonso, quite carried away by the idea.

It was seldom that a tip straight from the stable came the way of this unworldly man, but he knew how to make use of one. Hastening to the abode of the pious Lady Karin, Bridget's daughter, he told her all he knew. Prignano would be pope, however improbable it sounded. She, in turn, saw that there was not a moment to lose if the cause of her mother's canonisation were to prosper. She rushed straight to St. Peter's. No daughter of Bridget's could be content with doing things by halves, and so the startled Prignano found his way barred by a princess of Sweden abasing herself on the marble floor at his feet and showing him a degree of reverence which nobody had ever shown him before. It was a perplexing incident, the first of many that week, but deeply gratifying too. Respect, and respect from the high-born in particular, was what he craved for.

There were only four days to go before the conclave. The cardinals' houses were full of comings and goings, of rumours and cross-currents. No two witnesses could agree afterwards on who suggested what or who was swayed in which direction. Prignano was certainly mentioned, but with what purpose and by how many is extremely doubtful. It is tolerably clear that the cardinals intended to elect one of their own number. The odds were on Viviers.

To the growing disorder in the city, reactions were varied. One great prelate, in a sermon, asserted that a conclave held under these conditions would be invalid. Glandève, fussy as ever, made a solemn declaration before a notary to the effect that any vote he might give to a non-French candidate would be a forced vote and a void one. Geneva, we are told, set the blessed Bridget's censures at defiance by wearing armour under his ecclesiastical robes whenever he went out of doors.

By this time the whole business was beginning to get on Peter's nerves. It struck him that practically every soul in Rome was bent on ensuring, by fair means or foul, some result that should at least appear to be left to the Holy Ghost. When his confessor, the Prior of Santa Sabina, came scurrying down from the Aventine with a fresh crop of electoral exhortations and alarming rumours, he decided that the time had come to take a firm line.

'I assure you,' he told the Prior, 'I will not vote for anyone except of my own free choice. That is a fact. Yes, even if I have to die for it. And if it comes to that, why should I think it an unworthy end, to die at the hands of this people in this holy city, where so many thousands of saints have borne witness to the truth?'[6]

He spoke irritably and with irony. He was still not expecting any serious trouble.

Eleven days after Gregory's death, the cardinals entered their conclave. It was the first to be held in Rome for seventy-five years, and the Romans were clearly preparing to make the most of it. It was also the first to be held in the Vatican. As to what happened inside, it is safe to say that no other conclave has been so hotly debated. Few events in Church history have called into being such a mass of contradictory evidence, so many irreconcilable stories told by unimpeachable eye-witnesses, so generous a supply of oaths, death-bed confirmations and divine portents to uphold them. When good men start lying in a really good cause, facts vanish into thin air.

With this warning in mind we may approach the Vatican in the footsteps of Peter and his fellow-cardinals who assembled there on the evening of 7 April 1378.

The Vatican of those days, a not very satisfactory substitute for the burnt-out Lateran where the papal court had formerly resided, bore very little resemblance to what we see there now. It was something like an Oxford college of the more rambling sort, with courtyards and stone buildings of various dates and several tall towers. A large chapel and other rooms on an upper floor had been set aside for the conclave. The main gate of the palace stood next to Old St. Peter's at the top of the square, which of course lacked its present symmetrical shape and Bernini's colonnades.

The square was so full of people that Peter and his colleagues had no little difficulty in forcing their way through to the palace gate. The ebullient Trasteverini were there in force, mingled with several thousands of yet more pugnacious hillmen. All were shouting for a Roman or at least an Italian pope.

'*Romano lo volemo, o almanco italiano!*'

The crowd stank of garlic, sweat, cheap wine and mounting hysteria. A banneret struggled frantically to clear a path. There were some unsteady grabs at bridles as the cardinals and their conclavists rode by.

'If you lord cardinals don't,' a voice bellowed, 'We'll make your heads as red as your hats!'

At last they reached the Vatican doorway. It was none too soon for Peter's conclavist, a serious young Spanish cleric from Tarazona. Here they found the Bishop of Marseilles, the principal guardian of the conclave. With him were a banneret and an unimpressive citizen guard. The promise to keep the public at some distance from the Vatican had already proved illusory, and the usual recriminations inseparable from Italian public life were in progress. As the cardinals entered, a section of the crowd came in with them. They demonstrated. They insisted that the outer gate should stay open all night. Nor would they allow the inner doors and openings into the conclave itself to be walled up with masonry as the regulations prescribed, leaving only a hatchway for communication. They would not even let the door be locked. The Bishop of Marseilles was telling everyone that they had taken away his keys. The confusion went on for hours. Late that evening the bannerets were admitted to the conclave, despite protests at the irregularity, and harangued the cardinals once more in favour of a local pope. Only long after Their Eminences had gone to bed were the guards able to put a beam across the inner door.

Peter was confronted with an additional omen. The usual curious wooden cubicles or cells had been constructed, one for each cardinal, and each bearing its owner's coat of arms. But the previous night the building had been struck by lightning and his cell had been damaged. It was only a split plank. The carpenters had already repaired it. Yet Peter was superstitious about such things. It strengthened his resolve to play a relatively passive part in what might follow. He had no hard and fast intentions anyway.

Except for old Cardinal Tebaldeschi, who was heard snoring through everything, nobody had much sleep that night. The populace drifted in and out of the courtyard below and even into the ground floor immediately beneath the conclave. They banged on the floor-boards, shouted their monotonous slogan, clashed their weapons, and at last, having broken into the papal cellars, got drunk on the 'Greek wine, Vernaccia, Malmsey and various other good wines' which they found there—the stock so carefully built up by the Reverend Pierre Alamon on his repeated journeys. They stove in some of the casks, so that next day witnesses saw a pool of wine in the courtyard with planks laid down to bridge it. As anyone knows who has tried to sleep in central Rome, even a peaceable Roman night holds an astounding volume of noise. This crowd was not particularly peaceable. Did its behaviour amount to *violentia*, or was it only *vinolentia*? No doubt there was some of both.

Peter's young conclavist, Fernando Perez de Calvillo, was full of fond hopes that his master might be elected. He was sure that he was popular with the Romans, as he told him some time after midnight.

Peter quickly disabused him.

'If they asked for me and made all that infernal din about it, I would refuse their invitation with the last breath in my body!'

He tried to get some sleep. Towards morning the noise died down.

★

Soon after daybreak the sixteen cardinals attended the traditional masses. Before they were finished the words were drowned by renewed shouting outside. Then an unnerving, battering, brazen-throated clash-and-clang started up in the tower of St. Peter's close by.

'Why are those bells ringing like that?' the Cardinal of Brittany asked his colleague Tebaldeschi, who, as Cardinal of St. Peter's, might be expected to know.

'It is for the catachumens, or perhaps for the exorcism,' the old man answered vaguely.

In a momentary pause the bells of the Capitol could be heard in the distance, ringing in the same way. Cardinal Noëllet, who had been Geneva's predecessor in the Romagna, knew the sound and what it meant. It was a sound all too familiar in Italian cities. The bells were being hammered *a stormo*. It was the signal for the populace to rise in arms.

'I think I can guess who is going to be exorcised,' he remarked as steadily as he could.

Another cardinal sent his servant up on to the roof. The man reported that huge crowds were converging from every side.

The clamour continued and grew yet more insistent. The so-called guardians passed an urgent message through the window of the conclave. Their charitable advice, as Gibbon calls it, was that if those inside did not immediately choose a Roman or an Italian pope they would all be cut in pieces.

'Hurry! We can see the danger more clearly than you can.'

At first Cardinal Aigrefeuille parleyed with them. Then he and Orsini dragged the senior cardinal, Florence, to the window, and the three of them promised to satisfy the crowd's demands within twenty-four hours. The crowd howled its objection to any such delay. Orsini was the coolest. As they stepped back from the window, Aigrefeuille clutched at his cloak.

'Come along, come along, my lord! I for one am ready to elect an Italian or a Roman or the Devil himself, rather than die like this!'

Their colleagues made them go back and promise to satisfy the crowd that very day, if only they would withdraw from the court-yard or at least keep quiet, so that the cardinals could hear one another.

At that the noise abated a little. What happened next inside the conclave is, of course, disputed. It was an undignified and confusing episode, and, afterwards, the reticence of those who were there was more than matched by the inventiveness of those who were not.

Florence, due to give the opening address, declared that he could find no words to do so. Limoges and Peter said that to elect anyone under these conditions would only produce a schism. Cardinal Flandrin replied that to refuse to elect anybody would have the same result, for the Romans would kill those who refused and force the survivors to elect whomsoever they wished, whereupon the cardinals who had stayed behind at Avignon would elect an-other. If, on the other hand, they were to elect someone now in accordance with the crowd's wishes, they could re-elect him properly later on, when they were in safety.

Did Flandrin mean re-elect him, or hold a new election altogether?

Others objected. They could not agree. They rose to their feet and began to walk up and down the chapel. Several were in favour of yielding to the crowd rather than risk death. Seeing this, Limoges and Peter suggested Prignano. They had evidently been convinced by Flandrin's argument. The idea was well received, save by Orsini, who still refused to vote under these conditions. Noëllet said his own vote was obviously valueless because of the intimidation, and Florence and Brittany showed great reluctance.

Peter tells us that, though he had not intended to vote for an Italian, he was content at this stage that Prignano should be pope. If, however, the cardinals were unwilling to re-elect him properly later, he took it that Prignano would have to resign. But clearly there was no orderly, general discussion at all, particularly on this last point.

Someone, in all likelihood Aigrefeuille, called the meeting to order.

'My lords,' he said loudly, 'Let us sit down at once, for I am sure we shall very soon have a pope.'

Orsini disliked being steam-rollered, though he did not know the expression. He accordingly suggested a stratagem.

'My lords,' he proposed, 'let us postpone the election and deceive these Romans. I know of a reliable friar who will serve our purpose. Why not send for him, invest him with the cope and mitre, and pretend that we have elected him pope? Then we shall be able to withdraw to some safer place and hold a genuine election.'

Orsini's suggestion was felt to be too undignified. Things had not yet gone that far. But some Italian it must be. Florence suggested old Tebaldeschi, the Cardinal of St. Peter's, the only other Roman besides Orsini.

As the uproar outside was getting louder, Limoges decided to bring matters to a head.

'The Cardinal of St. Peter's is a good and saintly man,' he declared, 'but in the first place he is a Roman, and to choose one would be to yield too obviously to the populace, and secondly he is too old and infirm. He is therefore not suitable. You, my lord Orsini, are also a Roman, and apart from that you are too young and not impartial enough; it shall certainly not be you. The Cardinal of Milan comes from Visconti's territory, and the Cardinal of Florence too from a city which is hostile to the Church, so it cannot be either of them. In fact no Italian in the Sacred College is suitable. But I propose that we elect someone who cannot be seriously objectionable to the people and who, we have reason to hope, will be ready to follow our wishes. These conditions I can see fulfilled by one person alone, and that is Bartolommeo Prignano, the Archbishop of Bari. He is of mature age, well over fifty. He has great administrative experience, having spent more than fourteen years in the service of the Curia. His blameless life, integrity in office and upright character are well known. I therefore cast my vote for him.'

Did Limoges really say quite all this, with a riot going on just outside? It reads a little too much like a speech put into his mouth by somebody who favoured Prignano, which is what in fact it is. Yet it seems clear that he spoke the decisive words, whatever they were and in whatever sense they were understood (or even heard) by the others.

Did he add that he voted for Prignano freely, 'intending and willing that he should become the true pope'? And, if so, why? Were the words intended to rebut the idea that this was only a fake election, or a provisional one? And how many of the cardinals who followed him qualified their voting with these or other words, and what did each of them intend? And did they only vote for Prignano out of fear, as they claimed afterwards? And did they or some of them assume that the learned and docile Archbishop Prignano could not fail to understand that such an election was uncanonical, and therefore no election? And did they say among themselves, while still there in conclave, 'that as soon as they could they would move to a safe place, and then they would hold a fresh election'?

No one knows. All these questions and many others, after centuries of special pleading, still hang in the air. It all adds up to a great deal less than certainty.

At any rate, in one sense or another, enough of them voted for Prignano. There was no serious discussion of his merits, that is certain. Nor was there any secret ballot. Limoges was followed by Aigrefeuille and other Frenchmen and, the tenth to vote, by Peter. Orsini abstained, giving the obvious intimidation as a reason.

It was nearly lunch-time. They agreed not to announce the result at once, for they wanted time to hide their plate and valuables, and Prignano was not in the Vatican and would have to be fetched from some distance. Meanwhile rumours spread outside. The noise grew to a fresh crescendo. The panic-stricken guardians hammered once more on the door, imploring them to elect a Roman before they were all killed. Only a Roman would satisfy the crowd now. And indeed 'Romano lo volemo!' was the prevailing cry by this time; only a few still shouted for a possible Italian alternative.

Three cardinals went out on the balcony to reason with the mob. Orsini, linguistically the best equipped of the three, addressed his fellow-citizens. Did he say, as one right reverend eye-witness deposed: 'Listen, Romans, if by this evening you have not got a pope with whom you are pleased, I will let you tear me in pieces.'? Or did he, to follow the sworn evidence of another equally venerable prelate, remark: 'You Roman pigs, with your impudent demands, get out of here! When the conclave is over I am coming to chase you with my stick!' At any rate we can take it that he addressed them as Romans, and that his words had no perceptible effect. The Bishop of Marseilles was heard above the din, shrieking in his native French, *Allez à Saint-Pierre!* Thinking that he meant that Cardinal Tebaldeschi of St. Peter's had been elected, part of the crowd rushed off to plunder his house, as was the good old Roman custom.

Then Prignano and some other prelates arrived, fighting their way through the crowd. They ate in the Vatican but naturally outside the conclave. Someone noticed the Bishop of Marseilles treating Prignano with unusual deference. Doubtless the Bishop had heard the news somehow and was the first to tell him.

Lunch within the conclave was a confused meal. The food arrived late. They dined in small groups, Glandève and Viviers with Peter in his cell. Peter's conclavist sat next to the impressionable Glandève.

'Dean,' the latter burbled portentiously in Fernando's ear, 'I wish you to know that I have acted through fear. Yes, you have heard me right. I have acted as I did through the fear of death.'

'Is not Your Eminence exaggerating a little? My lord de Luna seems to be quite calm.'

'How can he be calm? How can anybody be calm? Have you not realised the danger we are in?'

When lunch was over a majority met again in the chapel and 're-elected' Prignano. It was Tebaldeschi's idea. Obviously they regarded the morning's results as dubious. But how could repeating the performance make it any more valid? The circumstances had not changed, except that this time seven of the cardinals were absent—Orsini, the three at Peter's table and a similar trio of Frenchmen.

While they were still engaged in this second election, the end came. The crowd began to shout, 'We have been betrayed! They have not elected a Roman!' mixed with other cries of 'Kill them! Cut them in pieces!' They took to throwing stones. Then they charged the doors. The luckless Bishop of Marseilles made a last attempt to calm them. A Roman drew his sword on him, screaming that he too was a traitor. The Bishop bolted to his own room and stayed there, the guard gave way and the howling mob surged into the Vatican. Some of the bannerets seemed to be leading them. Attacking the inner openings with heavy iron implements, they burst into the conclave itself like a tidal wave, entering from several points at once. They bawled threats and brandished weapons in the cardinals' faces.

'By the nailing up of God, we want a Roman! We have been cheated! Do you want to die, or will you make a Roman pope? *Romano lo volemo! Per lo clavellato di Dio!*'

'Quick! Into the inner chapel!'

Most of the cardinals and their conclavists took refuge there. Peter stayed where he was.[7] Five others dropped through a hole in the floor, where their servants had already taken their valuables. But there were Romans everywhere. They were caught and brought back to the chapel. The door of the inner chapel yielded too, as every other door had done, but not before Brittany had an idea. At his suggestion they instantly agreed to pretend that they had elected old Tebaldeschi. They had chosen Prignano in order to appease, when the cry had still been 'Roman or Italian', but the time for such half-measures was past. Nothing less than a full-blooded Roman would save them now.

Why did they not announce Prignano? Only someone who has never even seen a British football crowd in an ugly mood can ask such a question. Mobs do not stop to reason or accept compromises. Unless this Roman mob could be made to believe that its uttermost demands had been met, the lives of the French cardinals would not be worth a black penny of the Senate. And there had already been a rumour that morning that Tebaldeschi had been chosen. It would be believed the more readily now.

As the door gave way, with their backs to the wall, they pushed forward the protesting old man, saying that he was still unwilling to be pope and asking the crowd to persuade him. Amid delirious excitement he was clothed with the white mitre and the white silk cope and enthroned, still protesting ineffectively, while more and ever more of the populace squeezed into the chapel to kiss his feet and see if there was anything left to plunder.

His gout tortured him. His denials were inaudible. The Cardinal of Marmoutier held him down. He tried to shake off the mitre and succeeded once or twice, but the gesture was only taken for an edifying excess of modesty.

Again and again the Romans implored his blessing.

'*Maledetti siate tuttiquanti!*'

Only the nearest cardinals heard the senile execrations distinctly. The religious and patriotic ardour they inspired in all others present, however, served to cover the cardinals' retreat. Leaving everything behind, even their copes, they slipped out. Two or three reached their houses in safety. Four others never stopped until they were far outside Rome. The Cardinal of Brittany had the rings pulled off his fingers before he was half-way across St. Peter's Square. Reaching his house at last, he and his chaplain climbed on to the roof and hid behind a chimney, where the chaplain heard his confession while the mob broke into his rooms and his possessions were auctioned to passers-by in the street below. Late that night he and five others managed to reach the Castel Sant'Angelo in disguise.

Peter kept his head better than most. He did his best to calm the horde in the main chapel and left last of all. He was a small man and a Roman friend had to help to extricate him. Then an escort was obtained from the banneret and some of his more reliable followers. As they rode down towards the Ponte Sant'Angelo, under the walls of the castle, the French garrison thought he was being abducted by the Romans and tried to rescue him. Arrows whizzed through the evening air, the cry went up that the French were attacking peaceful Roman citizens, the alarm spread in all directions and the great bells of St. Peter's clamoured yet again. Eventually, after much ineffectual signalling by Peter and the banneret, the misunderstanding was cleared up, and Peter, refusing to take refuge in the castle, went on over the bridge and through the maze of narrow streets to his own house.

Prignano remained in the Vatican. Old Tebaldeschi had at last managed to make some of his compatriots understand that he was not really the pope. If anybody was, it was Prignano. He advised the latter to stay in hiding and not to leave the palace until things were back to normal. Prignano followed his advice. When some over-excited Romans suggested that he should be made to renounce his election, if indeed he had been elected, he could not be found. Some time later, when one of the guardians told him of this, the little Archbishop rejected the idea with unwonted vigour.

'They do not know me,' he declared. 'Even if they had held a thousand swords at my throat, I would not have renounced my election.'

When somebody told the Cardinal of Geneva of this answer, a week or so afterwards, he laughed for so long that the witness was amazed. Had he, perhaps, threatened poor Prignano with an even worse fate if he did not do what was required of him?

The riot died down and the Vatican grew quiet again, but Prignano did not sleep. He paced up and down in the dark in his little room in the almost deserted palace and hugged to himself the idea that he was pope. Had he not been waiting for years for the cardinals to treat him as a social equal? Now he was their superior. He tingled with excitement. The thing was beyond his wildest hopes. But not beyond his deserts! With what reverence must not a pope be treated? What could not a pope do? He, Bartolommeo Prignano, who had for so long been Their obedient Servant, he would show them!

# CHAPTER 3

# The Schism

WAS Prignano, as a result of these proceedings, the lawfully elected successor of St. Peter?

'This episcopal tumult,' writes Gibbon of an earlier turning-point in Church history, 'at the distance of thirteen centuries, assumes the venerable aspect of the Third Œcumenical Council.' That is the charm of Church history, how much it loses in dignity and gains in human interest when viewed close up.

Some previous medieval conclaves, before this one of 1378, had been almost equally remarkable. Several, for instance, lasted for over two years, one was interrupted by arson, and in 1271 divine inspiration only came after the impatient townsfolk of Viterbo had removed the roof from the building where the cardinals sat awaiting it. That a particular election was fantastic by our standards does not, of course, necessarily mean that it was invalid. On a wide enough view, it is possible that the Holy Ghost may work as effectively through a mob's frenzy or a roof's removal as through the sober deliberations of devout and single-minded cardinals in happier times. At least it would be impossible to prove the contrary, though it may strike some minds as being a shade less probable.

On the other hand the organised Church by the end of the Middle Ages had acquired a great many rules, set forth with a fair degree of clarity in the ever-growing body of canon law. What has to be considered is whether there was a breach of those rules as understood at the time. Even if we discount what seem to be embroideries and exaggerations, such as the story of spears thrust up into the conclave between the floor boards, or of faggots piled up ready to burn the cardinals, common sense would suggest that

E

there was such a breach. But here too the experts give us as varying answers today as they did then. Canon law, apparently, is a less exact science than one might imagine. In general Italians and the more fervent papalists say that the election was valid, while many French scholars and liberals say that it was not. When the experts disagree, can one take sides? Can we agree with the dictum that Prignano was elected 'in fear, but not through fear'? Noël Valois' opinion, that 'the solution of the problem escapes the judgment of history', seems less of a quibble.

Is it likely that the aristocratic French cardinals, if they had been genuinely free to choose, would have chosen the low-born Italian Prignano to be their master or have imagined that he would take them back to Avignon? A return to Avignon was certainly the most pressing issue at stake. And could even a medieval conclave stomach irregularities which would be enough to disqualify an election in the brashest of banana-republics or the most unwisely liberated of colonies today? May we not at least hold that, even in the Rome of 1378, no one had any right at all *at that stage* to be certain that Prignano was the true pope? Such is the view of modern Catholic scholars like Seidlmayer and Seppelt.

Unfortunately the cardinals bedevilled the issue still further.

\*

Among those present in Rome at the time was Nicolas Eymeric, the Inquisitor-General of Aragon. For the past forty-eight hours he had not left his lodgings. He was a man who had learnt how to take care of himself from long and detailed observation of those who had not.

His private network ensured that he was among the first to hear the news of Prignano's election. Soon after daybreak he sent a scout to St. Peter's Square. All was quiet. He set forth to pay his respects to the new pontiff, and found him walking in a covered gallery on an upper floor. Only two cardinals, Florence and Milan, were with him as yet. Eymeric had timed it nicely.[8]

'Ah! I am glad you have come, Inquisitor!'

The visitor got down on the floor to kiss the new foot, but its owner interrupted him.

'No, no! Nothing is final yet. But I am delighted to see you.'

They embraced as near equals. Eymeric noticed a constraint in the atmosphere. The two Italian cardinals were standing a little apart from their pope, as if bewildered or embarrassed. If there had been any conversation between them it had dried up. The Inquisitor, who never went anywhere without a purpose, judged the moment right to broach some confidential matter in which both Prignano and he were interested. Prignano interrupted him again.

'So far nothing is final, nothing is final. You must not speak to me about anything.'

Complete silence fell upon all four.

Presently another cardinal appeared and addressed Prignano.

'My lords say they are unable to come.'

'Why can't they come?'

'Because they haven't got their copes.'

'They haven't got their copes? Let them come in rochets, then. It is absolutely essential that they should come.'

The cardinal remained silent and stood his ground. So did everyone else.

After another long, uncomfortable pause, one of the bannerets arrived. He had plainly been sent on the same errand and had failed too.

Prignano called to some of the cardinals' secretaries at the far end of the gallery. He took hold of the cloak of the first man to reach him.

'This cope is good enough for a cardinal.'

He did the same to three or four others and raised his voice.

'Take them off! Take off those copes!'

He turned to the banneret.

'Take those copes to them! They must come, they must come. They must be made to come whatever happens!'

No one answered. No one took off his cope. Each person present seemed rooted to the spot and buried in his own thoughts. The Inquisitor judged that the right moment had come for him to leave.

★

In the Castel Sant'Angelo the situation was a parallel. It was clear to one person only.

Six French cardinals, utterly exhausted by their experiences, had sought refuge in the castle some time after midnight and had gone to bed. Having seen them arrive, the Camerlengo had made his mind up. Whatever else might have happened, this disgraceful scrimmage could not have produced a lawful pope.

Early next morning Prignano's first messsengers were knocking at the gate. The six cardinals were requested to come to the Vatican at once.

The Camerlengo appeared at the gate with a battle-axe in his hand. The Roman messengers repeated Prignano's words.

'What does the fool think he is doing?' asked the Camerlengo truculently. 'Does he imagine he is pope? He is no more pope than I am.'

Then his elder brother the Cardinal of Limoges appeared behind him.

'Be quiet. Of course he is the pope.'9

One thing at least was certain. They would not leave the castle. The streets were unsafe.

'I'll make them come,' said Prignano when he heard this news.

The bannerets had already accepted him as pope. At his bidding municipal officers were sent to all the various houses in the city where the cardinals lived. Soon they were knocking at Peter's door in the Via Tor Sanguigna.

Peter had not yet got up. He was lying in bed thinking hard about the previous day's work. The more he thought, the less he liked it. Prignano might make a good pope, but he would need a better procedure than yesterday's to make him a pope at all. One thing was plain. It would be advisable to see what the others did before he committed himself. After all he was the most junior of all the cardinals.

He asked young Fernando to tell them to go away. He was indisposed. But they insisted. Peter reluctantly got up and listened to floods of Roman oratory. As the stream of explosive *b*s and gritty *l*s battered at his ears, he thought it was the worst morning after he had known. He must come to the palace at once, they told him. Prignano was waiting for him, trusted him, looked on him as his

particular friend among the cardinals. At last they went away. Then
the worthy Don Alfonso arrived on the same errand. Then a second
municipal delegation, this time with an official request from the
S.P.Q.R. Again he made lame excuses. Finally a third delegation,
this time a banneret, two officials and a posse of fifteen armed
men.

'My lord, it is essential that you should go, and we have orders
from the Roman authorities not to leave you until we have brought
you to the Vatican.'

'What is the meaning of that? Do you mean you have orders to
take me there by force? You have no authority to do that, nor have
all the Romans put together!'

Fernando drew Peter aside.

'What are you saying, Your Eminence? Don't you see you are
endangering yourself and all the rest of us in your household too?
Why not make the best of a bad business, rather than put us all in
danger of death? Better still, Your Eminence, if you think it advisable, keep these Romans waiting here and ring the bell for the
horses to be saddled, and I will go quickly to the Castel Sant'Angelo
and find out what the other cardinals are doing.'

Peter agreed. When Fernando got there, the six cardinals told him
that if his master thought he could reach the Vatican without being
killed on the way, they advised him to go. For their part they had
sent a proxy empowering their colleagues to enthrone Prignano
in their name. Limoges' views had evidently prevailed over the
Camerlengo's.

When Fernando brought this news to Peter, he decided to go.
It was already past midday. He arrived 'very late', as someone
remarked disapprovingly, and found several of his fellow-cardinals
already there, and Prignano behaving pontifically and dressed for
the part. It only remained to do him homage, the more easily done
since Peter at least had voted for him sincerely.

Prignano's envoys went on working all day. At last they persuaded the cardinals in the castle to come too. The latter yielded,
as they explained later, 'because they had grown tired of refusing,
and because all their possessions and households were scattered about
the city, and because the castle would soon run short of food and
was not very safe'.

By now twelve of them had assembled. The other four, including Geneva and Orsini, had disappeared from Rome. The twelve went into the inner chapel with worried faces. In a few minutes they summoned Prignano and he walked firmly to the door. His diffidence, as several people noticed, was a thing of the past. After a very brief interval the chapel door opened again and the cardinals went through the ceremony of enthroning a pope. He took the name of Urban, a clear sign that the move to Avignon was off. Cardinal de Vergne, presumably as homesick as any Frenchman among them, proclaimed him to the people from the window.

'I have joyful tidings to announce to you. We have a Pope called Urban VI.'

After that the ceremonies continued daily, including one when a fresh bull of excommunication was published on the steps of St. Peter's against the Church's enemies, and they all snuffed out their tall thin candles and threw them down for a sign against the contumacious city of Florence. Peter had a long audience with the new Pope and emerged fairly hopeful. By a fortnight after the conclave the other four cardinals were back too, though with rather a bad grace, and all sixteen joined in the coronation and in the customary mounted procession to the Lateran.

The procession neglected none of the traditional observances. In the Campo dei Fiori the Jews offered the scroll of the Law and were duly rebuffed with Christian words about 'the blinded people of Judah', upon which the soldiers used their long leather whips and the pious crowd hooted the rabbis down the side-streets into the ghetto. The cavalcade made the customary detour near San Clemente to avoid that street of ill omen where, as everyone believed at that time, the unfortunate Pope Joan had given premature birth to her baby on a similar public occasion in the ninth century. And in the Lateran portico Prignano, or Urban as we must now call him, seated himself on the *sedia stercoraria*, the porphyry commode. This was a ceremony of great antiquity, popularly believed to have its origin in a physical inspection to make sure that the Pope Joan episode would not be repeated. The crowd went wild with excitement, and somebody trod on the Cardinal of Marmoutier's toe. They raised Urban from his embarrassing seat with the text, 'He lifteth the poor out of the mire', and the procession continued on its dignified way to revere the Apostles' heads in their silver reliquaries.

Finally there was a banquet. The Cardinal of Brittany was surprised that Urban drank so much and ate so little.

'And how are you this morning, my lord?' a Spanish prelate asked the still panting Glandève next day. 'Your Eminence had a lot of work to do yesterday.'

'Exhausted, quite exhausted. But for the chicken and the other refreshments which our lord the Pope gave us at the Lateran, and excellent wine above all, the worst, the very worst would have happened to us.'

In short, things were back to normal. That is the strange and deplorable fact. Outwardly at least the cardinals proclaimed Urban as pope and continued to treat him as such for the next three months, writing letters to Avignon and to the courts of Europe to announce his election, and soliciting various benefices and favours from him.

If electors acquiesce in the result of an unfree or dubious election, for the sake of peace and quiet or from any other unheroic motive, does that make the election valid retrospectively? Not according to modern ideas; too many dictatorships have started that way. Can it be assumed that the Holy Spirit acts retrospectively? Not with confidence. What does canon law say? Its voice is uncertain. But do the electors, having kept silent and misled the world, lose their moral right to rebel later on? Some authorities have held that they do. By accepting Prignano as Urban VI the cardinals did not make his claim a good one, but they greatly weakened their own case against him.

\*

'They say the new Holy Father is an alarming man,' wrote a worthy Italian abbot a little anxiously to Catherine at Siena. 'His manner and words fill people with terror. Apparently he has the utmost confidence in his divine office and therefore fears no man, and it is clear that his aim is to root out simony and the craze for magnificent living.'

He spoke less than the truth. From the beginning, life with Urban was extremely difficult. One might forgive the slight exaggeration in his first encyclical, when he announced that his electors had been unanimous and 'inspired by the Holy Ghost, with a concord rare indeed', if what concord there was had lasted for longer than the day after his coronation. On that day, during a service in the Vatican chapel, he stormed at the bishops who had come to pay him homage, calling them hirelings who had deserted their flocks. Many of them were senior Curia officials, absent from their titular sees (as they muttered to each other in the corridors afterwards) for precisely the same reason that Prignano himself had been absent from Acerenza and Bari. One of them, Martin de Salva, a Spaniard and an acquaintance of Peter, protested vigorously and offered to resign. Then a papal tax-collector who had come to present his accounts was denounced as a simonist and cursed with the text, 'Thy money perish with thee!' Addressing the assembled cardinals and prelates, the Pope condemned their way of life in violent terms, and soon afterwards cut their dinners down to a single course. He called Limoges a liar, Orsini a fool and Geneva a bandit. When the Prince Consort of Naples came to congratulate him, he deliberately kept him waiting on his knees at a banquet, holding out a cup until the pontiff might deign to take it from him. To the Queen's ambassadors he said that she ought to be put into a nunnery and her kingdom given to the French. He was capricious in money matters, delayed repaying a loan made by the Emperor, and refused ever to repay another loan of 20,000 florins made by the Count of Fondi; instead he took away one of the latter's titles and gave it to the Count's enemy. When the scholarly Cardinal of Milan dared to correct him on a point of law concerning excommunication, with which penalty he had been wildly threatening everybody in sight, he jumped up and screamed, 'I decree it! I can do everything!'

At another consistory he tried to beat Limoges, and Geneva had to hold him down on his throne to prevent it. Then he hurled baseless charges at Cardinal de Lagrange, who had been away negotiating with Florence. Lagrange was blinded by yellow money, he had filled his purse corruptly, he had prolonged war instead of making peace, he had committed every evil deed under the sun.

'Now that you have become Pope,' replied Lagrange to this tirade, 'I may not answer you back, but if you were still the *archi-episcopellus*, the little Archbishop of Bari, as you were not many days ago, I would tell the *archiepiscopellus* that he is a damned little liar!'

What had become of the hard-working, the pettifogging, the self-effacing civil servant? Was the sudden promotion from dogsbody to supreme pontiff more than he could take? Did the coronation ceremonies unhinge his reason? Had he been reading too much of Augustinus Triumphus?

Whatever it was, it could not be kept a secret. On the Tuesday after he became Pope a party of Curia jurists, marshalled by their senior, an Englishman named Robert Stratton, were trotting up the steps of St. Peter's. Suddenly the Cardinal of Milan appeared in the doorway and came down the steps towards them, his face showing unwonted agitation.

'Where are you all going?'

'We are going to do reverence to His Holiness,' Stratton replied.

'To him . . .!' exclaimed the gentle old Italian cardinal, raising both hands and his eyes to heaven. 'To him! Oh Lord, help Thy Church!'

★

Pierre de Gaudelin, Castellan of the Castel Sant'Angelo, was a professional soldier from the Dauphiné and a man of character. He took his cue from his friend the Camerlengo and refused to give up the stronghold to Urban. His depositions in Latin and Provençal make amusing and sometimes illuminating reading.[10]

Urban and his Roman allies wanted the castle badly. It contained the papal treasure, and its independence was a standing proof that all did not accept Urban at his face value. They tried fair words, bribery, everything. At last Urban sent his hostages to the castle—his own nephew, the Senator's, and somebody else's nephew for good measure. Then the Castellan made his way up to the Vatican.

'Welcome, my Castellan, I am really delighted to see you. I admire your prudence . . .' and the Pope moved on quickly to financial considerations. Despite his well-advertised aversion to such matters, he handled them in great detail. The Castellan heard him out.

'My lord, if I do what you ask, it will look as if I have given up the castle for money.' And he mentioned the oath he had taken not to hand over the castle without the consent of those cardinals who were still at Avignon.

Urban interrupted him.

'You are following the secret advice of those traitors the accursed Limousins. Do you know that I served under the Cardinal of Pamplona—Montirac, the Vice-Chancellor—for fourteen years, and I never had a good word from him? When he asked me to do some job he would never even deign to look me in the face. Instead of that he used to throw his orders at me with his back turned and mooing in that voice of his like a bull-calf. And I fear you will come to a bad end, Castellan, for one of these days the Romans will take all the cardinals and senior foreigners prisoner, and they will lead them in front of your castle and start chopping their heads off, and then you will have to surrender it.'

The Castellan's eyes opened wide. He saw how it had all happened. However, his immediate concern was the castle, not occupational psychology. He refused politely but quite firmly to bring dishonour on himself, even if Urban himself was going to lead the way. If anything like that were to happen, he explained, it would only make him join with others in a relentless struggle to destroy both Urban and his Romans.

The castle, less than half a mile from Urban's palace, remained a place where his writ did not run, a sign that his claims were not going to pass unchallenged.

*

Obedient to one of the more arbitrary decrees which came from the Vatican in these days, Peter had left his pleasant old house by the Tor Sanguigna and had moved into cramped and murky rooms next his titular church. It meant leaving a large building empty and displacing an elderly canon, but he was not going to argue about the minor follies of government. He spent much of his time in his new quarters, working by himself.

One morning young Fernando poked his long nose round Peter's door without knocking first. Peter had Gratian's *Decretum* open in front of him and was very busy making notes. He stopped and quickly put the paper away.

'Why are you trying to hide what you were writing, Your Eminence? I think I can guess what it's about. It's about the Pope and the cardinals, isn't it?'

Peter looked at the young man with some embarrassment. What a bad conspirator he, the Cardinal, would make. Like most of us until we try, he had imagined he might make rather a good one. Thank heaven no one else had found him at it.

'For the love of God, don't say anything about it,' he said very earnestly. 'Assuming that what you say is right, you must realise that it must not become known. If he or his Roman friends were to hear that I or any of my colleagues had doubts concerning his election, not one of us would escape. Seriously, Fernando, you must not breathe a word of this to a living soul.'[11]

This incident took place about three or four weeks after Urban's elevation. It is the first indication that Peter was beginning to share his colleagues' doubts.

The French cardinals were beginning to leave Rome. The city was already too hot, and one by one they obtained leave to go to Anagni in the hills. Before they left there were more outbursts of temper on Urban's part, and Geneva gave him a warning.

'It amounts to this, Holy Father. You refuse to treat your cardinals with the honour due to them, in the way your predecessors used to. You are undermining our status all the time. I must warn you, unless you stop it, you may be sure that we cardinals will do our best to cut you down to size.'

*Diminuere honorem vestrum.* It is difficult to do this to a pope unless he is repudiated altogether. But the cardinals acted with great caution. Even when they had all reached Anagni the twelve Frenchmen did nothing in a hurry, except to obtain discreet military protection from the Count of Fondi, that powerful landowner whom Urban had offended too. They held long discussions behind closed doors, got in touch with some reliable mercenaries and with their colleagues at Avignon, and put out tentative feelers in the direction of Paris. There, as their secret emissaries reported, Charles V and his advisers were far from enthusiastic about dethroning Urban, having other things to worry about, but at least they could be trusted to see that the French cardinals came to no harm. The news was disappointing, but better than nothing.

Peter, more conscientious than some of his colleagues and much slower at making his mind up, stayed on in his hot and cramped rooms in Rome. The more he thought about the problem, the more doubtful he grew. He had voted freely for Urban, and once they had all outwardly accepted him as pope, he had allowed himself to have great hopes that here was a man who would reform the Church. In fact he had come out strongly in his favour, and his early declarations of this kind, like a letter he made Fernando write to a friend at Avignon, have a slightly defiant ring about them, as if designed to forestall criticism of the new pontiff. But now his fellow-cardinals were dribbling away to Anagni, with guarded and highly confidential hints of their intentions, and he could no longer hide from himself the knowledge that Urban was not the man to reform the Church and, more important still, that if even a few of them besides Orsini had in fact not voted freely and genuinely for Urban, he had not been canonically elected either. And whether their subsequent behaviour could have remedied such a defect— that was a legal and a moral problem that defied his attempts to solve it.

Take Geneva's case. If anyone had been in favour of electing Prignano, in some sense, before the conclave started, it had been he. Yet as soon as it was over he had escaped from Rome and stayed away for well over a week. That he returned at all might well have been due to pressure. His remarks about Urban had been scathing. Had his vote for him, then, been a valid one?

Yet some of them, surely, must have voted genuinely for Urban. And Urban, though he was proving himself an unfortunate sort of reformer, was at least linked closely with the cause of reform. His most ardent supporters were Peter's new friends, people to whom religion meant more than a convenient ideology upholding the wealth and rights of great prelates. They were people whose sincerity Peter respected deeply and whose ideals he largely shared, though he thought them a little naïve as individuals. If Urban were truly the Pope, it would be infamous to desert him and them.

But Urban was incompetent. In a few weeks he had antagonised almost everybody who mattered, even many senior Italians, his natural supporters. He would not listen to a word of advice. Old Tebaldeschi, the only member of the College who still believed in him wholeheartedly, was dying. How could Urban hope to reform the Church or even to govern it effectively?

Peter was deeply interested in the theory of government. He had built up his career on his special knowledge of the subject. From this angle too Urban presented a problem. Given time, the professional bureaucrats might inherit the earth. But was this what happened when one of them did? If so, it was a bleak outlook. The bureaucrats would undermine hereditary power in its various forms, and all the idealists would support them. But what if the new rulers were unsuited to wielding supreme power by reason of the accumulated petty grievances they had to work off? Was there an Urban beneath every Prignano?

The summer wore on relentlessly, slowly paralysing thought. Through sticky Roman afternoons and unquiet Roman nights, whenever he tried to rest, the problem glared at him. Days and weeks went by and he could not decide. No news came from Anagni. Urban would do nothing. Every brain was addled. Even the futile war with Florence dragged on inconclusively. Rome was no longer venerable, but squalid. Those solid brown towers were a mockery.

Peter could face physical danger, but not uncertainty about fundamentals. He would have been lost in the world of today.

His idealistic friends kept pestering him. They were outside the inner circle and only saw Urban at a distance. What was the truth about all these rumours? He told the Prior of Santa Sabina that, in his own opinion, Urban had been genuinely elected, but that his conduct since then had been insupportable. But surely he was not thinking of joining the others at Anagni? asked Don Alfonso, as they walked in the little garden next his lodging.

Peter was at the end of his tether.

'Why should I stay here with our lord, when he does none of the things I am urging him to do? I would not even serve God, if he did not do something profitable for me!'[12]

It was a most unwise remark to make. Taken out of its context (as it very soon was) it sounds like a benefice-hunter's confession in a bad anti-clerical melodrama. Genuine benefice-hunters seldom talk like this, nor is there anything in Peter's life to make us think that he was that sort of person. So we must supply a context. Obviously they had been talking about the advice, whatever it was, that Peter had been pressing on Urban. To apologise to the cardinals? To resign? To submit to the decision of a General Council? Something like that. And Don Alfonso, in urging Peter to stay, may well have provoked the outburst by some innocent fatuosity, such as foreseeing a brilliant future for him at Urban's side.

At last he made up his mind to go to Anagni. As he told Alfonso he could serve the Pope better there than if he stayed in Rome.

And the Pope? The Pope was in bed and Dietrich von Niehein was reading to him.

Dietrich, as he tells us in his memoirs, had done his superior this little service for many years. Here they still were. Urban, relaxing after a day of rudeness and self-torment; Dietrich, dutifully reading. It is a curious glimpse, at once touching and a little absurd, like a second-rate fresco or an Edwardian snapshot.

Dietrich was about thirty, a Westphalian, round and solemn, dependable, owlish. He had been Prignano's personal assistant at Avignon, and now he perched loyally and deferentially behind the Pope. There was no change in the relationship between them, save that it was intensified. Urban exploited him, trusted him as he trusted very few and was fond of him in a curious way, while the basis of Dietrich's attitude to his leader was an unquestioning loyalty coupled with worry, worry lest a mistake of some sort should be made. He worshipped whatever was regular. In the meticulous routine of Avignon mistakes had been few, but now they were being made every day on a grand scale, and Dietrich's expression was more doleful than ever. He felt quite wrongly that people would blame him for these happenings.

He too had been observing the strange phenomenon of Urban with growing uneasiness. 'For a small man there is nothing worse than to rise to a great height unprepared,' he writes portentously. Now, after three months of it, very few cardinals were left—only Peter and the four Italians, in fact. Soon Urban, he feared, would be 'like a sparrow on the roof-top', left behind after the other birds had flown. But even then Dietrich would never dream of abandoning him. He had to a marked degree that peculiar, formalistic sense of loyalty still so common among his fellow-countrymen, a loyalty which transcends higher loyalties and common sense. Urban and he were *Schicksalsgenossen*, fate-companions. They would stay together whatever happened.

Peter had an intelligent Latin's loyalty to the workable truth. He had to find out whether Urban was truly the Pope. To do this, he must go to Anagni and interrogate his colleagues. There was no other way. If he found that Urban's election was valid, he would do his utmost to reconcile them to him. Urban must give him leave to go.

Both Peter and Urban had just received a letter from Catherine, and it is not unlikely that these letters had some effect on what they did. She wrote at least twice to Peter; her first letter was to complain about the Franciscans, but this second one shows that news of the crisis had reached her. Harking back without a doubt to their first conversation at Avignon, she tells him no less than three times to be a pillar which cannot be shaken.

> I have heard that discord has arisen down there between Christ on earth and his disciples. . . . I implore you never to give way for anything in the world, not even in the persecutions which are going to start up among you clerics. . . . Do not delay finding a remedy until the rock falls on our heads. . . . Be a man and a pillar which never gives way!

In her letter to Urban she assured him passionately of her own allegiance. The rest of it was so full of contradictions that even he may have noticed them. She told him to make peace with the Florentines, but never to trust a compromise. She told him to check his own hasty temper, but never to put ointment on a sore instead of burning it out with a red-hot iron. He must take firm steps to surround himself with a band of devoted helpers.

And here was yet another of them, trying to leave him?

Fortunately Urban was relaxed when Peter saw him. In that mood he seems to have realised that Catherine was over-fond of red-hot irons and that her gentler advice was the better. Peter received permission to go.

Peter was touched by his kindness—if it was that—but he found it exasperating too. Why had he not shown even a fraction of this dignity and wisdom earlier? It would have saved such a mountain of trouble.

Of course he knew nothing of schizophrenia. The concept would have shocked him deeply. A man had only one personality, just as he had only one soul. Anything else struck at the roots of Christian philosophy.

★

He left next morning. His small party rode through the Forum. Through the Arch of Titus, where he might glance up at that highly symbolic relief showing triumphant Romans carrying off the seven-branched candlestick from its place at Jerusalem, and with it the Church as well. Down the short slope towards the Colosseum. It crouched there in the dusty morning sun, a beast of prey, old, mangy, but still dangerous. On, as fast as might be, through the uncertain-tempered city, past the steel points glinting from observation posts and the dispirited parabolas of washing.

Out, at last, through a gaunt archway at the Porta Maggiore, where to Peter's great relief the guard let them pass without trouble. From there they made good speed along the Via Casilina, straight as a die towards the gap between the hills. The road was empty; only the broken aqueducts hurried back groggily in the opposite direction. As the road rose out of the plain they paused to rest the horses and drink bitter, watered wine from their goatskin bottles and to look back towards Rome, a blur in the heat-haze. How soon would he be back? It depended on what he found. Not very long, probably, in any case. They mounted again and went on at a comfortable trot uphill, and presently they met a patrol of the Count of Fondi's men, wild-looking fellows, shabbily turned out but well armed. These too let them pass. Some frontiers are deceptively easy to cross.

Geneva was there to welcome them at the gate of Anagni. Some of the College had thought Peter was never coming, but he knew better. A man cannot cut himself off from his own sort for ever.

At dinner everything was pleasant. The food was well chosen, the wines were French. Above all there was no sign of tension among the diners. Conversation was general and amusing. No one asked inconvenient questions. All made him welcome in the most natural way possible. Peter began to relax for the first time for months.

Back among his own sort. But was he? He thought hard about it as he went to bed that night. Yes and no. An irritating conclusion. Everything in life, it seemed, was yes and no.

Yes, because they knew how to behave. Three months at Urban's court had convinced him more than ever of the value of manners. Here at Anagni there was no need to fear that the social ground would give way under one's feet any minute, that some fissure would open and reveal squalid basements of the soul. Embarrassing at any time, and when that soul was the Vicar of Christ's it was more than one could stand. Here, up at Anagni, life could be dignified, at least on the surface. And that, to a Spaniard, is essential.

But no, because it was only on the surface. With their lack of foresight and principle, with their egotism and moral cowardice, these charming French noblemen, these gifted ecclesiastical careerists had split the Church, the one divine thing on earth, and they went on behaving like gentlemen. Not one of them felt remorse for his part in the dreadful thing which was happening. They were heartless. The whole age was heartless. At this moment, in that devastating revelation that comes to every sensitive person sooner or later, Peter realised that he did not belong anywhere, and never would. Montpellier had been too provincial for him (and he was ambitious). Avignon had been too corrupt (and he was fastidious). Rome was where he would have best liked to belong, but it was too chaotic for him (and he was neat). And Anagni? It would not last long enough to be worth the trouble of finding a suitable adjective. Then it would be either Rome or Avignon once again.

Next morning, after prayer, he looked at Anagni from a different angle. The question he had come to solve was not where he belonged, but to whom the lawful government of the Church belonged. There could be no 'yes and no' about that. Organised religion did not allow of 'yes and no'. There was a clear answer, and by training and position he was well qualified to find it.

He set to work. He argued with them, sometimes all together and sometimes separately, always systematically. They had two main arguments to support their case.

In the first place, only each one of them could know what it was that had moved him to vote as he did in the conclave. Somebody had to be believed, and there was no better evidence than the word

F

of each cardinal. And a majority solemnly assured Peter that the
motive force had been fear. Therefore Urban did not obtain the
required majority and had not been canonically elected. No
subsequent acts or omissions on their part could alter that basic fact.

Secondly, a General Council of the Church could not decide the
question because a pope must summon it, and there was no lawful
pope who could do so. To allow Urban to summon it, even if he
were willing to, would be an admission in his favour and would
prejudice the issue. Nor had a Council been called in similar circumstances in the past.

Peter took weeks with his researches. At length Geneva told
the Castilian ambassador that he was losing patience. They were
all agreed about Prignano, he declared, all of them save Peter de
Luna, and yet he wanted more time to study the question. He was
being far too conscientious.

The ambassador asked Peter for his view of the matter.

'Don Alvaro, my lord of Geneva is complaining of me and says
I am too conscientious. Naturally I want to see where the right lies
and to be absolutely clear about it. For I tell you truthfully that if
I were to agree with them now and go to Avignon, and later on
I were to discover that he was the true, lawful Pope, I should go
back to him on my bare feet if that were the only way.'[13]

No one else said anything like that.

It is the clue to Peter's thought-processes in these last weeks. In
Rome his mind had been running along political channels. He had
come to Anagni to reconcile the cardinals with Urban. Now he
saw that this was impossible. The only question that remained was
the legal one.

Morally he thought that the cardinals had rather a poor case
But he was a canonist, not a moralist. His legal mind could find
no flaw in their two main arguments, try as he might. They were
watertight. There was nothing for it. Urban was not the true pope
Peter went over to the anti-Urbanists and never looked back.

He never saw Rome again.

He sent letters to his friends there and asked that his confessor
the Prior of Santa Sabina, should come and see him. The Prior ha
left us a full account of the interview.[14] On arriving at Anagni the
good man found him alone in a small room, temporarily furnished

a cheerless place of transit in which the Cardinal's much-travelled cat struck the only homely note.

Peter, looking more wan than when he had seen him last, came quickly to the point.

'I have sent for you, Father, so that you may hear my confession and so that I may console myself a little in your company. But first of all I must ask you if you think that the man at Tivoli' (Urban had moved there) 'is pope? For if you believe that, I am afraid you will not be able to absolve me.'

The quiet tone in which he said this was more than the Prior could stomach.

'Holy Mother of God!' he burst out. 'What is all this? Have you called me here to bear witness to the truth? For what you have just said is a falsehood. And I have something else to say, my lord Cardinal. Do not imagine that the things you told me earlier, in Rome, were just words written in water. If all of you here, now that you have come to this place, were to tell me the exact opposite of what you said before, I would not pay it any more attention than I would to that cat there playing with the flies on the wall.'

Peter was fond of his cat and did not see why it should be included in this commination. His confessor glared at him as if he could not believe his own ears.

'What on earth do you mean, then? How can you go back on what you said earlier? On what you said then, speaking so calmly, to me, to your faithful friend, to your beloved son, to your fellow-countryman?'

Peter flushed and collected his thoughts for a moment. This was being even more difficult than he had feared it would be. The Prior was a Spaniard, as he had just reminded him, and once a Spaniard gets an idea firmly into his head it is next to impossible to make him change it. Peter had the same difficulty himself.

'It is quite true,' he replied at last, speaking slowly and carefully, 'that I came here intending to reconcile them with him, and for my own part I know that I gave him my vote freely and willingly. But since I came here and have heard what my colleagues have to say, I have been forced to recognise that he is not pope at all. That is what I now believe, and I shall never believe anything else.'

The Prior jumped to his feet. The Devil had led them all astray, and Peter too. That was his opinion. Peter admitted quietly that it was a possibility, since he was only human. He made the Prior sit down again and tried to get him to follow his line of reasoning, showing patiently that it was a matter of evidence and probability, that only the individual can say where the frontier lies between accepting a *pis aller* and being intimidated. But the Prior fastened on to a sentence of Peter's, to the effect that but for Urban's wild conduct they would all still be with him. Did not this imply, he asked excitedly, that they acknowledged that the election had been valid? In vain Peter strove to show him that it meant nothing of the sort; it only meant that they might have accepted him as pope, though they knew his election had been irregular, if he had shown himself fit to rule the Church.

Peter had expected no better outcome of the argument. But the prospect of a schism appalled him. He begged the Prior to take a message from him to Urban and induce him to renounce his office voluntarily before it was too late. He paid his confessor's expenses and sent him back to Rome. But the single-minded Prior, when he reported to Urban, only urged him to 'beat down the ambitious hosts of the Devil'. Urban, of course, said he would.

The news of Peter's defection saddened his friends in Rome, and Don Alfonso in particular.

'I really do believe he went there with the best intentions,' he concluded, summing up what they all felt. 'He wanted to go fishing and catch the others, but oh dear me, he got caught on the hook himself.'

Events now moved quickly. Old Tebaldeschi died in Rome. The three remaining Italian cardinals tried to bridge the gap and, significantly, went the same way as Peter. From Anagni all the cardinals issued a declaration denouncing Urban and giving their version of events. This document skates over a few inconvenient facts, but it is less disingenuous than the rival account put out by Urban, which soft-pedals the riot to the extent of declaring blandly that 'complete silence reigned both outside and inside the palace' during the critical moments. Not even modern Urbanists—for there still are some—can bring themselves to accept this.

All sixteen cardinals moved to Fondi for greater safety, and there, on 20 September, in the Count's palazzo, they held a short conclave and elected the Cardinal of Geneva as their pope. The three Italians did not vote, but they were present at the election and did not oppose it. The others were unanimous. The new pope took the name of Clement VII, after his predecessor who transferred the Holy See to France.

They crowned him with the papal tiara and all the regalia. The Camerlengo, with commendable foresight, had stolen them from Urban's treasury.

Two popes competed for the allegiance of Christendom. The Great Schism had begun.

# CHAPTER 4

# *Spain*

FACED with the problem of two rival popes, elected within a few months of each other by the same cardinals, a simple solution springs to the modern mind, namely that neither of them was unquestionably legitimate and that therefore a vacancy or interregnum followed until the succession had been conclusively settled to the general satisfaction. It is an amusing comment on the perennial pugnacity of churchmen that in the course of six centuries this solution, which incidentally saves the dignity of the Holy See better than any other, has scarcely commended itself to anyone. At the time people felt it was somehow self-evident that one pope or the other was legitimate, and historians up to the present day have joined happily in the game of taking sides. Italians and clericals strongly favour Urban; anti-clericals and Frenchmen tend to support Clement. It would be against human nature to deny them both.

In 1378 the two sides wasted no time in making matters worse. Urban, no believer in half-measures, created twenty-nine new cardinals of his own, all in a single day's work. Several declined the honour (wisely as it turned out) and Catherine raised objections to some of the others. But Urban had a fresh College of Italians, tied to him by patriotism and self-interest.

The autumn air crackled as his spiritual thunderbolts passed Clement's travelling in the opposite direction. As these missiles proved singularly ineffective, both sides hired mercenaries. The result for the first seven months was a stalemate, since the mercenaries drew their pay and took care to do nothing to endanger further instalments.

Looking farther afield, the two sides dispatched letters and envoys to the courts and universities of Europe. In this respect Urban was badly served; some of his first emissaries in France and Spain spoke secretly in favour of the cardinals. Governments reacted cautiously. Even France held back at first, '*car la matière estoit trop haulte et périleuse et doubteuse*'. In universities, however, the response was gratifying. A number of eminent scholars hastened to put aside whatever useful work they were doing and to engage in propaganda that nowadays would scarcely deceive a child of ten. For instance Baldo, the light of Padua's famous faculty of law, triumphantly produced the following line of argument in favour of Urban, among a host of others. In the first place, he said, the cardinals were free, because they were free to elect any Italian they liked. They complained of fear, though whether they really felt fear no one can tell. But by saying that they had elected Urban through fear they admitted that they had *elected* him, i.e., that it was a true election. The fear was doubtful, but the election was not.

In justice to Baldo it must be said that a good deal of medieval thinking was like that. One suspects that the reasons for believing fervently in Urban's cause are not those alleged. The real conviction behind Urbanism, ancient and modern, is geographical. The pope residing in Rome must be the true one.

If the schism affected scholars in this way, what energies would it not release in Catherine's case? For nearly two years her talents had been wasted. She had gone back to her native Siena and dealt with convents and village clergymen, recalcitrant hermits, local feuds, small sinners. Gregory in his last year no longer listened to her, and Urban had ideas of his own. Was the rest of her life to be an anti-climax? Then came the news, in a tendentiously Urbanist version, of the French antipope's election. For the second time her hour had struck.

She wrote immediately to Urban, assuring him of her support. She wrote to Peter, telling him he must be a pillar. She wrote a blistering letter to the three Italian cardinals who had joined the other side.

> You would have us believe that you elected Pope Urban out of fear. He who says this is a liar! I speak to you without any respect, for you do not deserve it. . . . Fools, worthy of a thousand deaths! Blind men! Liars! Idolaters! . . . You were

present when the demons elected a demon. . . . Christ on earth is
an Italian, and you are Italians, so that not even patriotism
prompted you as it did the foreign cardinals. . . .

Then she came to Rome. She watched the pope of her choice as
he launched a fresh salvo of anathemas from the steps of St. Peter's.
His greatly reduced court made her welcome and wondered what
to do with her.

Someone suggested sending her on a mission to Naples, whose
gay and fickle Queen had transferred her allegiance to Clement.
She was to go with the other Catherine, Bridget's daughter Karin.
Hagiography, which should surely have jumped at the chance of
describing a meeting between the two St. Catherines, is strangely
silent. Can it be that even Rome was not big enough for them both? At
least we know that Karin was fourteen years older than the Sienese
prophetess and that she altogether lacked her fiery qualities. And her
last meeting with Queen Joanna had not been a success. To Karin's
relief and Catherine's great annoyance the mission was cancelled.

Catherine's next plan was to make all the hermits and holy men
of central Italy come to Rome and demonstrate in Urban's favour.
To this end she dictated a fresh batch of letters. The hermits, however, showed a most improper reluctance to leave their meditations
and their cool forests in order to plunge into the dusty streets and
dubious polemics of Rome. An English hermit in particular flatly
refused to come. Catherine found this inexplicable. She was at least
as much of a political busybody as a mystic. To her a crisis in the
visible Church was all-important. Why should this Englishman
prefer his ilex-wood? 'There are woods here, too,' she wrote to
him furiously, glancing through her visionary eye-slits at the treeless
Campagna.

Another plan. Her faithful Fra Raimondo should go to France!
She saw the poor man off on the next boat to leave the Tiber.
When the news came that he had turned back at the French border
to avoid certain martyrdom, she was bitterly disappointed.

But Catherine achieved her own martyrdom, though in a less
spectacular way than she would have wished. In those seventeen
months in Rome as Urban's propagandist she literally drove herself
to death. If her judgment was indiscriminate, so was her courage.
She was a saint and a fighter.

Her letters went out in every direction. To the rulers of Florence, telling them to pay Urban what he said they owed him. To Urban's mercenaries, telling them they might keep their loot with a good conscience. To Queen Joanna, telling her of what awaited her in the next world if she died a heretic. To the Queen's ambitious and ungrateful nephew, telling him to come with a Hungarian army and conquer Naples from her; to the King of France, telling him that self-love is the root of all evil; to Fra Raimondo, telling him he had found a way to throw down his burden on the ground. One of her disciples gives us a glimpse of her dictating four letters simultaneously. 'She dictated now to one secretary and now to another, sometimes hiding her face in her hands, and then gazing up to heaven with her hands clasped together, and all the time she was wrapt in ecstasy, yet she went on dictating.'

It could not go on for ever. One day, as she entered the porch of St. Peter's and looked up at Giotto's mosaic of St. Peter as a fisherman, the Ship of the Church slid down out of the mosaic on to her shoulders, on to hers alone, and its weight crushed her to the ground. After this last vision the end came quietly. She was no more than thirty-three when she died. They buried her in Santa Maria sopra Minerva, the only Gothic church in Rome, built by the Preaching Friars over the shrine of a militant goddess.

*

The road south threaded purposefully through the hills. On either side the first of the almond blossom gave proof that the year had turned. Far behind, already out of sight, lay Fondi and all the intrigues and improvisations of a papal court in exile. In front the road to Naples unrolled at the discreet pace of two well-fed, well-trained animals bearing a bishop and a cardinal legate.

Each mile disclosed more that the two men had in common. Both were deeply thankful to have left Fondi, a headquarters half reorganised, overloaded with new fiats and constant changes of plan. Both found the relief and the spring day loosening their tongues. Both were glad they could talk at last in their own forceful, idiomatic Spanish instead of in Church Latin, a useful language in its way but a grey one, rendered cliché-ridden by centuries of bureaucratic usage and slightly embarrassing by the knowledge that humanist scholars were beginning to laugh at it. Both were on their way to Spain, to new and important tasks in their own country. They respected what they knew of each other and were anxious to learn more, for both perceived, as good politicians, that they would need each other in the months and years which lay ahead.

Until now they had seldom come together, for Peter had not left the Curia since his appointment, while the Bishop had been serving in the diplomatic branch. The Bishop's title and its emoluments were Gregory's last reward to a resolute if somewhat unimaginative envoy; the see, Pamplona in northern Spain, had once been old Montirac's before he became a cardinal. Absentee benefices were the normal means of providing a livelihood for papal civil servants. If the see was neglected, that was not the holder's fault. But though Pamplona saw nothing of Martin de Salva, headquarters saw little of him either. He was usually away conducting long and tedious negotiations with the Florentines or, latterly, short and explosive ones with Urban. From this last mission he had been lucky to escape with his life, for Urban, who had an excellent memory for that sort of thing, had marked him down ever since Martin had reacted sharply to one of his tirades in the Vatican. On that occasion Martin, reporting back from his arduous diplomatic exchanges, had not been willing to let Urban rave at him as a hireling shepherd who had deserted his flock in distant Pamplona—particularly since Urban himself, or Prignano as he had been in his civil servant days, had never dreamed of abandoning his own desk in order to visit his titular sees in the south of Italy. Martin had pointed this out in plain language, offering to take the first ship to Spain and more congenial duties at Pamplona if that was what Urban really wanted.

The storm blew over, but he was not forgiven. When he appeared several months later as the cardinals' envoy with an ultimatum, Urban's immediate reaction was to lodge him in the most toad-infested dungeon at his disposal, pending further penalties. Then, after a few days, with the unaccountability of a schizophrenic, he let him out again. And now his rival, Pope Clement, though less as a matter of principle than from a shrewd appreciation of where such a man could help him best, was sending the unchallengeable pre-schism Bishop of Pamplona to take charge of his own neglected bishopric at last.

For the crisis had brought about a sea-change in the lives of senior papal officials. Both sides were sending them out in all directions as missionaries to the hesitant governments of Europe. Who was to get which posting, and how he would be received when he got there, were virtually the sole topics of conversation in Rome and at Fondi. Some appointments carried promise of vast convivialities, others of something closely approaching martyrdom. All would involve much skilful pleading and hard work. Peter was the obvious choice for Spain, and was on his way there as legate *a latere* to the four kingdoms of the Peninsula.

In the course of their ride to Naples Peter and Martin de Salva became lifelong friends. In some ways it was an attraction of opposites. Martin was impressed by Peter's birth, by his rank in the hierarchy, and above all by his learning and his breadth of mind. Peter could see both sides of a question, a faculty which had brought him no little anguish of late as he had watched his certainties vanish into darkness. Martin, on the other hand, was a straightforward middle-grade civil servant from Navarre. He came from a small town in the smallest kingdom in Spain. Others call the Navarrese backward, they call themselves traditional. They are loyal to their friends and hate their enemies. It is as simple as that. Martin had a black-and-white view of life, he was staunch and dependable, and Peter soon found himself growing very fond of him.

Martin had never lost his way. On returning to Rome from the peace conference, he had found Prignano behaving insufferably and those who ought to know beginning to murmur that the election had been most irregular. From that moment Prignano had been the enemy. There was no darkness for Martin. Not even in the dungeon, for his captor left him some chinks of light to see the toads by. And naturally Martin hated him all the more for it.

To Martin the Cardinal's experiences stood on a suitably higher plane. He listened with close attention to the story of his intellectual wrestlings. There was, in particular, the argument that Urban's followers never ceased repeating—that the cardinals acknowledged him publicly as pope, and therefore never doubted inwardly that he was the pope, and in fact still knew it, only he trod so hard on their toes that they rebelled. Peter pointed out the two non-sequiturs in the argument, and how hard it was to see them, particularly if one disliked the cardinals to start with.

That brought them to their coming task in Spain. Together they gave it much thought, dropping all pretences. The hardest part was going to be explaining why the cardinals had behaved as they did. Why had they yielded to fear so tamely and delayed so long afterwards? Why had they shown themselves so irresponsible? Glandève, for instance, had never stopped talking about how the Romans stole his jewel-box when they broke up the conclave. He and some others seemed to be more upset over losing their plate and their rings than they were about placing an intruder on the throne of St. Peter. And having done it, they went on happily benefice-mongering under him right up to the last moment.

Peter and Martin could find but one explanation, that the erring cardinals were French. France has always been an incalculable country in Spanish eyes, admired and envied for its power and brilliance, despised as soft and rather heartless. The French, or their ruling class at least, lacked steadfastness and true virtue. They did not have to fight the Moors on their own soil. It was reasonable, then, to expect the conduct of French cardinals to be less than heroic.

They would take the line that the cardinals were only human. Yet now, to repair the damage and to pay the price, there was great need of something more than people who were only human. It would need saints. They must hope to find a saint in Spain who would help them.

★

Avoiding, somehow, the toils of Queen Joanna, who was on the look-out for an energetic and competent adviser to replace her former Prime Minister and lover Acciaiuoli, the two ecclesiastical statesmen took ship with a certain Captain Bernaldez and sailed from Naples. Martin soon noticed that there was something strange about the ship. She was small and remarkably fast, and on closer inspection she proved to be more than adequately armed. The Catalan crew, though excellent seamen all of them, did not inspire confidence. Captain Bernaldez smiled alarmingly through his many scars. Slowly it dawned on Martin, to his consternation, that he was a passenger in a pirate ship.

It was all the more remarkable that the Captain and the Cardinal were obviously old friends. Their dealings were by no means confined to this present voyage. In fact, as the Captain presently disclosed to the Bishop, his piety blending with his professional pride, the good ship had lately been undertaking some little commissions for the service of Holy Church. A short time before they left Fondi, Urban's legate-designate to Spain had arrived there mysteriously and been lodged incommunicado in a convenient tower. Martin like others had been puzzled. He now learned to his amazement that Peter and Captain Bernaldez had jointly planned the naval operation which had resulted in the schismatic legate being landed, c.o.d., on the coast near Fondi two days after he had set sail for Spain in another ship.[15]

Peter rose still further in Martin's estimation. The episode left the Cardinal with the unfortunate belief that such methods could be made to pay. Yet there could be no doubt that he and Martin were well advised to be crossing the Mediterranean under Captain Bernaldez's protection. The Captain had many competitors on this coast, mostly Italians whose links were with the Urbanist side—the Genoese corsair Basilio of Levanto, for instance, or a promising local boy named Balthazar Cossa, who was starting up business from a base on Ischia.

*

They landed at Barcelona on 6 April. It was just a year since the fateful conclave in the Vatican.

Martin, after staying a short time to lend Peter what support he could, took the road to Pamplona. Before he left, Peter had achieved what must be the first aim of any ambassador—and what nowadays, in an age of telephones, journalism, jet aircraft and all too mobile Premiers and Foreign Secretaries, seems to be the sole aim which has been left to him. He was honourably received. ·

This result was by no means automatic, for Urban had written to the King of Aragon imploring him not to let the 'messenger of Antichrist' land, or if he landed to imprison him without pity. The letter left Pedro the Ceremonious in some perplexity. It would be sinful not to take the right side in the schism, whichever that was. Politically, it would be most unwise to declare for one side and then to find that his powerful neighbours had decided differently. Moreover, he was distantly related by marriage to both the rival papal legates who were now on his doorstep. (Urban had promptly replaced his kidnapped bishop.) Religion, caution and family honour all joined in advising the King to tread carefully. He was still treading carefully when he died eight years later.

Naturally he made enquiries. To this end a special council was called in Barcelona. It met a mere four months after Peter had landed. Both legates addressed it at great length. Its report was inconclusive.

It took Peter a little time to adjust himself to the tempo of his own country. Even in this busy and outward-looking commercial port, where they speak clipped Catalan instead of the sonorous language of the uplands, the pace was so much more sedate than that of France or Italy. Each time he came back he found Spain more isolated and old-fashioned than he had remembered. It used to be comforting. Now, with so much to do, it struck him as more than a little tiresome. But that was the way it was.

Outside Spain events moved briskly enough. The mission to Paris, led by Limoges and two other cardinals, was completely successful. Disregarding the University's hesitations, Charles V of France pronounced officially for Clement. His ally, Scotland, followed suit with commendable speed, and the learned *Treatise of the Bishop of Galloway on the Schism, against his neighbours the English* was widely read and still more widely approved throughout the North. England, scenting French intrigues behind everything, decided immediately for Urban and refused Cardinal Malesset permission to land and put his case. In Ireland there was some little confusion. The same in English-held Gascony. Malesset was now trying to enter Flanders but was finding it difficult—Flanders was closely linked to England by the wool trade. Aigrefeuille had been stopped on the frontiers of Germany. All along that ever-discordant border ambitious prelates competed for rich sees and there was street fighting in cathedral towns. The Reich as a whole was Urbanist. There were some light-hearted changes in Bavaria. Savoy, Clement's own homeland, naturally took his side. Austria sold him her allegiance for 120,000 florins and then went back on the bargain. The north and centre of Italy were solidly Urbanist while the south, under Joanna, accepted Clement. And so on throughout Europe whose kingdoms, responding more to the balance of power than to the niceties of canon law, divided neatly half on one side and half on the other. The religious orders, too, in fact the entire Church, split along well-established lines of political geography.

Then bad news came from Italy. The Castel Sant'Angelo was starved into surrender at last, Clement's mercenaries were defeated. by the others egged on by Catherine; Clement himself fell ill, and before worse could befall he and his court were evacuated to Avignon. Catalan galleys under Captain Bernaldez achieved this Dunkirk, while the Roman senate and people started to tear down the Castel Sant'Angelo in their patriotic fury, and managed to strip off some of the more marketable marble facing before they tired of the exercise.

The aged cardinals who had stayed behind at Avignon, and all the city's tradesmen, greeted Clement with enthusiasm—all except Montirac the Vice-Chancellor, who was very cross. He was an old man and nothing so damned silly had happened before. 'Why did the cardinals write to us like that?' he grumbled. 'Why did they do such things and now say something quite different?' It was all most irregular. But naturally he too accepted Clement. Only the lesser breeds could take a creature like Prignano seriously.

Back in the Palace of the Popes and his health recovered, Clement returned to the offensive. Learned men all over Europe were coming forward with ingenious plans to end the schism. For instance there was the way of a General Council. But who should summon it, preside over it and ratify its decision? A Council of the Church is different from an international congress. To give it authority, these functions must be performed by a sole, undisputed and legitimate pope. There was none, and the rivals were unwilling to co-operate. Clement himself preferred another way, the Way of Action, that is of military action. The French King's brother, the ambitious Louis of Anjou, must evict Urban from Rome. The so-called Kingdom of Adria, hastily created on paper out of those parts of the Papal States which bordered the Adriatic, should be his prize.

Clement would also help to finance the operation. And Joanna of Naples, 'deposed' by Urban and threatened by Urban's champion, should adopt Louis as her heir. There were daily conferences in the Palace at Avignon and the couriers came and went without a pause.

All this news, as it filtered through to Peter, confirmed him in his opinion that it was going to be a long struggle. He would have time to develop his own plan of campaign in Spain. There, or course, nothing can ever be made to move as fast as outsiders would like. Indeed, at any given moment, to a non-Spanish eye, the country appears quite stationary. This is not so, as Peter knew. He worked steadily, but without haste or impatience, to win the four kingdoms over for Pope Clement.

Of these kingdoms the most outward-looking was his own. The barred flag of Aragon flew over many territories besides Aragon proper—over boisterous Valencia and canny Catalonia, over Roussillon and the Balearics, over newly-won Sicily and the Catalan adventurers in the Duchy of Athens, and efforts were being made to fly it over Sardinia too. Not a fish dared show its nose in the Mediterranean, they boasted, unless it had the bars of Aragon on its tail. But just because Aragon was outward-looking, its leaders were suspicious of France and hostile to French expansionists like the Duke of Anjou. Urban's envoys played on this mistrust. Then Urban himself redressed the balance by promising Sicily and Sardinia to others. Pedro the Ceremonious of Aragon stayed neutral.

The other kingdoms were scarcely more promising. Castile had an alliance with France but went its own way. Portugal, threatened by Castile, looked to England. Navarre was isolationist. None of them would be drawn into Clement's camp by French influence. Meanwhile the money due to the Pope went into the four royal exchequers.

Peter knew all this before he started. He saw his task as one of slow propaganda. Propaganda, that is, not so much among the masses as channelled towards the right people—weighty churchmen, men of learning, influential courtiers. Each one of them must be reached through some suitable introduction and handled the right way. If indifferent to the whole question, he had to be made interested; if interested, benevolent; if benevolent, an active member

AVIGNON, THE PALACE, TODAY
(*Photo Editions S. L., Villeurbanne*)

ST. CATHERINE OF SIENA
A contemporary portrait by Andrea Vanni
(*By courtesy of the Soprintendente alle Gallerie, Siena*)

of some pressure-group. Together, in time, they would tip the scales, always supposing that the general situation did not change for the worse and make the task impossible.

For this, if useful connections, social gifts and skill in argument were enough, Peter was the man for the job. But there are people so cussed that they remain unimpressed by these things. Spain, to her credit, has more than her share of such people. To move them he needed a lever of a different sort. As he had already foreseen, he needed a saint. He began to look round for one, and remembered Brother Vincent.

Peter knew Valencia well. He held a benefice there. He remembered meeting a lively young Dominican, some eight years his junior, with a broad forehead and big dark eyes. The young man's spiritual growth had been out of the ordinary. Since then he had studied at Barcelona, Lérida and Toulouse. Now he was back in his native Valencia. Already he had a great reputation as a preacher, and there were strange rumours of miraculous graces.

Brother Vincent had just written a treatise on the spiritual life. The age was full of such writings, but this one was different.

> There is no merit in a man's being poor, but there is if being poor he loves poverty. . . . The slightest wish for greatness, however cleverly disguised as service to others, is like a snake raising its head; one must stamp on it at once. . . . Try to convince yourself that the worst kind of criminal would have served God better than you have done if he had been given your chances.

When he read these words Peter knew that he had found what he had been looking for. 'Try to convince yourself. . . .' Here was a proud nature struggling to good purpose with the harder precepts of Christianity. Such a man would spare neither himself nor others. And here was something else. 'In religious activities one should prefer the will of others to one's own, so long as one is satisfied that theirs is good.' This man would accept Peter's leadership.

Notwithstanding what he had seen of Bridget on paper and of Catherine in practice, Peter had not lost faith in saints. Catholicism never has; it is one of its merits. 'In any great crisis of the Church,' wrote Peter about now or a little later, 'there always springs up some saint—Thomas Becket for instance in Pope Alexander III's time—

who shows forth the truth by his life and miracles while most of us are bogged down among the subtleties of the law.'

Peter sent for Fray Vicens Ferrer and they spent long hours together. Each had much to give the other. The Dominican renewed the Legate's awareness of the higher forms of prayer; for the most part, this last year or so, he had been praying for guidance in his perplexities and latterly, on a lower plane still, for success in his debates and lobbyings. And the Legate brought to this young Dominican, with his crisp intellect and his dedicated will, a new and immediate duty. The schism must be ended, and ended in the only right way, by the victory of the lawful pope. Peter gave him all the material in his possession and lent him his admirable secretary, Canon Francisco Climent, another Valencian discovery. The result was Vincent's treatise *On the Present Schism*, the classic presentation of the Clementine case, dedicated with gracious permission to His Majesty King Pedro of Aragon.

Leaving that cautious monarch to ponder the document at his leisure, Peter looked farther afield. By far the largest state in Spain was Castile. Up to now he had been forbidden to enter it, thanks to the Urbanist Archbishop of Toledo. But now there was a new King of Castile, a serious young man who decided to have the evidence sifted properly. Castilian envoys were sent to Avignon and to Rome, where they collected sixty-two contradictory depositions from those who claimed knowledge of the conclave.

Most of the Avignon cardinals answered their questionnaires rather wearily, but Glandève was thoroughly aroused.

> If I had been in safety, I would as soon have voted for the Sultan of Babylon as I would have for that Bartholomew Prignano. On that point I call heaven and earth to be my witness. . . . I never intended, for my part, to ratify that diabolical election. . . . As for the enthronement and the coronation, I wanted very much to hide somewhere instead of taking part, because it was altogether against my better feelings, but they forced me to come by threats and intimidation. And Cardinal de Luna came in the same way, as he told me afterwards. . . . If only I had been in a safe place I would never have taken part in any of these things. I have such a horror of all this diabolical violence and terrorism, which in any case renders an election utterly invalid.[16]

The Castilian enquiry was held at Medina del Campo in the King's presence. Peter came with his former conclavist Fernando, his secretary Climent and Brother Vincent. Immediately after the opening ceremonies Peter addressed the court, speaking in Spanish. He was followed next day by Urban's chief spokesman, an Italian bishop, whose arguments may have suffered from their being delivered in Latin. Each side then presented a written statement giving its own version of the facts. Each was confronted with the other's text. The sixty-two depositions were studied and compared and thirty-four Spanish witnesses interrogated. It was by far the most thorough of the various judicial inquests made at the time.

Peter was closely cross-examined on his own part in events. This was the crux of the investigation; Clement's case rested on how his Legate would answer these questions.

His answers had been preserved.[17] They are candid and illuminating, but add nothing essential to what the reader already knows. Peter was an excellent witness, drawing a clear distinction between what he saw and heard, how he interpreted it at the time, and how he interpreted it now in the light of fuller knowledge.

The most awkward questions were those concerning his own attitude immediately after the conclave was over. When Prignano asked him next day if he thought the election was valid, how did he answer?—He had delayed going to Prignano, he replied, until he knew that his colleagues in the castle were ready to accept him. As to what he told Prignano then, he would not commit himself exactly, but thought he had answered in the affirmative.

What were his feelings, then, on coming out of the conclave?— He could not remember having any clearly formulated opinion just at that moment. But he did remember very clearly how the sight of his colleagues enthroning and crowning Prignano had reassured him. Later on he heard them discussing it, and then his doubts arose once more.

And how had he reached the very definite opinion he held now?— He had spoken at great length with his colleagues, individually, and they had assured him that they had acted under the impulse of fear. They were cardinals, and their word was the best, in fact the only evidence of what went on inside their minds. Therefore they must be believed. If we reject their evidence, he concluded, we step into a labyrinth from which we shall never find our way out again.

Peter had come through this ordeal with credit. His answers and his arguments made a deep impression. The enquiry had lasted four months and it was time to reach a decision. The court gave its unanimous verdict for Clement.

Urban's advocate withdrew; he became the 'Quisling' Archbishop of Bordeaux under the English occupation. The King of Castile proclaimed his adherence to Avignon. Arrears of papal taxes would be paid to Clement. Forty Castilian prelates publicly took off the rings which Urban had given them. An Urbanist cardinal threw down his hat, rightly confident that Clement would give it back to him. Clement's personal observer wrote an ecstatic letter to his master praising Peter to the skies.

Peter went on to Portugal, where after many delays a similar though much less thorough inquest was held. At Santarem he used the same arguments, this time within a remarkable framework of biblical quotations, applied with all the misplaced ingenuity which the age demanded. Who would have thought that 'For I know that thou art gracious and merciful' referred to Clement, even if the last word is *clemens* in the Vulgate? The Portuguese, however, were going through their birth-pangs as a nation; with each dramatic turn in foreign policy they changed sides in the schism as well. A war with Castile and the landing of three thousand English archers under the Earl of Cambridge settled the matter for the moment, and after one more swing of the pendulum the decisive battle of Aljubarrota confirmed that Portugal would remain both independent and Urbanist.

From these travels Peter returned to his ancestral home in the bare torrent-eroded hills near Calatayud. The country looks like North Africa; the church towers are modelled on minarets and adorned with Moorish patterns in brickwork; they have not even bothered to change the town's Moorish name, Kal'at Ayyub. Clean poverty, high parched voices, ramming winds and a sledgehammer sun. At Illueca, some twenty miles out, the great castle of the Lunas stands thin along a knife-ridge among the savage red hills. Here he settled down to wait with oriental patience until the King of Aragon should die and give place to his son.

He had six years to wait. They were among the most contented years of his life. He was at home, among his own folk, in the dry invigorating country that he loved. He might have lived more splendidly in Castile, where his Pope was recognised, but he was better placed for the next move where he was, and happier too. He had plenty of time, time to go and talk to his sister Celestina, now Abbess at Calatayud, or to put up a simple inscription to his father's memory in the principal church. He was running his own show in his own way, far from the pressures and intrigues of head-quarters. His mission had not been a fiasco and he had reason to hope for further successes presently. Meanwhile he could be useful. He could devise admirable statutes for the University of Salamanca and sensible decrees to check concubinage among the clergy. He could keep an eye on Brother Vincent, who was conducting an over-exuberant missionary campaign among the Jews, and see that the latter were not subjected to pogroms. (The next big one came soon after Peter had left Spain.) Above all he had peace of mind, for he knew he had taken the right course. He had time to read, to write and to think.

At the end of the six years old King Pedro died and Aragon fell at Peter's touch like a ripe apple. As soon as the news of the King's death reached him, he went to Barcelona. The judicial enquiry, towards which some cautious preliminary steps had already been taken, now opened with one of those disconcerting turns of speed which Spanish officialdom can always achieve when it wants to. Seven weeks after Pedro's death Aragon recognised Clement. In the general rejoicings, only the Avignon treasury looked on a little sourly. For the Aragonese, more commercial in outlook than the lordly Castilians, were careful not to offer to forward their arrears of papal taxes.

Peter was now a power in Aragon. He found himself having to rescue the new King's mother-in-law, who was accused of having bewitched old Pedro and was about to be tortured. Peter obtained a pardon for her and himself went to let her out of prison. There was also a tiresome dispute involving his former secretary Canon Climent. Peter sent it to arbitration by a certain Gil Sanchez Muñoz. Many years later, this Muñoz was to wind up the tangled skein of Peter's own life.

Of the four Christian realms in the Peninsula, only little Navarre remained. Carlos el Malo had died and Carlos el Noble had just mounted the throne. Surrounded now by Clementine neighbours, he saw clearly that his small kingdom must follow the fashion. Pride dictated a decent delay. Navarrese pride was worth exactly three more years. Then he formally consulted his clergy, with Peter's friend Martin de Salva at their head, and found them unanimous. An invitation went out to Peter. At Pamplona, on 6 February 1390, the last of the Spanish states accepted Clement. A week later King Carlos, whose coronation had been delayed all this time lest a schismatic should profane it, was crowned by Martin in Peter's presence. Peter had written to Avignon and the reward came. Vice-Chancellor Montirac had died and there could be a new Cardinal of Pamplona. As a special favour Martin received his red hat from the Legate's hands.

These events called for oratory on a generous scale. The congratulatory address which Peter delivered in Pamplona cathedral when he presented the hat has been preserved in full. As he composed it, he reflected that everyone in this provincial little place knew all about Martin. Why then bore them with biography? Better to dazzle them.

He based his remarks, as always, on a strict framework. This time, to everybody's surprise, it was the woman clothed with the sun in Revelation, chapter xii. Her crown of twelve stars prefigured Martin's twelve virtues. Their enumeration in impeccable Latin took an hour and twenty minutes and enabled the Legate to quote from a galaxy of classical authors, most of the Fathers, his own favourite devotional work the pseudo-Dionysius (to which Brother Vincent had introduced him) and a number of moderns like Boccaccio and John of Salisbury. He worked in a compliment to the King and a reference to Clement, but mere biography was rightly ignored.

Hardly a soul in the cathedral can have followed the Legate's allusions. But all were deeply impressed with the performance. How profound!

Actually, though Peter had been reading widely, his knowledge of ancient authors was probably not quite so encyclopaedic as that. But, like most great men, he had found an excellent secretary. And, much more to the point, he had known how to bring about a political change in Spain.

\*

While Peter was living at Illueca and waiting for Aragon to make a move, Dietrich was very busy seeing Naples systematically. In later life he wrote his memoirs;[18] they show him in that spring of 1384 plodding earnestly round the recommended sights, his pockets bulging with classical references. He penetrates the grotto at Posilipo and the catacombs of St. Januarius. He turns away from the dancing blue curve of the Gulf to burden his memory with useless statistics. We catch a glimpse of him as he peers myopically into the little semi-extinct volcano called La Solfatara; he goes scrambling obstinately down to get a closer view and is nearly boiled alive.

After this last experience, Dietrich decided to make his cultural *Ausflüge* in the company of like-minded colleagues and compatriots. For few but Germans remained in the less honorific strata of Urban's court. They all went out to Torre Annunziata to taste the wine in the archbishop's cellars there. One of them, a proctor of the Rota and 'a discreet sort of man', passed blissfully out of consciousness until the next day, when he woke up with no memory of what had happened. 'At which I marvelled greatly. Though whether it was from some weakness of the brain, or merely from drinking too much, I do not know.' There speaks the authentic Dietrich.

Urban had moved with all his governmental apparatus to Naples. He too, like Clement, believed in the Way of Action. Charles of Durazzo, husband of Queen Joanna's niece and heir, had risen in rebellion with Urban and Catherine backing him. He brought a Hungarian army. Joanna, her ladies and two new Italian cardinals of Clement's all took refuge in the Castel Nuovo. Frantic messages were sent to Clement's champion Louis of Anjou, but he held back. Joanna's Prince Consort tried to raise the siege, but was captured within sight of the walls. Joanna, bombarded by nauseating projectiles and her food-supplies at an end, surrendered. Three days too late Louis' ships arrived from Provence. They were too few to attempt a rescue. Joanna refused to come to terms with Charles and was presently murdered in her prison—'suffocated between the pillows in the bed where she had found her highest joys', as one of her many clerical detractors informs us.

In the wake of Charles' army came Urban's implacable legate, Cardinal Sangro. He made a clean sweep of the Clementine clergy in Naples. The venerable Archbishop of Salerno was burnt at the stake, other prelates were tortured, thirty-two bishops and abbots were removed in a single day, and the two captured cardinals were forced to burn their hats in Santa Chiara.

At last Louis of Anjou's army, financed and blessed by Clement, came marching down the Italian peninsula. But for some unaccountable reason Louis by-passed Rome where Urban sat practically defenceless. He missed the rendezvous with his fleet on the Naples coast and occupied the heel of Italy instead. He died there two years later. Avignon never forgave him.

In the meantime Urban moved to Naples. Part of the bargain with Charles had been that large tracts of the kingdom should be given to Urban's nephew Francesco Prignano, commonly known as Butillo or 'tubby'. As Charles showed no haste in implementing this arrangement, Urban decided against his cardinals' advice to go and intervene in person. For Urban, though he had a genuine dislike of simony, saw nothing wrong in a little nepotism.

Naples that season held plenty for Dietrich to marvel at. There was Urban, behaving more strangely than ever, summoning 'that son of perdition who calls himself the King of France' to appear before him in a matter of days, quarrelling openly with his new set of cardinals and spurned by Charles, who had gone off to deal with Louis. There was Charles' Queen, regent of Naples in his absence, and a lady of character as one would expect of Joanna's niece. Dietrich looked on in horror while 'she ruled tyrannically, sitting her horse astride like a man as she rode about the city, turning night into day while she played at dice with whomsoever she wished, and on some days staying in bed until lunch-time'. There was Butillo, who set the whole city in a ferment by abducting a nun of noble family and shutting himself up with her in his lodgings for several days, while Urban excused his forty-year-old nephew with the words, 'He is only young'.

Then there were the seventeen new cardinals, the latest batch whom Urban had recklessly appointed. The many Neapolitans among them did not dare to take office. 'But they stayed hiding in their dwellings in Naples like wolves in their lairs, lest they should be derided by the populace,' while the ladies of Naples greeted each other playfully with the words, 'I hear your husband has been made a cardinal'.

And then the cardinals of earlier vintage, nattering rebelliously in corridors. Six of them, including the Cardinal Sangro who had persecuted the wretched Clementines and an Englishman, Adam Easton, put their heads together and began a rather pedantic debate on whether they would be justified in putting a pope like theirs, who was little short of a madman, under some form of restraint. Most unwisely they set down their scholastic findings on paper. A colleague betrayed them and Urban arrested all six, confining them for the moment in a disused rainwater-cistern at Nocera.

For by now the Roman Curia was at Nocera, out in the wilds far beyond Vesuvius. Urban and Butillo set up house in the huge strong-hold which guards the pass to Salerno, leaving the Vatican officials to find quarters in the slatternly village outside.

At first all went tolerably well. Dietrich gives a lyrical description of the Nocera countryside, of its vineyards and giant chestnut trees, of the nut-fattened pigs and the superb ham they yielded, of the capons which were the biggest he had seen, of the excellent wine, of how cheap everything was. 'And therefore the papal officials pre-ferred to remain there, so long as they were safe.'

Yet morale in this earthly paradise was low. 'Their position seemed open to doubt on many counts, and for that reason there was much murmuring every day among the civil servants of the Curia.'

Then a rumour spread that the Queen Regent's unruly troops were coming to plunder them, and they all ran away. Urban sent for Dietrich to find out why his civil service had disappeared.

'They are delicate men and unwarlike, as Your Holiness knows quite well. Could not they have rooms in this enormous castle, where they would feel safer?'

'This castle is scarcely big enough for me and my suite,' the pontiff replied irritably. 'Don't stand there arguing, Dietrich. Go and bring them back!'

By this time the luckless bureaucrats had reached Castellammare

on foot. There the civil governor took away any weapons they had
and told them to move on. They fell inevitably into the hands of
the local boatmen who, pretending not to understand their Italian,
took them far out to sea. At a pre-arranged signal Catalan pirates
from the Isle of Capri (for Captain Bernaldez was back on his beat)
boarded their craft and relieved them of everything they had. They
were then landed penniless at Naples.

Dietrich, obedient and unimaginative, had stayed at his post
serving his lawful tyrant. For this he received an appropriate
reward.

One evening, early in January, Urban sent for him.

And when I came he immediately gave orders for the gates of
the castle to be closed. Seeing which, I began to be afraid, for
I thought he intended to do me some injury. Nor could I
ascertain for some time why he had sent for me. But a highly
placed friend of mine, seeing my uneasiness, whispered in my
ear, 'What a pity you came at all! But do not be afraid, *you* are
not in any danger. Only be careful, I advise you. I cannot say
any more.' On hearing this I began to recover my confidence to
some extent. And after I had been standing there alone for a
considerable time, at last Pietro da Alatri, our lord Urban's
secretary, appeared, and then Basilio of Levanto a well-known
pirate of Genoese origin, and Master Paolo da Giovinazzo di
Puglia, who was later a notary to the Apostolic See, and Benedetto a leading canonist who had a most distinguished academic
career at Padua and whom Urban afterwards placed in charge of
the Treasury, only he died a few days later, and last of all some
titular bishop, a Domincan and a relative of Basilio's, so they
said. They had all been deputed by Urban, with me, to examine
the imprisoned cardinals. So as soon as we were all assembled
we all trotted along into the castle keep. . . . Once inside, we
went first to where they kept Cardinal Sangro. The cell was
so narrow and cramped that the Cardinal could hardly stretch
out his legs. Butillo accompanied us and began to exhort the
cardinals to make a full confession of all they had done, promising by his knighthood (by which he set great store) that they
had nothing to fear even if they had sinned grievously against
Urban, for Lord Urban did not wish them ill or seek their
destruction, but rather wished to forget everything and let
bygones be bygones and to treat them mercifully—adding that
he himself would certainly spare no pains to induce Urban to
view their case in a favourable light. And so we went one by

one to all those cardinals, for they were kept apart in separate rooms, and we found them loaded with chains. We conducted the examination in general terms . . . for the Pope had not cared to give us any specific instructions.

After the interrogation we went back immediately to Urban and told him all we had learned. And two of us, Paolo and Pietro, standing there in that bleak little room at the foot of Urban's bed, wept bitter tears before him and could not gasp out a single word for their sobbing. But Urban, furious, jeered at them saying, 'Why are you crying like a lot of feeble women?' On which they rushed out of the room.

Dietrich was scared. Left alone presently with Urban, he put first things first, imploring him not to expose his faithful officials to all these dangers but to leave the country before their enemies could strike back. He added a charitable plea for the cardinals.

But my words were in vain, for the more I said the angrier did Lord Urban grow, until his face became like a blazing lamp and his voice grew so hoarse that he almost choked. Seeing this I was disconcerted and I stopped just in time. He told me I was very badly informed about what was being plotted against him, but that I should soon be made wiser. Then he shouted for Butillo's secretary, Fino of Amalfi was his name. When he came he asked him where he had put the Bishop of Aquila's confession. To obtain it he had had the Bishop inhumanly tortured on the rack the day before, and for fear of the torture the Bishop had confessed to various things and had declared that several of the cardinals were implicated. When I read through this confession, extorted from the Bishop under torture, I said to Urban, though I was very much afraid, that the cardinals' case ought not to be prejudiced by such a confession. . . .

On the third day Urban gave orders that his disciplinary commission should examine the cardinals again and 'put them to the question'.

And in the evening, as darkness fell, he directed me and the others whom he had nominated to proceed to a large cellar in the castle which had been constructed by my lord Otto Prince of Taranto when he reigned in those parts. And when we were ready, Cardinal Sangro was brought in by some attendants with shackles of iron on his feet, wearing a long tunic without any girdle and a strip of towelling wound twice round his body, because there were very cold winds always blowing through that castle, which stands on an exposed site on a hilltop. When he had almost reached the far end of the cellar, he saw the ropes hanging down from above in the shadows, ready for him, and the same attendants who had led him in quickly stripped him of his clothes, leaving him only his drawers and vest, and he was bound tightly to the ropes by those butchers. At which sight Butillo, who was standing there close by, laughed immoderately. But I, who was attached to the Cardinal, began to tremble and to suffer, for there was no place where I could run away and hide. But why do I linger? The Cardinal, who was a middle-aged man, tall and heavily built, was tied to the strappado like this and was hoisted up to the ceiling three times, and after that he seemed to have little life left in him. Seeing this, I said to him in the pause when they had let him down to the ground, 'My dearest Father, do you not see how your soul cries out to God? Save yourself by saying something, and you can get out of their hands this time!' He replied, 'I don't know what to say.'

So when the torturers wanted to start again I said to them, 'Stop! He has said enough to me already.' They wanted me to tell them what he had said, but I answered that I must write it down first and that I would tell them later on. And so they did not torture him any more for the moment. Instead they carried him to the door of the cellar and laid him on a bench where he could get some fresh air. When he had recovered, he said to us who were standing round him: 'Look at me, Brothers. Before this I was a famous man, one of the great men of the age as you saw for yourselves, but now I am the most wretched of all. . . . And it is the judgment of God, because when I was acting as our lord the Pope's legate in this kingdom I did not spare all those prelates and churchmen but rather acted as I did, without regard for their age or cloth, because I thought I should please him by doing so.'

Then Butillo assured him that he had no need to fear our lord the Pope, and that our lord the Pope only wished to treat him gently, and much more rubbish besides. But the Cardinal would not take comfort, for he greatly feared that memorable pontiff's cruelty.

Basilio the pirate enjoyed his work. 'For he was of a malignant disposition and had a natural hatred of clergy and ecclesiastical persons.'

Next morning it was the Cardinal of Venice's turn. Urban told Basilio that this time he must hear the Cardinal's cries. Once more Dietrich and his miserable companions filed into the torture-chamber. 'We obeyed because we could do nothing else.' They tortured the poor old man all that morning until lunch-time. Each time the strappado raised him by his wrists he repeated the words, 'Christ suffered for us.'

> And meanwhile, in the garden outside, Urban paced up and down reading the office aloud, so that we who were inside might hear his voice, for he wished to remind Basilio not to be slack in carrying out his orders.

Dietrich invented a headache and was given leave to withdraw. He escaped, as those with any sense had done long before, and reached Naples—'although I was robbed of all my goods by bandits and, as well as that, two young assistants of mine received wounds from which they nearly died'.

Charles of Durazzo decided that it had to stop. He sent a force to besiege Nocera under the Abbot of Monte Cassino, one of those sabre-rattling prelates for whom the period gave such ample scope. Three or four times a day, we are told, the Pope came to the window of the great keep and solemnly excommunicated the Neapolitan army with bell, book and candle. In return Charles offered ten thousand florins for Urban, dead or alive.

The siege, being Neapolitan, was quite remarkably inefficient. Urban escaped with ease, dragging his six cardinals and his other prisoners with him along the mountain tracks, tied on horses under the July sun. The Bishop of Aquila, his limbs broken in the torture-chamber, could not stand the pace, so one day Urban had him killed. His body was tumbled into a nameless hole by the roadside and the party, like Arab slave-raiders in Africa, continued on their dusty way to the coast. In this manner they crossed the ankle of Italy to Trani, where they embarked in a Genoese galley. Coming up northwards again, off Naples, the Pope discharged another anathema at Charles, a long shot over the horizon. Then he landed at Genoa and settled down there for the next fifteen months.

Before moving on again he had five of the six cardinals murdered. Their bodies were destroyed in quicklime, one rumour had it. Anyway, nothing was ever seen of them again. The sixth, the English Cardinal Easton, was only saved because his sovereign Richard II pleaded for him with Urban. He outlived Urban and has a fine tomb in Santa Cecilia in Rome.

A story spread through Italy that the five bodies were salted and dried in an oven and that in Lord Urban's cavalcade, as it moved slowly south towards Rome in that spring of 1388, there were five mules each bearing a coffin surmounted by a red hat, as a warning to the others.

This last item is legend. The rest, sad to say, is not.

Two Italian cardinals deserted to Clement from Genoa. Dietrich on the other hand, rejoined him. In spite of everything, he thought to himself, Urban and he were 'fate-companions'. And Urban was glad to see him again. In spite of everything, he could recognise a trustworthy official when he saw one.

# CHAPTER 5

## *France*

THERE is a low ridge near Avignon, where the roots of stunted pines and junipers twist out of the parched earth and the wild thyme crawls boring for moisture between the hot flat stones. Away in the distance the sunlight glints yellow on a meander of the river and rests steadily on the Palace of the Popes, so that it stands out against the dark plain beyond. The view was there in Peter's day and when Corot came to paint it.

Just in front of one's feet, the dust and the pine-needles hold a small frenzy. An ants' nest has been kicked open. At first the ants run frantically in every direction, colliding and turning at right angles. Then two streams carrying eggs start to flow out of the chaos, going in opposite directions. The eggs are large and white and obviously they matter most. Presently there is something like order again, and the beginnings of two new ants' nests.

Peter was back in Avignon, after two years in Italy and eleven in Spain, and he did not find it amusing. Some of his colleagues had died, others had grown middle-aged, and there were many new ones. Most of them had relapsed into a comfortable inertia, well aware that any change would jeopardise their careers and incomes. They had a vested interest in the schism.

It was a short-sighted view, because nobody outside the cardinals' *livrées* shared it. The Pope and his party stalwarts worked for victory, which meant the confounding and liquidation of the other Obedience. Everyone else outside wanted the schism healed, no matter how. And governments were beginning to come round to the same opinion.

Nevertheless, the Curia had its own peculiar momentum. The mill had been set up once more on the banks of the Rhône, where at least there were no Luddites to disturb it, and it had been grinding merrily for the past decade. The water rushed over the wheels and the great stones went round and round, as they always would unless you smashed something. Bulls, provisions, legal awards and dispensations; fees, annates and *servitia*. The mill existed to provide all this. Did it help the Christian life in the world outside? Was the flour nutritious? A foolish, ignorant question. The mill ground on. It had taken control of the millers.

These are perennial troubles, if a Church is highly organised. Usually they can be hidden. The schism drew wide attention to them.

Peter's tour of exploration reached the Treasury and its head the Camerlengo. There he learned that the water was not coming down the mill-race quite as it used to do. The resources were halved, it had become far more difficult to collect the income from their own half, and when collected most of it was being spent on fighting the other half. The latest French expedition to Naples, for instance, had cost the *Camera* 600,000 florins to date.

In short, as Peter soon realised, they could not go on like this much longer.

The Pope's own way out was the so-called Way of Action. Clement's faith in it remained undimmed. He pulled wires unremittingly; an unbroken line of grandiose, rickety, wire-supporting structures rose and sagged again across the years. Each plan was first hinted at in the strictest secrecy, then carefully leaked out to very important people, then suddenly proclaimed from the house-tops, then superseded and abandoned for a fresh one. It was treason to speak of it, to speak of anything else, to suggest it could possibly fail, to suggest that it had ever seriously been entertained. One had only to lose touch with Clement for a moment and one no longer knew which was the correct attitude.

Naturally he gave Peter a warm welcome. He was very much aware of the great debt he owed him. No one else had brought in three kingdoms. It was the greatest comfort to him personally to know that his oldest and most faithful colleagues such as Peter and Jean de Lagrange and Guy de Malesset had stood there behind him all the time, like rocks.

Clement had aged well, in spite of all his disappointments. His

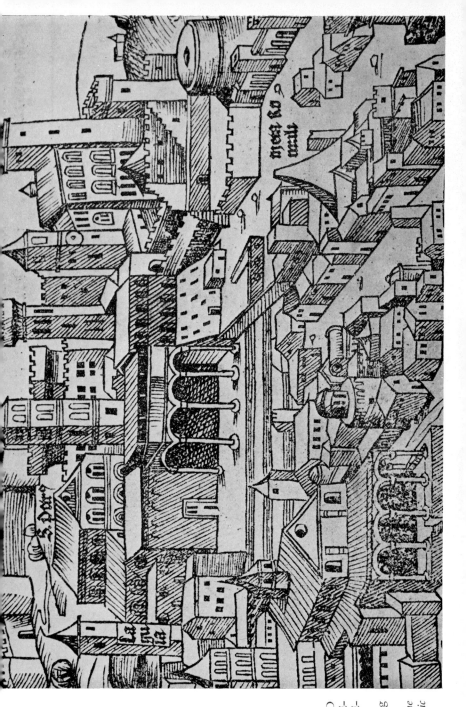

ST. PETER'S AND THE VATICAN BEFORE THEIR RECONSTRUCTION
From the Nuremberg Chronicle

(By courtesy of the Director, Brighton Public Libraries)

A POPE BY THE CASTEL SANT'ANGELO
Painting by Giovanni di Paolo
(*By courtesy of the Conservateur of the Louvre*)

character as well as his face and figure had rounded out. As Pope he had shed, to some people's surprise, all but a few vestiges of his military bearing and turns of speech. What they did not realise, perhaps, was that he had not started his career with them either. They had been the outward sign of an avatar, of the comparatively few years when he had seen himself as the predestined strong man in the College, successor to that great trouble-shooter Cardinal Albornoz whose castles still frown over so many townships in central Italy. Robert of Geneva, as Clement was then, never did things by halves. He had thrown all he had into sustaining the role. Now he was doing the same as Pope Clement VII. Yet the effect, though creditable and even dignified, was not exactly papal. Peter no doubt puzzled over this and could not put a name to it. Translated into modern terms, Clement resembled a distinguished wartime general who has been appointed to rescue some great public corporation from approaching bankruptcy.

For the moment his every thought was turned towards the projected expedition to Italy. It was due to start in March and would settle everything. There would be full-scale French participation, a thing long dreamed of and never achieved before. The King would be going in person, also the Dukes of Touraine, Berry, Burgundy and Bourbon, and they were inviting the Duke of Brittany as well lest he should start some intrigue with London while they were all away. That made five Dukes, plus, of course, the Comte de Saint-Pol and the Sire de Coucy. Of course all these names and their political connotations were already familiar to Peter?

Peter knew just enough about France. Clement's enthusiasm was touching, but not infectious.

On such occasions, as Peter left Clement's study in the Tour des Anges, he used to pause deliberately in the antechamber to look once again at the tapestries. They never failed to raise his spirits, and he felt much in need of that. He stepped into a world of action and colour. The glowing russet tones recalled the earth of his native Illueca. Some of the subjects were biblical, but his favourite was *The Voyage of Brut* with its jumble of ships, each ship packed with gallants and trumpeters and pensive ladies in tall conical hats. The ships were tall cogs built for northern seas and *The Brut* was an English legend, linked with their national hero King Arthur. Why

H

not go north, to Paris and Flanders and England? Perhaps it was an omen for his next mission. He could not stay at Avignon very much longer.

★

The great French expedition, of course, was countermanded. It was a young King's romantic dream. He was just twenty-four, and a courtier in Clement's pay had given him the idea. '*Et mieulx, Sire, ne povés employer vostre saison.*' But weightier counsels prevailed. If he went, denuding the country of troops and leaders, the English might well be tempted to break the truce and open another round in the Hundred Years War. To make sure that he did not go, and perhaps win Italy, they proposed a peace conference. Richard II would meet him at Boulogne. The Italian venture was postponed. Then Richard did not come.

Charles VI, spoilt, inbred, and living too fast, had something like a nervous breakdown. He recovered, and then it happened. As he was riding at the head of his troops through Le Mans forest one stifling August morning, a page's lance clashed accidentally on a helmet. In an instant the King was a maniac and laying about him with his sword. A minute or two later he was prone on the ground in an epileptic fit, but not before he had nearly killed his younger brother Orleans. After several weeks of violent insanity he was better again. These fits, often lasting much longer, continued intermittently for the rest of his life, that is for another thirty years.

When he was ill he had a horror of water and of the Queen. Medical science could do nothing for him, except to send in a gang of men with black masks to give him a bath, followed by a young lady in waiting who took the Queen's place. The Queen observed, sensibly enough, that she was more grateful to her than jealous, and the Bastard Dunois, Joan of Arc's comrade in arms, was born of this strange union. In his sane intervals Charles had six more children by the Queen. Joan's Dauphin was one of them.

This personal tragedy was a blow to Clement's hopes. In any case, it may be argued, the French could not have dominated Italy. But could they not have set Rome to rights, at least? Clement, not unnaturally, blamed them to the end of his days for never having

tried. In his view two very real opportunities were missed, one by
Louis of Anjou (the elder) when he marched down through Italy in
1382, and the second one now, nine years later. Such a military
stroke might have succeeded, if the rival pope's authority and his
supporters' morale had been at a low enough ebb.

Morale in Rome was certainly not very high. Urban had ensured
that. In fact another opportunity, a better one in every way, had
presented itself in October 1389 when he died. This was the
moment for which Europe had been waiting. One might well have
thought that Urban's cardinals, of whom fourteen survived at
his court out of the sixty or more who had acknowledged him at
various times, would have paused before they elected a successor.
At least they could have negotiated with Avignon. Instead, they
set a bad precedent by electing one of their number pope within a
fortnight.

Their nominee, who took the name of Boniface IX, was a tall,
handsome Neapolitan in his early thirties. They had chosen him
most understandably for his amiable manners. In other respects he
was a curious choice. Dietrich, who needless to say went on serving
under him, found many faults to criticise.

This event disturbed the more intelligent people in Clement's
Obedience. Up to then it had always been possible to hope that
Urban's death would solve the problem. Now, with a rival pope
younger than Clement, the schism looked like lasting indefinitely.

There remained the Way of Action. What did Peter think of it?
He would have been puzzled by our moral hesitations before the
use of force, which arise because we have re-interpreted Christianity
in the light of modern humanism. His Christianity had not the
slightest objection to the use of force in order to coerce honest but
mistaken belief. The medieval Church did not consider that error
has rights. Nor do we, quite. What has changed, and changed so
vastly for the better, is the kind of error we are prepared to tolerate.
But if Peter knew the text, 'Compel them to come in', he also
knew, 'Put not your trust in princes'. He can have had few illusions
on this subject. He knew that his dealings with Spanish princes had
only been successful because he had been able to persuade them
that their interests coincided with his. As an experienced diplomat
he could appraise French interests realistically. And to France, by

this time, a pope at Avignon was more of a liability than an asset, and the conquest of Rome had at best a very low priority.

The Way of Action in fact was an attempt to conduct military operations without troops or reliable allies. Only a Clement, with his relentless drive, could have kept on following it. His optimism never failed. He went on talking success. If the royal government were unco-operative for the moment, there was still the Duke of Anjou, whose house had ruled in Naples for well over a century. The young Duke, a boy of twelve, was there at present with an army financed by Clement and with Clement's legate at his side. Naples had changed allegiance in the schism for the fourth time, and would change it again before long. Meanwhile Clement had other irons in the fire. His zest undimmable where politicians were concerned, he intrigued with Gian Galeazzo of Milan and with his son-in-law the Duke of Orleans, who was the mad King's brother and a rising power in France. For Orleans' benefit the 'Kingdom of Adria' was once more taken down from the papal shelf and carefully dusted.

*

Peter spent over two years at Avignon. He settled in. Wherever fate might take him, he believed in unpacking. His old house, far away in the southern part of the town, was unsuitable for a senior cardinal, and he had taken a better *livrée* as soon as one fell vacant, though it was some years before he returned to occupy it. His new place stood exactly on the site of the present Préfecture, which has even copied the original plan by once more bridging over the narrow lane which divides the site into two. From this street, in Peter's time, you entered a courtyard with a well in the middle, finding the stables on your left and a long wine-cellar or storeroom on your right; above the cellar was the *tinel* or dining-hall, a hundred feet long, and above that a chapel, while from one end of the hall the bridge-room led back across the street to the more intimate quarters on a smaller courtyard. It was one of the best *livrées* in Avignon, though his furniture was solid rather than opulent and almost ascetically uncomfortable in the eyes of his French fellow-cardinals.[19]

From the window of the bridge-room one looked down into the Rue de la Bouquerie. The people below moved briskly and were well dressed, but the town's great days were over, never to return. Peter had been just in time to see the tail end of them under Gregory. Avignon was still a capital then, as rich and sophisticated as any in Europe though on an intimate scale. Now it was only a prosperous provincial city. Most of the Italian bankers had gone home and the more enterprising goldsmiths had moved to Lyons or Dijon. Of the floating population, only the benefice-hunters and litigants were left. A shadow of impermanence, a faint odour of illegality, hung over everything. No, not illegality! Disintegration.

And the reason? Public opinion was slowly turning against them. His French colleagues said so. This was something that he found difficult to grasp. He would look down from his bridge-chamber at the passers-by. Were *they* public opinion? What did they know about it? Or care, unfortunately, so long as their bills were paid? Anyway they had no standing in the matter. Right and canon law must decide, not laymen and their public opinion.

He must get out of Avignon, for a time at least. He must find another mission, something big to get his teeth into.

Could he go to Naples, perhaps? No, his junior colleague Cardinal Thury was there already, and doing well. A hard, ambitious man, Thury; he had met him at Medina del Campo and taken a dislike to him. There was another Italian outpost on the other side of Rome, but Peter did not covet it either.

News from this outpost filtered through only intermittently, for it was a partisan district inside enemy territory. A day's ride north of Rome you entered an ill-defined tract of hill country held by Gascon soldiers of fortune, the debris of many Italian wars. So long as some modest retaining fees reached them from Avignon they were more than willing to be Clementines. The small hill-towns in the neighbourhood bought a minimum of peace on the same terms. These arrangements, which had a certain nuisance-value and from which Clement hoped great things, were supervised by a resident legate.

Clement looked on Cardinal Pileo di Prata as a personal triumph. He had started as one of Urban's many cardinals. By the time Urban reached Genoa, Pileo had had enough. He set fire to his hat in the public square of Pavia and took the road to Avignon, where he was fêted and reappointed cardinal. Then, as 'Legate in the Patrimony of St. Peter in Tuscany', he was sent back to Italy to advise the partisans. He held court at Montefiascone for a year or two, but Rome, now that the amiable Boniface IX was there instead of Urban, looked infinitely more inviting. So Pileo tried to betray his stronghold and, foiled by the townsfolk, slid down a rope from the battlements into the Roman Obedience once more, leaving three of his fellow-conspirators behind to be killed. Duly rewarded for his agility, he went through the rest of his life as the Cardinal with Three Hats.

His defection, though mortifying, was no great loss. The district remained more or less Clementine for years. It was an insignificant item in the ledgers of an Obedience which stretched in a great arc across Europe, from Scotland to Cyprus and Corfu.

Italy being closed to him, Peter looked northwards. Could he do anything in Paris, where the court was undependable and the University openly disaffected? Or in England, which had been resolutely Urbanist from the start? Or in Flanders, ruled now by the nominally Clementine Duke of Burgundy, but anti-French and linked with England by the wool trade and therefore still mainly Urbanist? Peter spent much time in the library, reading up these countries and Clement's bulls concerning them. The Chancery, he noticed, had lost none of its technical ability to strike precisely the correct more-in-sorrow-than-in-anger note.

> Clement, etc., to Our beloved son the most noble Duke of Burgundy, etc. Since it has come to Our notice that certain persons dwelling in the Duchy of Brabant and the County of Flanders have for some time past adhered to Bartholomew Prignano of damnable memory whilst he was alive, and now, alas!, adhere to that disciple of perdition Perrino Tomacelli, falsely known to some in this lamentable schism by the usurped name of Boniface, We, moved solely by paternal affection and desiring nothing more than to lead back such misguided persons to the path of salvation, recalling them benignly from their errors . . .

In Flanders, a few years back, the English had tried out the Way of Action in a characteristically empirical manner. The Bishop of Norwich, a prelate of exceptional bigotry and drive, had somehow

induced Parliament to give him command of an army. An in-
flammatory bull from Urban, *Dudum cum filii Belial*, was published,
the City approved for its own reasons, War Office protests were
overruled, the crusaders took the cross in Westminster Abbey and
the expedition landed at Gravelines. There they massacred everybody without waiting to hear which pope their victims preferred.
They then besieged Ypres, an Urbanist city, which appealed to
Rome against the Bishop's spiritual missiles and to Paris against his
temporal ones. At last a French army appeared and there was a
quick Dunkirk. The City cut its losses and threw the Bishop to the
wolves in the War Office, who devoured him remorselessly.

Some English interventions in Portugal had also been labelled as
Urbanist crusades. They too had stopped. The English were inactive
concerning the schism. From a usually reliable source in Rome came
the report that they were in arrears with their payments of papal
dues to Boniface.

Peter, sitting beneath a tall Gothic window in the library, pon-
dered this curious episode and its sequel. He knew very little of the
English, though he had come up against their hostile influence in
Portugal and had acquired an exaggerated respect for it. England
was a self-contained country like his own, tough as the leather
jerkins of her archers but without nobility of soul. With his clear
Latin logic he saw what must have happened. The English were a
tenacious people; if they genuinely believed in Urbanism, they
would have gone on fighting grimly for it despite this reverse. But
no, they had found that Urbanism did not pay, and had perfidiously
thrown it over. It has always been well understood on the Continent
that English foreign policy is dictated exclusively by commercial
considerations.

Peter now felt confident that he knew how to handle England.
With a little encouragement, the English government would be
willing openly to declare its neutrality. No more could be expected
at the moment from such materialists, but later he would discover
and present some cogent economic argument for joining Clement,
and victory would be complete.

His confidence was strengthened by what the Prior of Salon was
able to tell him. The French and English had been holding conversations at Amiens, and the Prior had been able to broach the

subject of the rival popes with the formidable Duke of Lancaster. John of Gaunt's reply had been insular, as was only to be expected; but though he would hear nothing of Clement and his claims, he admitted to the Prior that Boniface's authority rested on a slender basis, and further declared that the Church would not recover its unity until an Anglo-French peace treaty had been signed.

In fact the schism, in the English view, was no more than an aspect of the Anglo-French quarrel. Peter hastened to report his discovery to Clement.

Next year he was there at the peace conference which met at Leulinghem near Abbeville. In a long eulogistic document Clement had appointed him his Legate to France, Flanders, Hainault, Brabant, England, Scotland and Ireland. Peter set forth for these waterlogged countries with high hopes. But the interview with John of Gaunt did not go well. Peter was told that England would continue to stand by Boniface, being rooted in the true faith. Either directly or indirectly—the accounts differ—he was refused permission to cross the straits.

'And since you speak of this malignant schism,' thundered John of Gaunt, 'Know that it has no authors but yourselves.' Once peace between the two countries had been signed, he added, the cardinals would be forced to restore unity. Otherwise they would be exterminated, if he had any say in the matter.[20]

\*

Peter was now Legate in Paris. If he found the English unpredictable, he could predict only too well how the rebellious University would behave.

Nicholas de Clemanges was its Rector, a brilliant young man, more of a Latin stylist than a serious scholar. Peter got on with him excellently on the personal level, but in their approach to Church politics they differed widely. Peter was a canonist, loyal to Clement and a stickler for constitutional niceties. Clemanges was a publicist, and public opinion was impatient to end the schism at whatever cost to papal dignity and to the pet theories of church lawyers. Already the University's views were hardening. Arbitration? An Œcumenical Council? Too long and too uncertain, both of these ways. The two popes should be forced to do their duty and resign. This was the Way of Cession. Every self-respecting leader of thought felt compelled to write a pamphlet on the subject. Even the great Professor Langenstein himself, who had first proposed the Way of a Council a dozen years ago, now came out for the Way of Cession. His latest tract, *An Invective against the Monster of Babylon*, had made a deep impression at Paris.

Clemanges, therefore, organised a poll of academic opinion, perhaps the earliest of its kind on record. It was taking place at that moment. Every senior member of the University was being asked to put his suggested remedy on paper and to drop it into a big box in the cloister. It was felt that this new technique represented a great advance.

Naturally Peter could not agree. Why had the Curia not been consulted? Particularly since Clemanges had been careful to obtain the government's approval. It was too late to stop it now, he was told. When all the answers had come in, it would take the committee several months to analyse all the proposals. Well over nine thousand answers were in the box already, Clemanges announced proudly. And how many senior members, with masters' degrees, did the University have on its books? About a thousand. The science of psephology was still in its infancy.

Peter waited with misgiving for the result to be announced.

The University of Paris, which plays a leading part in the rest of this story, had reached the very height of its prestige. In matters of philosophy and theology its rulings were normally accepted throughout Europe. Strange to say, neither the popes nor the Italian universities saw anything wrong with this state of affairs. They, with their more practical bent of mind, preferred to concentrate on canon law. Bologna, pre-eminent in canonist studies, enjoyed nothing like the independence of Paris. Much influenced by the Curia and browbeaten by their own students (for Bologna was an extreme case of undergraduate democracy), the Italian professors dealt with a subject which is by its nature conservative and unexplosive. In theology, on the other hand, reputations are made by finding something new and arresting to say. It is curious that the popes, with their centralising mentality, were content to hand over so dynamic a subject to a distant band of under-paid publicists responsible only to themselves.

Though not an organ of the Church, the University could easily be made to look like one, being a semi-clerical body with an international membership. Its weakness lay in its organisation, which was little short of chaotic by modern standards. Long after Abelard's time it still owned no buildings at all. In one way this was an advantage, for in disputes with town or crown it could threaten to move elsewhere. By Clemanges time, however, there was enough ballast in the shape of college buildings to make this threat unrealistic; the professors could still go on strike, but strikes are a two-edged weapon. For the rest, the Chancellor had lost all semblance of control, and the elected Rector (poor Clemanges) presided ineffectually over four jealous faculties and four antagonistic 'nations'. Majority decisions were seldom regarded as binding, and endowments were so few that the lecturers, subject to a constant rapid turnover, were only kept there at all by hopes of special patronage and favours from the pope.

To earn such favours, on the other hand, would be unthinkable, an act of intellectual treason against the prevalent Ockhamism. The long deadlock in the schism made the pope vulnerable. The hand that fed them could be bitten in safety at last. The University plunged into an all-out struggle to impose its policies on Avignon.

The first step was to obtain an audience with the King. Peter's first step was to try to prevent it.

This brought Peter up against the other main factor in his fortunes, the French court. The young King's sanity being intermittent, France was governed at this time by an ill-assorted committee of royal dukes. None of them, in Peter's opinion, was a reliable ally. Berry was a dilettante, Bourbon too quiet, Burgundy intent only on his own advancement. The King's younger brother, Orleans, might be worth cultivating, but at the moment he was lying low after a misadventure typical of him and of the court as a whole.

It happened when one of the Queen's ladies in waiting, twice a widow, was daring enough to marry a third time. This event offered the court an opportunity to borrow and improve on the ancient peasant custom of *charivari*. As midnight struck the lights were dimmed and the King and a group of courtiers entered the festive hall dressed as 'wild men'. They were covered with long hair made of tow, stuck on to skin-tight undergarments with pitch. While they were capering round the bride with horn-blowings and indecencies, a parody of folklore that verged on the genuine, Louis of Orleans arrived with an escort of torch-bearers. He seized a torch impetuously and ran towards the mummers. They caught fire. The Duchess of Berry saved the King's life by throwing her cloak over him. Five others were burnt to death.

Louis of Orleans was therefore in eclipse. Some other potentate must check the University. For lack of anyone better, Peter spoke to the Duke of Berry who was a personal friend of Clement and the Duke forbade the audience and threatened to have the unruly dons thrown into the Seine. They rushed to the Duke of Burgundy. He arranged for the University to have its audience.

Its proposals were based on what had resulted from the opinion-poll. Clement and Boniface, treated on an equal footing, should be offered the alternatives of cession, arbitration or a General Council. If either of them dared to refuse, he should be disowned by his own Obedience.

This was a call to revolution. Peter dashed from one Duke to another. He was able to impose delay. The University was silenced once again by the Duke of Berry and indignantly went on strike. In defiance of the ban long letters, composed in Clemanges' best Latin, were sent to the King, to Clement, and over Clement's head to the College of Cardinals.

Clement opened his letter in the presence of the courier who had brought it. Besides its general recommendations, which were daring enough, the letter contained a barbed attack on the Camerlengo, whom Clement had sent to Paris on some unavowable errand. Half way through, the Pope could contain himself no longer.

'This is a disgraceful letter!' he exclaimed in Latin. 'It's poisonous!'

Then his eye fell on the startled messenger.

'Do you know Latin?'

'Well enough for that, Holy Father.'

Clement got up and left the room, while the courier beat a hasty retreat in the opposite direction. The Pope's agitation grew when he learned that his cardinals were taking their letter seriously.

✱

Meanwhile, at a second peace conference with the English, Peter tried suggesting the way of cession to John of Gaunt. This *ballon d'essai*—there is no reason to suppose it was anything more—failed to obtain him his permit to enter England. But it did earn him a reputation for being in favour of the way of cession, even though he strongly opposed this policy in his official dealings with the French Dukes.

When he returned to Avignon, this reputation had preceded him. Clement received him coldly.

Peter was deeply hurt. He had done his utmost in Paris and at Leulinghem. He resented Clement's action in sending the Camerlengo to Paris on a separate mission. Clement brushed his protest aside. They also had some argument concerning the possibilities of a meeting between the rival popes, an idea which Peter was beginning to favour. Clement would not listen, and obviously distrusted him.

Peter spoke angrily of leaving Avignon and going back to Spain. He felt that his career in the Curia, after nearly nineteen years of devoted work, had reached a dead end. Why had he given his best years for this? He would go.

Four of his fellow-cardinals persuaded him, after a great struggle, to stay on. He remained at Avignon, nervy and depressed.

The strain on Clement was worse. He had endless discussions with everyone. To his mother and a few close advisers he even spoke of resigning. Then the Camerlengo returned from Paris with news of fresh discord between the Dukes and the University. Clement's optimism revived at once. He started to plan another Italian expedition. It was a pity, though, that he felt so poorly. For three days he stayed in his room. Then, on the morning of 16 September 1394, he got up and went to hear mass as usual. As he walked back to his room he suddenly felt very weak. He asked for some wine, but before they could bring it he was dead.

The news took only six days to reach Paris. The King, whose mind was normal again at that moment, consulted his advisers and sent off a reply that same evening in which he strongly urged the cardinals to delay electing a successor. The royal messenger covered the 440 miles in four days, an extraordinary physical achievement, arriving just in time to find the cardinals going into conclave. He handed the King's letter to the Cardinal of Florence, one of the last to enter. Then the conclave was sealed.

★

They began by debating whether the letter should be opened and read. Peter quoted the appropriate passage in canon law which expressly forbade it, and the letter remained unopened.

Their motive for haste is obvious. Without a new pope, their position *vis-à-vis* Paris would be very weak indeed. They could guess what the King had written. Were they to read his advice they would find it impossible to reject it. The papacy would then remain vacant indefinitely while the Antipope Boniface in Rome refused to resign; he had already proved himself intransigent. The end was not hard to foresee. Avignon would be liquidated under French pressure. They would have to choose Boniface or be disowned.

Whether from an austere regard for canon law or from tactical motives, Peter had refused to join his colleagues in their preliminary lobbyings. But once the conclave had started he dominated it by his legal learning and force of character. The Cardinal of Saluzzo proposed that they should either adjourn without electing anyone and open negotiations with Rome, or else elect Boniface outright. In Peter's eyes these were craven suggestions. Without wasting time by arguing their political demerits, he objected that Boniface and his anticardinals had been excommunicated and were therefore under a legal disability from which only a new pope could free them. Until then they could neither vote nor be voted for. Peter's argument may seem over-ingenious to us, but it was sound in theory, and his colleagues snatched at it. There had to be a new Avignon pope.

As a concession to Paris, they agreed to impose on themselves a conclave oath or 'capitulation'. The *cedula* containing it was drafted by Martin de Salva in the following terms:

> I promise on the holy gospels to work for unity with all my strength and not to do or say anything which could hinder or delay it. If I am elected pope, I will follow all profitable and suitable ways to unity, including the way of cession if the majority of cardinals at the time considers it appropriate.

The actual text of the *cedula* in its deplorable church lawyers
jargon was over three times as long, but that is the maximum o
meaning that can be squeezed out of it.

Peter and several others objected to this oath. It served no pur
pose, they said, for it only obliged a future pope to do what it wa
his duty to do in any case. It was also undignified, an unworth
concession to 'public opinion'. And they all knew quite well tha
any electoral pact made by a pope and tending to limit his freedor
of action was null and void in canon law, which was unusually clea
on this point.

There was a long argument, but the majority was in favour of th
*cedula* as it stood. If Peter raised so many objections, they insinuatec
did that mean he thought he was elected already? He protested tha
so great a burden was beyond his desires or his capabilities. At las
to put an end to an undignified wrangle, he agreed to sign. The
all did so, except the three tellers.

Next morning an Italian colleague asked Peter why he ha
found it so hard to sign the *cedula*.

'My dear Albano,' came the answer, remembered years late
'considering what a desperate state the Church is in, don't yo
think it would be a wretched sort of man who would refuse to giv
us peace and unity unless he had made some promise or taken som
oath?'

Of the twenty-one cardinals present, a dozen were Frencl
Apparently none of them, not even the ambitious Thury, relishe
the prospect of becoming pope against the King's will. The hal
dozen Italians could see no personal advantage in it either. If thing
went wrong, Boniface was not likely to treat an Italian competitc
generously. Saluzzo, a Savoyard, was equally unwilling. There onl
remained the two Spaniards. The senior of them was chosen b
secret ballot with only one dissentient voice, his own.

Protocol prescribes a decent hesitation. Peter, whether fro
genuine modesty or out of still more genuine caution, resisted muc
longer. Not for two centuries, a contemporary declared, had suc
resistance been seen in a conclave. At last he accepted. He was Pop
St. Peter's two hundred and second successor.

# CHAPTER 6

# The Way of Cession

PETER himself was as surprised, or almost as surprised, as anyone. Nobody could have foreseen that Clement, a vigorous man of fifty-two, would die so suddenly. Peter cannot have been planning to become pope. If, therefore, he had recently become known as one who favoured (or was supposed to favour) the way of cession, this had not been part of any deliberate, self-interested electoral strategy. He had only been feeling his way, as he always did. He could recognise a problem's existence before most people, but was slower than most in finding a solution. Then, his decision once taken, he would never go back on it.

When Clement died, however, he saw his chance. Why should he not aim that high? He had good cause to believe that no fellow-cardinal had greater abilities, a stronger character or better intentions than he had. Avignon's just cause was in the melting-pot; he was the man to rescue it. As a cardinal-deacon he was low on the list, but seniority of that kind mattered little. Only four of them were of an earlier vintage than he was, and only two, Malesset and Lagrange, were of the same date. Unless some Frenchman were willing to risk his King's displeasure by becoming pope, the odds were short indeed.

At such a moment, with the election only a few days ahead, it would be unreasonable to expect a candidate to disclaim any advantage he might have in the eyes of his electors. In so far as Peter's reputation for favouring cession rested on a misunderstanding, it was not for him to clear the matter up. By opposing the *cedula* he showed that he thought a pope should have full freedom of action. If, after that, the cardinals believed he would be their willing tool, they had only themselves to blame for their lack of judgment.

Actually, at that time, few if any of them were wholeheartedly in
favour of the way of cession. Certainly not if it meant throwing over
the cause they had upheld for sixteen years and risking their own
careers and emoluments. Their aim was much simpler. They wished
to resist the meddlesome professors and politicians without breaking
with the King, on whose good will they were dangerously dependent. To this end they elected Peter with all convenient speed.
Any other version of their motives and expectations is pure hypo-
crisy. This is important, in view of what followed.

Peter's first act as Pope was to choose his own name. In spite of
the pressure of events, he would not have been true to character had
he not given the choice a little thought. It would be wise to take
a name which had already been held by an Avignon pope. Of
these, Urban was impossible, and the consequences of Gregory's
mistake were still with them. Rather than be merely innocent,
which sounded too much like a sacrificial victim, or clement, which
suggested reserves of power he was unlikely to enjoy, he would
prefer to be blessed. His choice was therefore Benedict. The last of
that name had been the strictest and most reforming of the Avignon
popes, a strong opponent of simony.

Soon after midday they took him to Notre-Dame des Doms, the
unpretentious cathedral, and proclaimed him as Benedict XIII. It
was Monday, 28 September 1394. He was the first Spanish pope.[21]

His first task was to read the King's letter.

Its contents were exactly what they had expected. His Majesty
trusted that his *très chiers et especiaux amis* would have the good sense
to postpone the election.

Peter—it will be convenient to go on calling him that—spoke to
the Cardinal of Amiens, Jean de Lagrange, a worldly Burgundian
bull of a man who had close links with the royal court. He and two
colleagues had sent the King the news of Clement's death, to which
this letter was the reply. They shaded their eyes and wrote to His
Majesty again.

*Nostre très redoubté Seigneur,*
  We know that, moved by the devotion which you have
always shown towards our mother Holy Church, you will take
pleasure in hearing news of her welfare.   We therefore beg to
inform Your Majesty that . . .

And now that he has recently been in France and has lived at your court he has become entirely devoted to you. Consequently, in his new position, he is determined to make you his leader in all his endeavours, and so to continue, diligently following all profitable ways to end the schism, according to your good pleasure and advice.

Meanwhile it was best to lose no time. Next day Malesset ordained him a priest. And on Sunday, 11 October came the day of his coronation. The ceremonies lasted all the morning in the great Gothic chapel of the Palace. He was consecrated as a bishop. He received the robes, the mitre and the ring. The cardinals paid him homage, and then into each kneeling cardinal's mitre, held out before him, he dropped a small leather purse symbolising the customary largesse, which on this occasion was set at 4,000 florins. Heaven and the Camerlengo knew how and when it would be paid. In fact it never was paid.

The ceremonial reached its climax. They led him to the Window of the Indulgence, where he could be seen by the crowd which packed the courtyard. The senior cardinal deacon placed the venerable tiara on his head. Peter gave his blessing as Pope.

Next day the first formal bulls were dispatched.

In those addressed to Paris he spoke of his intention to work for unity in co-operation with the King, but carefully avoided any specific undertakings and any mention of the conclave oath or *cedula*. Not a word, either, about making the King *son chef*. These omissions did not pass unnoticed in Paris. But there they were good politicians too. Having failed to prevent the election, they wrote fulsome letters expressing the joy they felt at its result. A special envoy followed, bearing the royal congratulations.

Pierre d'Ailly, Chancellor of the University and confessor to His Majesty, was sent on this dignified errand. He was a remarkable man in every way. In fact his reputation preceded him, and Clemanges was unusually naïve in thinking that a personal letter of introduction was called for.

> For among your illustrious subjects you have one who is a most learned scholar, a man who has won the highest praise for his faith, his discretion and his upright character, a man burning with zeal for the Church's unity. Chancellor Pierre d'Ailly is the light of our age. . . . You must single him out, cultivate him,

I

receive him with open arms, trust him with everything as if he were your other self. And there can be no doubt whatever, you will not lose by doing this, nor will you repent of having chosen such a master.

Peter smiled to himself and thought about what else he knew of d'Ailly. He had not been privileged to see him in action as an ambassador until now.

D'Ailly's adaptability in these situations was already something of a legend. He had appeared at least twice before at Avignon, first to conduct a highly illogical case against the Dominicans, and then again to press for a certain youth of sensational piety to be canonised at once on the ground that his miracles offered the clearest possible proof of Clement's legitimacy. And this in spite of his own well-advertised doubts on the subject.

Peter, still in Spain at the time, had missed both these performances. More disappointing still, he had missed meeting the saint, an aristocratic teenage bishop whom Clement had patronised and even made a cardinal. At eighteen the prodigy had died, and less than two years later d'Ailly was standing here before Clement, claiming 2,128 miracles to the holy boy's credit, including thirteen persons raised from the dead, fifty-seven healed of blindness, fifteen of deafness, eight of dumbness, six of dropsy, the Duke of Burgundy's chamberlain cured of a tournament injury and the Duke of Bourbon's master baker from being struck by lightning. To Clement's credit, he refused to be swept away by d'Ailly's uncritical statistics and by the shallow piety in high places which lay behind them, and the saint, Pierre de Luxembourg, was only beatified by Clement's double a hundred and forty years later. This refusal, incidentally, shows that Clement was more than the self-seeking politician of some modern textbooks.

As Chancellor, d'Ailly's powers over the University were almost nil, but he would be blamed if anything went wrong. Privately, as he watched the University coming up to the boil, d'Ailly looked forward to exchanging the Chancellorship for something less unstable; at present he was only an ornamental lid on a kettle. He therefore made himself the leading theorist of the reform movement, and as such he had been attacking Avignon up to a few weeks ago. Now, however, as he stood before Peter's throne in the

Avignon audience-chamber, honey dripped from his mouth. The new Holy Father's superlative qualities were the admiration of all. Nowhere were they admired more than in Paris. A golden age would return; nay, was it not with them already?

Why the sudden change? Peter wondered, as he listened with a certain unwilling admiration to the convolutions and cursus-endings of the Latin. Was it because one of Clement's last actions had been to give d'Ailly a rich canonry at Rouen? If so, how easy everything was going to be. No, it was the King speaking, or rather, since the poor King was hardly in full control of policy or of himself, these high-flown compliments represented the latest eddy in that carp-pond of royal dukes. The next splash, when Burgundy's fins broke the surface, might be very different.

D'Ailly was always a jump ahead, though whether ahead of his own party's thinking or of common honesty was a matter of opinion. Yet this strange man was more than a mere careerist. He was one of the foremost intellectuals of his day. A book of his on spherical geography inspired Columbus. But before all else he was a liberal theologian, an Ockhamist, one who rejected the proofs and certainties of the last generation and looked on papal claims with a sceptical eye. Theologians of his school tended to back the bishops and princes against the Curia and to support the dangerous theory that a General Council stands above a pope.

The schism, of course, gave them every opportunity to indulge these notions. They had already produced a whole literature of tracts and pamphlets, to which d'Ailly had lately contributed an amusing *Letter from the Devil*. Peter had admired it and disapproved of it. D'Ailly, he thought, would be a most dangerous enemy. He must be won over or at least neutralised. A start could be made at his private audience, due in a few days.

*

Peter had inherited a pleasant study in a tower, part of the additions made some forty years earlier by his predecessor Clement VI, who considered that a pope should live well. Above it this Clement had built a private chapel, profusely adorned with soft-hearted Italian angels, the most reassuring sub-species he could find.

Below it was a bathroom with copious hot water, a reckless innovation which in the opinion of more conservative churchmen smacked of the errors of Islam. The study itself was equally designed to banish care, being lit by two ample windows and having the entire wall-space covered with delightful frescoes, lively scenes of hunting, shooting and fishing in an idyllic countryside.

In this room, then, Peter received Pierre d'Ailly. The famous reformer was in no way disconcerted by the décor. Their discussions lasted several days and ranged widely. It was an excellent opportunity to examine the problems that lay ahead.

Before long they reached the critical subject of finance. It was easy enough to agree that simony must be checked. But what did the term include? The taxes payable on appointment to a benefice, for instance? Hardly; the Holy See must raise funds somehow, and this was now one of the established methods. Peter had been having some hair-raising talks with the Camerlengo, François de Conzié, whom he hastened to confirm in his job. He was an indispensable man who would restore the papal finances to health if anyone could, but no one could expect him to do so without *servitia* and annates. On the other hand, Peter decided, certain unauthorised gratuities and extortions would go. (Their suppression did nothing to make him more popular with his cardinals.)

Clement had left his finances in a desperate state. Rumour said that the tiara had been fetched out of pawn for Peter's coronation. The truth was nearly as bad.

D'Ailly perforce agreed that papal taxes must stay. Seeing his advantage, Peter counter-attacked. What about all those clerical appointments in lay hands? The seven hundred and fifty benefices which Clement in his difficulties had seen fit to place at His Majesty's disposal? Surely His Majesty's ambassador could see the urgent need for some generous and tactful measure that would restore these appointments to the Church, where they rightly belonged?

As the great reforming churchman remained strangely silent, Peter passed on to other matters. Relations with the University. These were now much better, on the surface. He had delighted the University delegates by telling them, as he took off his cope, that it would cost him no more effort to lay down the papacy if duty so demanded. They happily ignored the little qualifying clause. Yet Clement had made the same remark once when receiving a group of Carthusians, and the popularity it brought him had been of the briefest.

D'Ailly approached the subject of Church unity with great discretion, behaviour which was not lost on Peter. Peter's immediate aim was to consolidate his position. His chief argument, which formed the corner-stone of a memorandum[22] he was drawing up for the papal nuncios to Paris, was that there must be a true pope in existence and that without one there could be no unity worth the name. The argument begged the question, but ingeniously. The final section of the memorandum made it clear how far he was prepared to go.

> ... And after dealing thoroughly with that suggestion, and driving their answer home in conversation with the King and his uncles and everybody else—which is something they can surely do, with God's help and with their own knowledge and tact— the nuncios will come finally to the principal object of their mission, explaining that our lord the Pope, in so far as it is granted him from on high, is altogether determined to unite the Church and to root out this pestilent schism, and that he intends to take no important step without the advice and good will of the King and the Dukes.

He asked them to send a special team of experts, to give their views in detail and join in the planning. He was ready to adopt any reasonable and practical way they could suggest, so long as God and his conscience allowed it.

Peter's memorandum is tense, repetitive and anxious. There are some last-minute marginal corrections, very possibly influenced by his visitor. As d'Ailly listened to Peter, he could not avoid feeling a little sorry for him. This brisk little Spanish Pope, for all his ability and character, had his back to the wall.

And what sort of proposals would be regarded as unreasonable and unpractical? Those which only took him into account, and not the usurper. They must all join in putting at least as much pressure on the rival pope as some would like to put on their own one.

There was something in that.

It was time for d'Ailly to return to Paris. Their conversations had not been unfruitful. Peter gave him leave to send in his own little roll of personal requests. He was sure there could be no hint of simony in that.

★

The roll appeared very promptly on Peter's desk. In it d'Ailly asked for permission to cumulate benefices himself (something he had already been doing to good purpose) and went on to suggest a number of lucrative sinecures for his many friends, including Clemanges and other leading spirits in the reform movement. Peter looked at the document, so neatly and correctly drawn up, with the utmost distaste. There was nothing for it; he dipped his pen in the ink and wrote the necessary formula. The action revealed to him, in a clearer light than ever before, the necessary immorality of power. How much farther along this road would he have to travel? He felt badly in need of advice from someone nearer to heaven than he was, and remembered Brother Vincent.

Brother Vincent, as it happened, stood in equal need of help. For several years he had been promoting a great movement to convert the Jews. The excitement it engendered throughout Spain had led to some unpleasant outbreaks of violence since Peter had left the country; in fact it was a turning-point, the beginning of that narrowness and intolerance which has stained the Spanish Church ever since. Vincent did not mean it to be that. Partly to counteract these excesses, partly for its obvious propaganda advantage when preaching to Jews, he had developed the theory that Judas Iscariot died penitent and was therefore in purgatory rather than in hell. The Inquisitor-General for Aragon disliked this notion, perceiving that its consequences could touch him professionally, and a process for heresy was opened against Brother Vincent.

Peter sent for the papers. On the surface they showed a clear case. The Church taught that Judas was in hell and Vincent had publicly contradicted this teaching. Could he of all people really be guilty of heresy? Or was the charge only another example of bureaucracy run wild? In the privacy of his own study Peter looked up Judas in Holy Writ. What he found puzzled him greatly; as a lawyer, he found it impossible to reconcile the two accounts of Judas' end given in Matthew and in Acts. The former was clearly the source of Vincent's theory. At the same time Peter made a still more puzzling discovery. Judas, though already perceived to be a traitor, had been allowed to take part in the Last Supper. Who in the world, then, could be excommunicated? This was a startling idea to a medieval churchman. How much more of current ecclesiastical practice might crumble away if one started referring to the Bible? Peter, no theologian and not even a priest until very recently, felt out of his depth. Yet something told him that this was vitally important. At any rate, he thought, I will use excommunication as little as possible, whatever the temptation. It has been used too often and too carelessly.[23]

Peter knew better than to give his enemies a handle by making his unorthodox researches public, as John XXII had rashly done when he proclaimed his own pet theory of the Beatific Vision. Instead he found a practical way out of Vincent's difficulties. He burned the papers and quashed the proceedings. When Vincent arrived he made him his confessor.

A little later the Inquisitor himself arrived, having been kicked out of his job. It was the same canny Nicolas Eymeric who had been the first to congratulate Urban. He was an old man now, grown crotchety and unpopular through having served the Church too well. Peter felt he owed him a refuge and allowed him to stay in the Palace, giving him an easy post in the propaganda department. He was a great talker. In time he learned to keep off heresy, which Peter found an uncongenial subject, and talk about magic instead. Old Eymeric had written three books against necromancers and was a great authority. Peter found his queer stories an interesting diversion.

Peter stood much in need of Brother Vincent. He wanted someone more than an ordinary confessor. As a man of action, entangled each day more inextricably with power and enjoying it thoroughly too, he knew that he was in danger of losing touch with the deeper side of religion. It had been better in those spacious years in the castle at Illueca; then, he had been able to take some hesitant steps along the path of contemplation as mapped by his favourite author, Dionysius the Areopagite. But in France latterly he had lost ground, and now, in the papal apartments in the Tour des Anges, the door that led that way was locked. His fate was a different one. He may have derived some wry comfort as he looked at the charming hunting scenes frescoed on his walls and reflected that obviously no one expected a pope to be a mystic. One such experiment had been enough. Just a century ago they had dug a contemplative hermit out of his cave in the Abruzzi mountains and had made him Pope Celestine V. But he had failed to combine the two roles and, instead of revitalising the Church, he soon resigned in favour of that hard-boiled politician Boniface VIII, whose pride provoked a reaction which led to the move to Avignon. . . .

*Resigned*. The word, never far in the background, brought Peter back with a jerk to his more immediate problems. He had fenced cautiously with d'Ailly and others when the way of cession and the conclave oath or *cedula* came up, since he had not yet made up his mind about them. But the subject was seldom out of his thoughts. Did the *cedula* oblige him to follow the way of cession rather than any other way? He hoped not, for these last weeks had brought a strong sense of purpose into his life again. There was so much crying out to be done, and he could do some of it. But he was a scrupulous man and the thought nagged at him.

There was one loyal friend whose expert advice he would value. He sent for Martin, the only Spanish cardinal at Avignon, and put the question to him. After all, Martin had drafted the thing.

Together they examined the text of the *cedula*, well aware that a great deal depended on what they found there. They were both of them godfearing, scrupulous men and canon lawyers of unusual distinction. Under the glare of four eyes, holes began to appear in the *cedula*. Soon it was leaking like a sieve. In fact it was even less watertight than most legal documents. Had Martin made it like that intentionally? There is no way of telling.

In the first place, a majority of cardinals must recommend the way of cession. They had not done so yet; perhaps they never would. If they did so recommend it must be their honest opinion, not a move induced by fear or favour of Paris. Even then Peter was not bound to follow that particular way to unity alone, but only to give it equal consideration with other ways. Moreover, it must be 'profitable and suitable' in the political context of that moment, and Peter was the judge of that. And lastly, no agreement tending to restrict a future pope in the free exercise of his sovereignty was valid in canon law.

Now what was left of the *cedula*?

If some of these arguments appear unconvincing or even verging on the deceitful to us, that is only because we are all of us latter-day liberals and firm believers in round-table bargaining. We must forget these preconceptions and put ourselves back into the fourteenth century. Peter and his fellow men were not equals. He was their sovereign lord the Pope. His power did not come from them and it could not be negotiated away.

The cardinals to decide when he should abdicate? The Sovereign Pontiff bound by a majority vote like the chairman of one of those Italian banks? The very idea was absurd. It was illegal too. Gregory X's law of 1274 declared any conclave pact invalid, even if confirmed on oath, and as recently as forty years ago Innocent VI had rightly refused to be bound by one.

But Peter had signed the *cedula* before his colleagues elected him. Was he not under some moral obligation at least?

No, for what the Church had made illegal could not be moral. The cardinals were not ignorant of canon law. They had chosen him, a Spaniard, because they wanted a pope at once and none of them had the courage to become one. Which showed the sort of men they were and what their advice was worth. Why should the first Spanish pope in history make himself their servant, and through them France's servant, dismissable at a moment's notice?

By these and other such arguments Martin and Peter convinced themselves that he had a completely free hand. There can be no doubt at all that they believed it sincerely. If there was a flaw in their reasoning, its origin lay in the nature of the institution itself, and not in any perversity of theirs.

But if the right and the duty to govern were Peter's alone, he had still to decide what policy to follow before others tried their hardest to decide for him. By choosing the way of cession, he could make himself the most popular man in France. Some months back, in Paris, he may have thought that the idea had possibilities. The trouble was, it meant putting the papacy into the hands of the Dukes and the University. That was bad in itself, and great harm might come of it. If Peter were to bind himself to abdicate, the

Italian usurper would harden his heart. Seeing his rival in a weak position, he would laugh at the idea of abdicating too. And then one of two things would happen. Either the French would be craven enough to give way, and then the true Pope would have retired in favour of the false one and the genuine succession would be lost. Or else the French would order the cardinals at Avignon to elect another pope, making sure this time that he was an obedient little Frenchman—willing, for instance, to let French princes steal the Church's property.

Peter and Martin believed that there was a connection between the way of cession and despoiling the Church. Events would show that they were right.

So the way of cession would have to be resisted. Peter would be accused of inconsistency, but that could not be helped. He must stand fast against it.

Did either of them realise how hard that was going to be?

★

Peter's nuncios asked the King for advice. The King's reply was to call a synod of the French clergy to meet in Paris and discuss how the schism should be ended. This was not what Peter had meant. If the Pope consented to do nothing without the King, the King should do nothing without the Pope. Peter's one-time conclavist Fernando, now Bishop of Tarazona and rising fast in the Curia, was sent hurrying to Paris with this message. The King assured Peter that the synod's findings would be sent to him for information only.

The synod's president, Simon de Cramaud, saw things very differently. His was yet another canon lawyer's career—the Duke of Berry's chancellor, a royal judge, a quick succession of little-visited bishoprics, much real estate acquired in Poitou, and so Latin Patriarch of Alexandria and head of the French clergy. As such he never walked across the street from one palace to another without a train-bearer. Peter loathed him so heartily that he had stopped Clement from making him a cardinal, something which Cramaud did not forget.

The synod met in the Sainte-Chapelle. A hundred and nine

dignitaries attended it, with the University's delegates well to the fore. Under Cramaud's chairmanship they rejected all ways except cession, voting that it should be imposed on the Pope if the King agreed. Peter had encouraged his French friends to attend, but they were few. Their spokesman, Élie de Lestrange, could only muster nineteen votes. The King, going back on his word not to impose a ready-made plan, accepted the synod's proposal, which thereby became the official policy of France.

Peter did what he could to meet the challenge. He made d'Ailly a bishop, thus detaching the most respected of the reformers from the extreme party. He appointed d'Ailly's moderate and able follower, Gerson, to take his place as Chancellor. And he made at least eight of his cardinals give him their opinions in writing.

What they wrote was revealing.

Thury and Jean de Lagrange proposed arbitration by six cardinals. To ensure that these had no inconvenient loyalties, the King should nominate Peter's and the Emperor Boniface's. This was a recipe for short-listing Thury and Lagrange as candidates for the united papacy.

Cardinal Giffone, a slippery Neapolitan, produced a long list of arguments against cession, arbitration and a Council, proposing instead that the two popes, plus those cardinals who had been present at Urban's conclave, should be locked up in a room by the King until they reached agreement. This was a delightfully ingenious recipe for a victory by Peter. Only four cardinals would qualify, all of them his, and Thury and Lagrange would be excluded.

The remaining cardinals, that is the majority, wanted a conference between the two popes, which was Peter's own solution. Provided, of course, that the King wanted that too. Froissart has put his finger on what concerned them most when he makes them urge obedience to the King's wishes, 'or els he wyll stoppe fro us the fruites of our benefyces, without the whiche we can nat lyve'.

*

In Paris it was decided that three royal Dukes in person should present the King's plan. A procession of gaily decorated boats bore down the Rhône. At the head of the flotilla came Berry, Burgundy and Orleans, then came seven royal counsellors, then the three suites

of gentlemen-in-waiting, notaries and secretaries, and lastly, inter-
mingled with the numerous maîtres-d'hôtel and fruiterers, came ten
socially browbeaten delegates of the University. Tents were pitched
on the bank each night, and for a whole fortnight the ambassadors
gave themselves up to the delights of Lyons. At last, on 22 May
1395, they reached Avignon.

Peter received the three Dukes graciously. They introduced the
gentlemen of their entourage. There were the customary osculations
and letters of credence. Refreshments were provided. Conversation
flowed. The University delegates were kept waiting in an anteroom.

Presently, as the last quail's tongue disappeared, a courtier murmured something to the Duke of Berry.

*Ah! Ce pannier de crabbes!* He had forgotten them. He now feared
he must beg His Holiness to extend his benevolence, if only for a
moment, to this academic appendage which some mischance had
attached to their mission. No one regretted the necessity more
infinitely than he did.

The Dukes took their leave and the ten dons were ushered in.
Their tempers had not been improved by the wait or by the detailed
instructions concerning protocol which the master of ceremonies
had been imparting to them.

'We paid as much reverence to that Pope Benedict XIII as we
would have paid to God in Heaven,' the most radical of them,
Master Jean Petit, complained afterwards.

The royal mission took up residence in the spacious buildings of
Villeneuve across the river.

Peter had already met the three Dukes in Paris.

Philip the Bold of Burgundy, who ruled over semi-Urbanist
Flanders from Clementine Dijon and maintained a vast network
of relations with the Urbanist princes of Germany, was only too
anxious to end the schism on any terms which his academic hangers-
on could devise. He himself was no theorist, only an astute, methodical, hard-bitten politician whose family aims were too big for France.
He had heavy features, a mouth like a trap, a long fleshy nose and a
very cold eye.

His brother John, Duke of Berry, gave most of his thought to the
arts, in so far as they could be made to serve his own magnificence.
In such cases he was a lavish patron, in fact his whole life was one

long succession of *très riches heures*. The open-handed Clement had been his personal friend, but now that there was this legal-minded Spanish Pope who tried to balance his accounts, Berry's puffy, peevish face showed plainly in unguarded moments that he thought the fellow was a bore.

There remained Louis of Orleans, much younger than the other two; he was the King's brother while they were his uncles. He had lived down the accident in the ballroom when five courtiers were burned to death and had quite recovered his normal over-confidence. He was a typical French prince of the period, gay, intelligent, extravagant, ambitious, unsteady and devout. He had the long nose and the determined jaw of the Valois, but an open face and frank eyes set wide apart. He was serious about poetry, love and politics, but far from systematic in any of them. His ambitions were vague Italian ones, conflicting with Burgundy's. He had married Valentina Visconti, daughter of the expansionist despot of Milan. The Queen Mother disapproved and had banished her from court, so he was ready for anything. He might even fall again for the 'Kingdom of Adria', mused Peter.

The mission soon got down to business. The Dukes, who disliked the effort of making formal speeches in Latin, used a certain Gilles des Champs as their mouthpiece. Their first move was to demand to see the *cedula*. Peter, who felt that the whole episode of the *cedula* was undignified, had not mentioned it in any of his dealings with Paris. In this he made a serious mistake, for in the absence of the authentic text his enemies had circulated an apocryphal version committing him to follow the King's dictates. He now had the true text read out; it did not mention the King at all.

But it mentioned cession. There followed a series of meetings at which the Dukes urged this course and Peter urged his own plan for a conference with Boniface. He was sure that in such an encounter he would be able to confound his rival and emerge victorious. Was he not both an unchallengeable witness to the facts of 1378 and an unrivalled advocate as to their interpretation? The other side would make as poor a showing as they had done at Medina del Campo. What better way of serving justice could the Dukes suggest?

The Dukes stuck to their brief and repeated their demand for cession. It was the King's choice, they explained. Peter replied quietly that he had asked the King for advice, not for orders. Would they care to give him the details of the King's plan in writing, so that he could consider it further?

'There is no need for anything in writing,' replied Berry acidly. 'The proposal is contained in the one word, *cession*!'

Peter said he was not prepared to treat so important a question so summarily. The Dukes knelt briefly and withdrew. Before leaving the building, they invited all the cardinals to meet them that evening in Villeneuve, on French soil.

This was a high-handed breach of etiquette but a most effective move. The College was instantly in a fearful flutter. Some asked leave to go, others did not. All went, except one aged cardinal who was ill.

They met in the pretentious mansion that Cardinal Giffone had built for himself in Villeneuve; his arms are still there by the gate. From the large mullioned windows on the *piano nobile* they watched the setting sun briefly gild Peter's towers across the river. Then the Duke of Berry called the meeting to order.

His opening remarks were short and precise. He demanded to know what each of them thought. Was cession as proposed by the King the better way, or was a conference as suggested by the Pope? His notary sat ready to take down the answers in full. This time it suited Berry to have it in writing.[24]

They all looked at their senior, Corsini of Florence.

'It is already rather late,' quavered the old man unhappily in his high Italian voice. 'One can see that my lords are very tired. Perhaps, if Your Graces wish to discuss this so difficult affair, we may give you our answers tomorrow morning?'

'We are not in the least tired. We would like your answers now.'

'Ah well, dear me, if it were possible, the Church today finds herself in a more miserable state than she has been at any time since holy St. Peter, the Prince of the Apostles. And there are many reasons. . . . Yes, to be sure, Your Graces demand which is the best way and the quickest way. . . . We should strive to work by every way. . . . Yes, indeed, Your Grace, I think perhaps the way of cession might be the swiftest and the holiest way.'

'Thank you. Have you got that down, Master Notary? Now, Your Eminence of Poitiers, please. You are next.'

'The best way is the way which is most pleasing to the Almighty,' began Malesset a little more boldly. He had taken over Peter's *livrée* and felt that his dignity was at stake. '*If* the way of cession is really that, and if the Church can really obtain peace and unity more speedily by that way than by any other, then I would consider it preferable.'

Jean de Lagrange's opinion was a foregone conclusion.

'The way of cession is better, quicker, easier, more honourable and more pleasing to God and to public opinion. There is no other way. I am willing to wager my share in paradise for this plan. There is no need to go into details now, but I am sure we all agree in principle.'

Albano, an Italian, felt this was going too far.

'I think one could well find some way that is better than this way of cession, some way more honourable for the Church, the Pope and the House of France. I know of certain people whose only object is to have His Holiness deposed. I cannot think Your Graces really wish him to abdicate unless it is for the peace of the Church. I take it your plan is for the usurper to resign first?'

Neufchâtel, a blunt young Burgundian nobleman in a cardinal's robes, said simply that he accepted cession because it was the King's plan and the Dukes'.

Aigrefeuille agreed, provided that the Church really obtained peace and remained free. Most others gave qualified answers like this.

Only Martin came out uncompromisingly against cession, and he as a junior had to speak after most of the others. He protested vigorously against the whole affair. It was without precedent that the cardinals should be interrogated behind the Pope's back. Their answers, obtained in this fashion, were null and void.

'Given the basic fact that our lord Benedict is the true Pope, shepherd of the Church and Christ's sole Vicar, our plain duty is to support him, to defend him and to drive out the usurper. The real way to get peace and unity for the Church, in accordance with God's will and justice, is to expel the usurper by military action or at least destroy his power. It is unfair and unreasonable, it is against God and justice, to take refuge from this duty in a so-called way of cession which places the Pope and the usurper on the same footing.

Nor does it reflect any honour on the royal House of France, for when your enemies see you forcing your Pope to resign, they will say that you knew you had been in error.'

But he spoke too late. Auch tried to follow his lead, but his courage failed him. The rest did not even try. Giffone was the most abject of all. The notary finished writing and Berry gave them leave to go.

\*

Two could play at that game. Fernando was dispatched at once with Peter's invitation to the Dukes. Would they be kind enough to call on him privately, one of them on each of the next three days?

To Burgundy he complained of threats which his suite had been making. He added that one of the cardinals who had declared for cession had already come privately to urge him never to accept it. What he said to Berry is unknown. With Orleans he got down to business. If this storm could be weathered, they would both go to Italy. Orleans became his secret ally.

If the cardinals were an uncertain quantity, so were the Dukes.

Relations grew steadily worse. The Dukes complained that Peter should not have put forward a plan of his own unless the King had approved it. Peter complained that they would never have treated a French pope like this. A wooden section of the famous bridge was mysteriously burnt, and the Dukes, having tried crossing by boat in the mistral, moved to the same side of the river as Peter. Cardinal Giffone, who wished to forget the long document in Peter's support which he had drafted only a few weeks back, declared that the Pope's familiars had burnt the bridge. Peter recalled that the Cardinal had burnt his own hat at Naples in 1381.

An eccentric Englishman in the Curia, John Hayton, chose this moment to publish eight closely reasoned *Propositions* showing that a pope's only judge is his own conscience and that those who presumed to coerce him were heretics; they should lose their degrees if doctors or their authority if princes. The University was a daughter of Satan, a mother of error, a nurse of sedition and an enemy of Holy Church. Peter, in the face of furious diplomatic protests, admitted in an off-hand way that these conclusions might be slightly exaggerated, but he gave Hayton shelter within the strong walls of the Palace.

The cardinals, even the more friendly ones like Albano, pressed him to accept the King's terms. Resistance was useless. If it went on they would all lose their benefices.

'And if I were to resign,' exclaimed Peter, losing his patience at last, 'Have you thought where I should be? I should find myself sitting on a footstool!'

'On the contrary, Holy Father,' replied Albano smoothly and disingenuously, 'You would be the most glorious man in all the world.'

'You think so, do you? Well, you will never see it happen!'

He issued two bulls making his position clear. To a royal counsellor who dined with him one day he was even more explicit.

'Before God, Messire Guillaume, I will never accept that way of cession so long as I live, not even if I were to see the coals blazing and the fire ready. I would let myself be burnt rather than accept it, not because I want to live for a long time as Pope, for I am already old enough at sixty-six, but because if I accepted I would deny my just cause and open a trap-door through which the Church would fall to destruction. You can tell them all that!'[25]

The Dukes had a last audience, but he remained adamant.

'Rather than adopt this way of cession, which would strengthen the usurper's position, I would prefer death.'

The Dukes saw that they had wasted seven weeks. They would not even stay to dinner.

'*Assez de repas!*' they replied to his invitation, strutting out after the briefest of genuflections.

Before leaving the town they engaged in a strangely un-ducal piece of public relations technique. They held a protest meeting in the Franciscan friary and gave their version of the mission's failure to the assembled citizens. Then they set out for Paris.

★

There can be no doubt that Peter was right not to give way. Whatever one's views concerning the Church's government, one thing is clear; at no time has the King of France received a divine

K

commission to exercise it. Peter, on the other hand, believed not altogether unreasonably that he had. His notions of sovereignty were strict and thoroughly medieval. His rights were absolute. They could not be shared or compromised.

His opponents fell back on the idea that the Church, as a community, has a right of self-preservation. If the Pope would not act to save them, they must save themselves. They did not stop to ask whether they had given their new Pope a fair chance to act. Instead, they claimed a right of resistance in an emergency—a right which, not yet fully accepted by the modern liberal state, has no place at all in any 'high' theory of the Church. There can be no right of resistance against the divinely commissioned head of a divinely established society. The notion that any such right existed was derived, of course, from Aristotle. There a doctrine of equity, as against law, could be found; it had a magical name, *epieikeia*. With the aid of this magic the Church's constitution might be stood neatly on its head.

Only trained philosophers could venture to talk about *epieikeia*. Most of Peter's opponents were not philosophers, they were merely Gallicans. Again, a national revolt against papal taxes, centralism and obstinacy has much to be said for it, but not if you believe that the Church on earth is a divinely constituted monarchy, something more than ordinary men trying half-heartedly to be Christians and organising themselves as best they may. And granted even the doubtful expedient of a royal supremacy over a national church, on the Gallican or any other model, the French King had no right to impose his policy on the whole Avignon Obedience without consulting the other countries which belonged to it.

The Kings of Spain were quick to take offence. They hardly needed any prompting from Peter, though he sent his nuncios to make sure that the finer points of the French insult should not escape their notice. The King of Castile complained at once; in fact he was so angry that his Spanish accent coloured his French spelling.

These protests won Peter a long respite. The University clamoured for immediate action, but the government realised that measures against the Pope must be co-ordinated with other powers. Cramaud was sent to England, others to Germany and Spain. They achieved little.

Peter used the respite to take stock of his organisation. The cardinals were broken reeds, but at a lower level the great Avignon machine was still in good order. The imperturbable Camerlengo, François de Conzié, was still there at the head of his department, methodically straightening out Peter's tangled finances, ready at a word from him to get the Apostolic Collector in Aragon to send 'two or three mares and as many really good-looking mules, with harness and saddles', or, a little later, ten crossbowmen to serve the Holy Father in his Palace. The Holy Father knew better than to acquire his mules and crossbowmen locally. He also perceived that, admirable though it was, his civil service would scarcely stand up to an intensified struggle with France. For one thing, it was still largely staffed by Frenchmen, beginning with the excellent Conzié himself.

He therefore began to build up a private organisation of his own, loyal to him personally and superimposed upon the much larger official machine. They were his eyes and ears, his confidential envoys and his M.I.5. An early recruit to this inner organisation and in all probability its head was one Simon Salvador, a Spaniard naturally, who drew his official salary as secretary to the *magister cere*, the highly respectable personage who supervised the supply of candles. Another was a quick-witted Italian, Domenico Masconi. Yet another was Martin de Alpartil, who came from a village close to Peter's ancestral home.

There was also a special propaganda department, busy just then answering an impertinent questionnaire of the 'have-you-left-off . . .?' type which the University had sent to Peter. 'Why hath Satan put it into thy heart to practise deceitfulness?' began the ex-Inquisitor Eymeric promisingly in his reply. Hayton and Pierre Blau backed him up.

Even in Paris Peter found a defender. D'Ailly, no longer Chancellor, kept very quiet; his new bishop's mitre acted as a candle-extinguisher, which was what Peter calculated when he placed it on his head. The new Chancellor, Gerson, was d'Ailly's pupil in liberal theology but not in careerism. He remained for many years the most moderate, far-sighted, consistent and honourable among the French reformers. He now wrote that cession was useless unless it was accepted in Rome as well. If Peter's abdication would not end

the schism, he was right not to abdicate. The University would harm
its own cause.

\*

Peter turned to his own plan. If he could open up direct negotia-
tions with Rome, the wind would be taken out of his critics' sails.
He wrote to Florence expressing hopes for a conference with
Boniface.

> If he emerges victorious from these discussions, I will pros-
> strate myself at Pope Boniface's feet and place my own future
> in his hands; and if I win, I will welcome the former usurper and
> his anti-cardinals at my court on the most favourable terms.

The Florentines passed the message on to Boniface and urged him
to accept, while their Secretary, the famous scholar Coluccio Salutati,
began a literary correspondence with Peter concerning the text of
Plutarch.

At this point the Italian section of Peter's secret service took a hand
in what was going on. He had inherited this section from Clement.
There was a network of confidential agents, discreet Pisan bankers,
daredevil Gascon soldiers of fortune and discontented landowners
like the Count of Fondi. They were all paid out of a special
reptilian budget, to whose existence the Camerlengo ostentatiously
closed his eyes. At the moment the organisation was hardly worth
its keep, but Peter, who had been sceptical while it worked for
Clement, was not unhopeful of it now. Anyway, it knew too much
to be dissolved out of hand.

The trouble about a secret service is that it is hard to control. It
does not readily respond even to instructions given by short-wave
wireless sets. Without any such inventions, and operating at about
six or eight weeks' time-lag by medieval courier, Avignon's agents
in Central Italy had a virtually free hand. Their achievements proved
a constant source of embarrassment. This time, just as Boniface was
wondering how he could well refuse to meet Peter, his own M.I.5
produced one of his most trusted bishops caught in the act of
plotting a wildly impracticable *coup d'état* in Rome with Peter's
myrmidons. Boniface, like Mr. Khruschev on a similar occasion,

grasped happily at this proof of the other side's bad faith and refused Peter's envoy a safe-conduct.

Presently Boniface heard strange reports from France. He was understandably puzzled by the French attitude to their pope and wished to know more about it. He sent an emissary of his own to Avignon, choosing a Neapolitan knight who was so fortunate as to be the brother of a Roman cardinal and the cousin of an Avignon one. The Cavaliere Brancaccio kept his ears open and his mouth usually shut, although once, in conversation with Peter's trusted Fernando, he threw out the suggestion that the two pontiffs should agree to divide Christendom until one of them died, whereupon the survivor should become sole pope. Why not? one wonders. Why not leave such a decision to Providence for once? But Don Fernando was still young enough to be shocked. It was a damnable idea, he replied, and would make of the Church a two-headed monster.

Peter was sure that Boniface had something more to say, and that Brancaccio was holding it back. Detaining the Cavaliere at Avignon, he sent off Fernando in hot haste as his ambassador to Rome. With him went a legal expert, a secretary, and the Italian Domenico Masconi of the secret service. The Camerlengo gave Fernando 1,000 florins for his expenses and looked Masconi, to whom he had just given a great deal more, straight in the eye. Four weeks later they landed on the Italian coast at Terracina.

The Count of Fondi sent an escort to meet them. Masconi saw to it that the inhabitants waved olive branches as they moved off. Fernando sent a message to Brancaccio's brother. Soon a safe-conduct arrived, though with the irksome proviso that they must not leave the Lateran while they were in Rome. Fernando overruled Masconi's objections and they descended from the cool Alban hills towards the city of the plain. After a very long wait by a tavern near some broken arches of the Acqua Claudia, the reception committee appeared and the Count's lancers handed them over. Entering by the Porta San Giovanni, they were only able to acknowledge the cheers of a small group of bystanders (at whose appearance Masconi looked triumphant) before they found themselves behind the stout doors and rusty bolts of the Lateran.

Two days later they were granted an audience. Fernando has left us a verbatim account of what happened.[26] As they waited in an anteroom, an agitated official hurried in to ask how they proposed to greet Boniface.

'I shall greet him in the same way as I should salute a distinguished prelate or a great baron.'

'But why won't you do him reverence according to papal protocol?'

'I trust I shall not be asked to bow down before an idol,' replied Fernando.

'I admit you may be right not to kiss his foot,' the baffled official conceded. 'But you ought to be on your knees when you make your speech.'

'I shall not do that, because a papal nuncio does not kneel even to a king or a cardinal.'

'But to a pope?'

'Only to his own pope.'

'You must wait a little while I go and tell His Holiness.'

Fernando glowed when the official reappeared after a few minutes, shooing before him a resentful gaggle of German visitors, who were being removed from the presence so that they might not witness the refusal to kneel.

With bared head ever so slightly inclined and using the expression 'Most dread Father' as a form of address and 'Our lord who is at Avignon' when referring to Peter, Fernando surmounted his difficulties. These foolish things are the heart's blood of every absolute court.

Next day there was a private audience. Boniface, a pleasant enough man in private life, broke the ice.

'Have we met before?'

'Not unless you were up at Bologna in my time, Most dread Father, but if you were, I think you must have been a freshman.'

'No, I was at Naples. I was one of the youngest cardinals my predecessor made, and as you have noticed I am not all that old now. Your master is quite elderly, I understand? Oh well, we all come to it! He is a great man, upright and very learned, a man with a clear conscience and many virtues. A very great man indeed. Well now, let us see what way he considers best in order to obtain unity.'

'Most dread lord, it was you who first sent an envoy to us. In taking this step you must have had a certain way in mind. May it please you to expound it, and I will tell you what our lord at Avignon thinks of it, for he will agree to any lawful and honourable way so long as it does not take too much time.'

'Your master, my dear ambassador, has been thinking of this problem much longer than I have. I hear on all sides how brilliant he is. His knowledge of canon law is far more profound than mine. I am sure he would not have sent you all this way, and you a prelate and a doctor as I hear, unless you were fully informed of his intentions.'

'Most dread Father, you were already discussing these matters with our lord's predecessor when our lord was away in Paris as legate. Please do not refuse to tell me your way.'

'Very well, tell me why your master will not restore obedience to me.'

'How can you ask for something to be restored which you have never possessed?'

'How can you deny that we possessed it? Was not my predecessor Urban freely enthroned and crowned by the cardinals, after they had got over their baseless fear which they allege?'

The fear was not baseless, Fernando protested. He had witnessed it himself. Boniface had been wrongly informed by interested parties.

'Oh well, I have no wish to argue with you. Let us go on. Please suggest some way out of our difficulties.'

'I expect your lordship has heard of the various ways suggested by the University of Paris, and how they all boil down to . . .'

'Don't speak to me of that impious University or its ways! Abdication is definitely wrong. I agree with your master there. So is a Council, there are too many difficulties. So is arbitration too; you cannot arbitrate or reach a compromise about sacred things.'

'It is true that laymen cannot, most dread Father, but clergy can quite well. If you would only consent to meet at some convenient place on the borders of the two Obediences, I believe that with God's help you would soon reach agreement.'

'That would only endanger both of us. We should have to place ourselves in the power of some prince or city-state, and they would force us to do what they want or else take us prisoner and maltreat us.'

'You have the Doge of Genoa in your Obedience. The Cavaliere Brancaccio says he is devoted to you. Why not go to some castle on the Genoese Riviera where you and your suite can live in safety, and our lord will come to Nice or some such place near there? For our lord trusts in the Almighty, and if once you come together unity will soon be accomplished.'

'But if we don't agree, and I fear we won't, what then? He and I will be in greater danger than ever. I am afraid that does not appeal to me.'

Fernando suggested arbitration.

'That way is no good either, ambassador, because my men will always be for me and your lord's will be for him and they will never agree.'

'I know my lord would choose godfearing men. If you choose men like that too, then with heaven's help . . .'

'Those are only words.'

They got no further at that interview. Things looked neither very promising nor altogether hopeless. Fernando's spirits rose when, some days later, he was asked whether Peter would be willing to come to some place near Rome under the Count of Fondi's protection. He answered that he thought he would. After that a fortnight passed in total silence. The confinement began to get on his nerves. At last he was summoned again, and on entering the room the reason for the delay was plain. The Cavaliere Brancaccio was there, back from France. He smiled unpleasantly at Fernando, while Boniface and his cardinals spoke angrily of being led into a trap. Fernando was told to leave Rome the next morning.

'My greetings to your master!'

It was only too obvious that Brancaccio had brought back news of how shaky was Peter's position in his own Obedience. As the wise Chancellor Gerson had foreseen, the University's campaign had spoiled all chances of unity by negotiation, at least for the present.

As Fernando's party left the Lateran Masconi, the secret service man, took a new lease of life. At his insistence they called at Civitavecchia, and there they met Boniface's Prefect in disguise, offering to sell the strategic port to Peter for a mere 12,000 florins and even to proclaim him in Rome if he would deposit a still larger sum and come in person. Did Peter realise, he asked, how well the

Romans remembered him ever since those happy days in 1378? Proof of it? They had never defaced his coat of arms on his old palazzo by the Tor Sanguigna. Was that not enough proof, between gentlemen?

Or would the Prefect sell Peter to Boniface? Fernando wondered, as he settled down to write his report.

Peter's thoughts when he read it were similar. But he studied every word that Boniface had said.

\*

Once again a stalemate had been reached. Though too weak to carry out his own plan, Peter had managed to check the rebellion against him. This was confirmed at a second synod held in Paris that summer. It was a feeble affair. Less than half the French prelates attended, the King was ill, Burgundy was absent, even Cramaud was away in Spain. Louis of Orleans took the chair and side-tracked the University's proposals.

Both sides were searching for allies outside France. The English were induced to send a mission to Avignon at last. It was not very effective, for a French source tells us that the 'Abbot of Voost-moustier' could not bring himself to salute Peter in any manner at all and therefore returned to London without having seen him. Later on a joint Anglo-French-Castilian mission visited both popes but achieved nothing.

Peter found his ally in the new King of Aragon, then campaign-ing in Sicily. Martin the Humane was not, unfortunately, a very warlike prince. It was a little difficult to imagine him campaigning at all, and almost impossible to envisage him storming the walls of Rome in person on the rightful Pope's behalf. He was forty-one and excessively stout, so stout that he was loath to travel except by ship or boat. He was an authority on church ornaments and relics, said his hours like a priest and heard mass three times a day. His palaces were crammed with religious bric-à-brac and his speeches with learned quotations. In spite of all this he had a certain vigour and dignity, was strict in enforcing the law and treated Jews and Muslims decently. His wife, to whom he was devoted, was a Luna, a not too distant cousin of the Pope's.

Another cousin, Antonio de Luna, was immediately sent to Sicily to persuade King Martin to visit Avignon on his way home. It was out of the way, but fortunately on a navigable river. Soon seven great galleys lay in midstream off Arles, while the monarch landed and paid his respects to the relics of St. Trophime. Smaller boats with determined rowers brought him upstream to Avignon, where gifts and honours were showered upon him—a relic of the True Cross, the title of Gonfalonier of the Church, plenary indulgences for every member of the royal family alive or dead, and then the highest award of all, the Golden Rose. With this last in his hand he rode through the flower-strewn streets, as was the custom. Then he knelt and paid homage for Corsica and Sardinia, which he would hold (if he could conquer them) as vassal of the Holy See. And there were valuable political discussions before he left.

It is time to introduce Peter's nephews. The word, in a papal context, may be taken to include any relatives deemed capable of advancement. The new Queen of Aragon and Count Juan the head of the family were clearly outside this category, but there were others. Cousin Antonio became Rector of the Comtat Venaissin, governor, that is, of the papal enclave round Avignon. There were also three nephews in the strict sense. The eldest, Pedro, was a blameless cleric at Valencia; the next, Álvaro, had other fish to fry; and young Rodrigo, growing up as a soldier, was later to become the nephew *par excellence*.

None of these could be promoted to the Sacred College. But other helpers had earned it and would be useful there to counterbalance the older cardinals of doubtful loyalty. Pierre Blau, his first nuncio, had already received the red hat. Now six more were added. The first of them, needless to say, was Fernando. The next pair were fellow-countrymen too, Boyl from Valencia and Anglesola a Catalan. Then an expatriate Italian, the protonotary Ammanati. The last two were absent and likely to remain so; Serra was the leading prelate in distant and changeable Sicily, and Bar, a cousin of the French King, had large estates in eastern France. He was included to make the list acceptable in Paris.

Every one of them, except the make-weight Bar, was a canon lawyer. Peter was growing suspicious of theologians and scholars. The Church was not a debating-society, it was an engine of government. Canonists were the trained artificers it needed. Any question could be thrown at them and they would deal with it. A local Provençal chronicle[27] tells how one day about this time a donkey gave birth to 'two male offspring, so formed as if they had been born of a woman'. The village concerned, feeling that only the highest authority could safely decide whether they ought to be baptized or not, sent all three to Avignon for a ruling. *Papa Benezeg* was apparently busy drafting controversial memoranda and could not be disturbed, but Cardinal Blau was available. He was newly promoted and a Provençal too; if anyone's leg was to be pulled, it had better be his. He descended reluctantly to the Palace courtyard and examined the miraculous family. Then he gave his orders. The children should be baptized, the village priest was to call on his bishop, and when he returned everyone in the village, without exception, must go to confession. His servants would take care of the donkey.

★

France made a final effort to get the way of cession adopted internationally. King Charles, in his next lucid interval, would meet the German Emperor Wenzel. If the two greatest monarchs in the two Obediences could agree on a common policy, they could surely impose it on everyone else. At the news that Wenzel was coming to Reims, optimism was unbounded. He really was coming; Louis of Orleans had lent him 30,000 francs for the expenses of his journey.

Wenzel was an extraordinary creature, large, amiable and feckless, extravagant and penniless at the shortest intervals, usually drunk. In the imagination, far away in some vast German pineforest with his hounds and his crossbow and his flask, he sounded rather jolly. In the flesh at Reims, against a background of soaring towers and civilised sunlight, he was indecent. On the morning after he arrived, when Berry and Bourbon called on him to invite him to lunch, they were already too late. He was drunk for the day and was retiring to sleep it off. Next day his *chef de protocol* just managed to get him to a banquet. At the end of forty courses the two arbiters of Europe felt sufficiently fortified to broach the subject of the Church's future. French spokesmen afterwards claimed that they reached the statesmanlike conclusion that, if one pope resigned and the other one survived, either France or Germany would be bound to lose face; both, therefore, should be forced to resign. Whether their minds actually met to this extent or not, there still remained much to be settled. But next morning another attack of Charles' madness was seen to be imminent and he was hurried off back to Paris. Orleans discreetly took his place and soon convinced Wenzel that resignation was better not mentioned at all.

Instead, would Wenzel please receive d'Ailly, Peter's newly appointed Archbishop of Cambrai, who wished to pay homage for his see which lay inside the Empire's border? In the œcumenical atmosphere, genially brushing aside his own Urbanist prejudices and the claims of sundry clerics within that Obedience, Wenzel accepted the homage. This generous act, being irreversible, lifted a weight off d'Ailly's mind. D'Ailly's priorities were strictly Brechtian. His temporalities safe, he was able to attend to his next task, which was to visit Peter as Wenzel's special envoy.

Froissart gives a lively but quite fictitious account of this mission and of the clash between prelate and Pope. In actual fact, d'Ailly never even mentioned cession. Why should he? He felt at peace with God and man. *Il enveloppa ses conseils dans le langage le plus onctueux, le plus caressant*, writes M. Noël Valois, who detected Froissart's mistake. For d'Ailly knew he had got Cambrai only just in time. Moderate reformers were at a discount. His friends were all leaving Paris and finding places to hide in. Gerson withdrew to a dim deanery in Bruges, while Clemanges, forced out of his rectorship, became Peter's librarian. The extremists, burly Norman doctors for the most part, were left in power.

France decided to go it alone. The country would stop paying papal taxes and would block papal appointments. Economic sanctions would bring the Pope to his knees. Peter, on his side, refused to renew the annual agreement which allowed the Crown to tax the French clergy. Under these conditions neither budget could be balanced.

The collision could not be long delayed. Over Christmas, which he spent at Pont-de-Sorgues with a few loyal followers, Peter considered taking refuge in Aragon. But that, he saw, would mean abandoning France without hope of recovery. He must hold out at

Avignon, somehow. It was his duty. The Camerlengo must get in stores and engage more crossbowmen from Aragon.

He held a last discussion with all his cardinals. As Boniface had rejected cession out of hand, he argued cogently enough, that way was no longer even possible, let alone desirable, and they were no longer bound by any promise to press for it which they might have given to the Dukes. Instead, they should rally to him. For their part they gave warning that France was determined to overthrow him. If France withdrew obedience all would be lost.

'Your benefices in France would be lost, you mean,' he replied. 'Though only for a time. But as for me, let them try it! St. Peter was no less pope for being denied obedience in the Kingdom of France.'

# CHAPTER 7

# The Siege

'IT is a great presumption on his part,' wrote the Duke of Berry furiously to Peter, explaining why Martin would not be received as nuncio in Paris, '—*grant presumcion à lui de vouloir soustenir une si mauvaise opinion contre le college et la deliberacion des roys*'. 'And,' he added still more pointedly, 'when you say that he enjoys so high a reputation everywhere, in truth it may be that before he adopted this deplorable opinion he was of good repute, as were others too. . . .'

The Dukes felt they had been trifled with long enough. The University had a ruthless confidence in its own logic. Together they represented France, that fusion of power and intellect which, in crises like this one, has the right and the duty to show the way to Europe. France was going to break Peter. For anyone, even a non-French cardinal, to take his side was presumptuous.

One tiresome preliminary remained before they could get down to business. Opinion in the French Church must be prepared and manipulated. This meant calling a third synod in Paris. The first two had not been notably successful, but this synod would be different. Dukes, not bishops, would preside and direct it.

Simon de Cramaud, who saw himself becoming a Patriarch worthy of the name, delivered the opening speech and gave the synod its marching orders. His remarks were brief, superficial, mendacious and to the point. They were no longer bound to obey that perjurer Benedict XIII. Instead, they must obey the King, who had taken over his powers for most practical purposes.

'The King has convoked you to advise him whether, in order to promote the way of cession, he should withdraw obedience or adopt some other course. Although he could have decided the matter himself, he has deigned to consult you. *Pour Dieu, soyez diligents!* For if you are not, he will know how to act. It is forbidden to re-open discussion of the way of cession, which has already been adopted in principle, irrevocably.'

The Patriarch went on to explain that he knew for certain that if France withdrew from Benedict, the kingdoms supporting Boniface would likewise withdraw from him, and unity would be theirs by Christmas.

On this note of hardy falsehood the proceedings opened. Cramaud, Gilles des Champs, Pierre Plaoul and the Abbot of Mont-St-Michel were the heavy guns on the one side. Against them were pitted two courageous French bishops, Pierre Ravat of Saint-Pons and Élie de Lestrange of Le Puy, together with Jean de la Coste, a professor of law from Toulouse. For some obscure reason, it was Normandy versus Languedoc.

Though Cramaud had done his best to canalise discussion, it still ranged widely. Should obedience be withdrawn altogether, or only partially, or should Peter be summoned again first? Gilles des Champs argued that Peter had 'put himself outside the Church' and was no longer Pope, but this sounded too revolutionary, even for a gathering like this. Later speakers shifted their ground. To withdraw taxes and appointments from Avignon, they said, would only be to restore ancient rights which had been usurped from the French Church. Money was a weapon in the hands of an obdurate pope; deprive him of it, and he would have to see reason.

This was partial withdrawal. Bishop Lestrange called it indecent. The Bishop of Albi failed to see how they could refuse obedience and taxes to the acknowledged head of the Church. The Abbot of Chaalis and the Prior of La Charité-sur-Loire failed to see how unity would come, even if they did so. Ravat made the point that if all were free to disobey a sovereign because they thought his policy was wrong, anarchy would result and would spread to the civil sphere. The Dukes found this thought a disturbing one, and Pierre Plaoul tried to reassure them, explaining deftly that they were true rulers, whereas spiritual rulers such as the pope were only public servants. The discussion circled round to money again, as discussions in France usually do, and some prelates glanced enviously at the lower rate of papal taxes paid by England. The Archbishop of

Tours pointed out that the English had no great reputation for orthodoxy to keep up. A really orthodox country must expect to pay Peter whatever they thought of him.

Up to this point the debate had been far from conclusive and cannot have given much satisfaction to its promoters. The Norman don, Plaoul, spoke more incisively than before. If they kept to canon law, he said, the schism would go on for ever. They must apply natural law instead. Natural law is a highly elastic concept, useful when one wishes to disregard the obvious meaning of the ordinary law. Doubtless natural law said that Peter must go. Cramaud went further; Peter, by keeping the schism alive instead of surrendering, was guilty of heresy. The best minds of the period such as Gerson rejected this line of reasoning, which begs several questions and blurs the distinction between schism and heresy. It may be doubted whether many of those present found it convincing either.

It was time to reach a decision. The presidents had followed the debate and its reception closely. They now decided, with considerable worldly wisdom, that the voting should be neither secret nor open. The voters entered a room one by one and told the presidents how they voted, handing in a note to the same effect. If a voter opposed withdrawal, the presidents argued with him. This took ten days, followed by a five weeks' interval while the presidents discussed in private what the result of the voting should be. It was Louis of Orleans against the rest.

At the end of July the poor King had a lucid interval. His Chancellor, Arnaud de Corbie, explained the synod's deliberations to him in guarded and very general terms. Charles declared that he had every confidence in his uncles and in everybody.

Did he agree, then?

'Lexé moy pincer et fetes sela que voldrés.' 'Let me think, and do what you want.'

Though the words betrayed some natural confusion of thought, officialdom was satisfied. The King had given his decision. They were covered.

Next morning the Chancellor spoke from a balcony of the Louvre. A large majority, he announced, 247 out of 300, had voted for immediate and complete withdrawal. Any criticism would be severely punished. There was none, until 500 years later, when the distinguished French historian of the Schism, M. Valois, found the original voting slips among the Chancery archives—for civil servants never destroy such things, even when they ought to—and revealed that the resourceful Arnaud de Corbie had converted a very narrow majority into a large one and concealed the fact that more than half the higher clergy had voted the other way.

★

With the falsified vote of an uncanonical synod behind them, the rulers of France published their decree withdrawing obedience from Peter. Cardinals Thury and Lagrange, tidying up the loose ends of the conspiracy, wrote to the Duke of Burgundy with some *petits advisements des choses qui leur sembloient de faire*. Then two royal commissioners appeared at Villeneuve and advanced across the bridge towards Avignon, stopping just short of the chapel which marked the papal boundary. There, to the thin sound of trumpets, they read out their decree, threatening the citizens (who were not French subjects) with the direst consequences if they stood by Peter. And any clerics who did so would of course lose their benefices.

It was the parting of the ways. That day or the next, seventeen cardinals and all but seven of the French officials of the Curia deserted to Villeneuve. Not even the Camerlengo had the courage to stay. Another notable deserter was Cardinal Blau, who had received his hat from Peter's hands. Two other cardinals left Avignon but did not join the rebels. The Cardinal of Neufchâtel stole the papal seal, and lesser fry looked after themselves in their own fashion—one of them went off with a substantial sum from the Treasury.

Five cardinals remained loyal. They were Martin and Fernando, Anglesola of Gerona, Boyl from Valencia and the Italian Ammanati. A sixth, Serra of Catania, stood by Peter too though absent from the Curia. All except Martin owed their promotion to Peter. All save one were Spanish. When trouble started they left their houses in the town, which were promptly pillaged, and joined their leader in the Palace.

From deserting the Pope to making war on him was a short step

L

for medieval cardinals. One of them, Albano, called on a wrathful
Holy Father during the final *sauve-qui-peut*, a courtesy omitted by
most of the others. Finding the passages full of Spanish crossbowmen,
and hearing from Peter's own lips that he would have Lagrange
arrested and punished, the Neapolitan divine recalled what Urban
had done at Nocera, glanced round him anxiously for ropes hanging
from the ceiling and took his leave at the first opportunity. Yet it
would be wrong to accept the cardinals' argument that they took
up arms in self-defence. What could Peter do to them once they
were across the river on French soil?

It is more to the point to ask what the government in Paris
expected from them. Officially it disclaimed any part in the siege
which followed. But the cardinals could not have conducted it for
a day without at least the tacit approval of Paris, and when their
zeal seemed to be flagging the King (or rather Arnaud de Corbie
in his name) wrote to them brusquely enough.

> *Tres chiers et feaulx amis,*
>     *. . . Nous avons entendu, non pas sans grant desplasir, que aucuns
> de vous se sont departis de la ville d'Avignon et transportés por leurs
> plaisirs acomplir, sans necessité aucune, en divers lieux, et encore se
> disposent les aucuns autres partir. Lesquelx departemens, si ainsi se
> faisoient, porroient estre un grant esclandre de vous et de l'eglise . . .
> Faites les tantost et sans delay retourner!*

Clearly the government expected them all to stay at their posts
in the front line. Several did in fact sneak away, though probably
less to accomplish their pleasures than because they disliked what
was happening. Malesset, Albano, Saint-Martial and Auch belonged
to this moderate wing. The rest were content, while rebelling
against the Pope they had elected, to be treated like subordinates by
the rulers of France.

The citizens of Avignon were not willing to risk royal displeasure
either, though they lived outside the King's dominions and depended
on the Pope for much of their prosperity. News came that a warrior
named Boucicaut was approaching with an armed force on the
cardinals' behalf and that his men, meeting one of the Pope's
officials on his rounds through the district, had killed him with a
casual lance-thrust through the neck. On hearing this the leading
townsfolk met hurriedly in St. Didier and agreed to change sides.

They opened their gates to Boucicaut, plundered the papal granaries outside the Palace, appropriated some warlike stores which had foolishly been left there and began mobbing any Spaniards they found on the streets. Perhaps they did not distinguish clearly enough between the two Boucicauts, any more than Froissart did afterwards. The great Jean Boucicaut, Marshal of France and hero of the recent crusade of Nicopolis, took no part in these events; in fact some years later he became a personal friend of Peter. It was his deplorable free-lance brother Geoffrey who led the attack. A government memorandum makes it clear that he came by arrangement with Paris.

'And so from this time,' writes Peter's faithful chronicler, 'the diabolical College assumed control of the city and of the Comtat Venaissin.' The defences of this miniature papal state in Provence crumbled at the first breath of war. The same thing commonly happened in Italy. Medieval popes, like the modern British, had a well-worn tradition of losing the first round. Only very seldom, when led by an Albornoz or a Cesare Borgia or a Julius II, did a papal army reach average standards of preparedness. Peter was no such war-lord; in that autumn of 1398 his only military ambition was to hold out in the Palais des Papes.

To this end, over the past eighteen months, he had devoted a good deal of thought and preparation. As early as the February of the previous year we find a certain Bernardo Bonini being engaged to put the artillery in working order. Froissart observes that Peter 'had of longe tyme purveyed his palays with wyne, corne, larde, oyle and of all other thinges parteynynge to a fortresse, and wolde nat be abasshed for a lytell thynge'. The rebel cardinals too had the effrontery to complain of the 'crossbowmen, sailors and pirates' who guarded the building and of their 'engines, bombards, catapults, javelins and artificial fire'. The pontiff had assembled all these horrible things, they said, 'not beholding God before his eyes, but rather urged on by some unbridled and headstrong fancy of his own. Not thus did Christ teach the holy Apostles, not in this wise has St. Peter instructed us, not by means such as these does a wise and good shepherd govern and control his flock.' True enough, but to follow this advice would have meant getting rid of the Temporal Power and transforming the Church into a loosely organised, disendowed, voluntary society, something resembling the vision for which the Spiritual Franciscans had been savagely persecuted a few generations earlier, but something utterly beyond the imagination of Pope or cardinals in September 1398.

Peter had just over a hundred professional soldiers in his Palace, virtually all of them recruited from the Kingdom of Aragon. His young nephew Rodrigo was among them. In addition close on two hundred of the Palace staff stayed loyal—servants, cooks, grooms, artificers, clerks, officials and ecclesiastics of all ages. The great majority were Spaniards too, though there were some Italians and Germans and a few exiles from the English possessions in Gascony. A fair proportion were fit and willing to undertake garrison duties, to which holy orders were no insuperable obstacle; the roll includes, for instance, *Arnaldus Vich, presbiter et bombarderius*. So small and unevenly trained a force could not be used offensively, of course, not even in the streets of Avignon against the town watch. But it might be enough to hold the Palace.

The building, though not strictly a castle, was obviously planned with military considerations in mind. The huge projecting towers enable defending archers to fire along the face of every wall, while the tall arched recesses which run up the whole height of the building and give it a vaguely Islamic appearance are by no means merely decorative. At the top of each blind arch is a vertical slit commanding the face and the foot of the wall. The windows, it is true, are larger and more numerous than a castle's, but most of them are set high, and the garrison walled up the lower ones at the first hint of trouble. The main weakness, and a serious one, is the cramped site in a town. Only from the two longer sides are there modest fields of fire across gardens or open spaces. To the north the old Romanesque cathedral is less than twenty yards away, while at the south end the houses almost touch the walls across the Rue Peyrollerie.

As one stands looking up doubtfully at Viollet-le-Duc's restorations or loses one's bearings so easily inside, it is hard to believe that about two hundred combatants were enough to defend every danger-point day and night. A sudden, determined assault with scaling-ladders, directed against several sides at once, might well have settled the matter very quickly. But it would have cost casualties, particularly during the first minutes when the attackers were like flies on a window-pane. Boucicaut's troops were mercenaries, not fanatics. They preferred siege-craft to scaling-ladders.

Indeed for the first three weeks there was not even a proper siege. It was possible to send Brother Vincent out to preach in the churches of the town and make it clear to the fickle inhabitants that the Holy Father was not going to yield. As a gifted propagandist, Vincent's place was outside. His modern hagiographers, who are pained by the saint's association with 'the Avignon antipope', imply that he went out because he disapproved of armed resistance, but this is to attribute modern humanist ideas to a medieval Dominican. Vincent was no pacifist, and he gave many proofs of his loyalty to Peter. None the less he had an unusual outlook, and this time he seems to have put Christianity before churchmanship and deliberately taken the opposite path from St. Catherine's. A little later, obtaining Peter's leave to do so, he started off once more on his missionary journeys, a large lame man with an enormous crucifix and a small patient donkey, disappearing slowly up the valley and into the Alps. The hagiographers skate over his next phase even faster, for his preaching revived the flagellant mania which had been mercifully dormant for many years. Fortunately he left behind his more politic-ally minded brother, the Carthusian Boniface Ferrer, to take a leading part in Peter's struggles.

Peter himself kept remarkably calm. He was thankful to see his Palace empty of that throng of half-enemies and fair-weather friends. Outside they could disgrace themselves if they must. The versatile Cardinal Giffone might compare him with Simon Magus and Julian the Apostate. The Cardinal of Neufchâtel, appointed Captain of Avignon by his colleagues, might parade brashly through the streets on a war-horse wearing a combination of scarlet robes and plate-armour and equipped with a sword and a com-mander's baton. ('Like those awful prelates in Italy do,' wrote Martin in disgust.) The townsmen might build barricades round the Palace, and Boucicaut's soldiery bawl obscene threats against *ce Pierre de la Lune et du soleil*, or swear to eat his liver and lead him to Paris with a chain round his neck like a dog. These various noises, coming in through his study window high up in the Tour des Anges, only sounded as if the vegetable market was working overtime. He had taken his decisions, and could only await results.

He had abandoned the other study next door, where Clement VI's gay hunting-and-fishing scenes seemed more inappropriate than ever, and now lived and worked in the old papal bedchamber, a soberly decorated room with narrower windows and stronger walls. Here, for some inscrutable reason, birdcages were depicted on the sides of the deep embrasures. At least they suited his present circumstances better. For his own part he had recently added a framed picture, the only work of its kind he is known to have commissioned. The picture's subject was typical of its patron. Apparently it has not survived, and at this distance it is not altogether easy to visualise just what a Late Gothic paintbrush made of *The Intrusion of Prignano*. If only Peter had lived a century later! What would not Raphael have done with so splendid a theme? But no doubt Peter's picture was dramatic enough in a spiky way. At any rate it satisfied him as he sat there beneath it calmly collating new bishops to vacant sees in distant lands. For that is how he spent those weeks. Disregarding the vague uproar outside, he methodically appointed one to Barcelona, another to Cordoba, another to Dunkeld. His letter to King Martin concerning the Barcelona appointment is a masterpiece of restraint and only alludes in passing to the 'various difficulties and vexations' which the writer is undergoing. By way of contrast Fernando's letter, written at the same time, is an agitated summons for help, chock full of military details and amateur strategy.

★

At the end of the month the fighting began in earnest. A few Spaniards held the gate in the town wall commanding the bridge. After four days' bombardment at point-blank range, this outpost fell to the rebels.

Within the Palace all was ready. There was a regular system of watches, relieved every four hours. Curial accountants checked the piles of arrows beside each loophole, and Spanish abbots presided benevolently over cauldrons of boiling oil. The loyal cardinals went their rounds; Anglesola and Boyl from sunset until midnight, then the Bishops of Segorbe and Imola, and Fernando from four until daybreak. The preparatory stage of war changes little with the times. There was the same boredom and vague apprehension. At night the moonlight would cut through loopholes on to grotesque sprawling sleepers. By day one might see a group of tonsured archivists clustered round some piece of military ironmongery in which, as educated men, they could feel very little confidence, while their ears were assailed by the unreal, immemorial jargon of the professional *bombarderius*.

'This here weapon,' came the words in medieval Catalan, 'has a high trajectory and a steep angle of descent.'

Then theory gave place to practice. On every rooftop within range the enemy had mounted catapults, bombards, mangonels and other engines, some of them taken from the Pope's own granaries. At a given signal they all opened an alarming but erratic fire on the Palace. Peter, informed at once of what was happening, came out of his study and climbed a tower to see for himself. While he was encouraging his forces and looking through an embrasure towards the bishop's palace, where Neufchâtel had his headquarters, a splinter of stone from a bombard struck him on the shoulder. Luckily it was no more than a bruise. He forbade his own gunners to reply 'out of respect for St. Michael's Day', as his companion and biographer Alpartil tells us, though perhaps self-control and psychological insight had more to do with it than the calendar. Useless gestures only serve to discourage one's own friends. The same thought, powerfully reinforced by what he had learnt from the story of Judas Iscariot, kept Peter from indulging in the pointless vulgarity of solemnly excommunicating his besiegers.

As it chanced Neufchâtel did not long survive his lucky shot with the bombard. 'For on Tuesday the first day of October our Saviour, not wishing to allow such sinful disobedience and *lèse-majesté* to remain unpunished, struck down the aforesaid Cardinal with a pestilent fever and innumerable glandules and carbuncles, so that on the following Friday he perished most miserably and his tyrannical dominion with him.'

On either side artillery fire was much more a matter of luck than aim. Bombards, the primitive cannon of the day, were no more than tubes of uneven bore reinforced hopefully with hoops, clamped

down on to large blocks of wood and charged very gingerly with
home-made gunpowder. At long intervals they coughed up small
sooty cannon-balls and prodigious clouds of smoke. Sometimes they
burst. Less temperamental, but still not really effective against
massive stone walls, were the catapults, which sent sizable boulders
hurtling through the air in high, uncertain arcs. Small-arms fire
with crossbows was less spectacular but considerably more
dangerous. The enemy archers in the cathedral tower were feared
by all.

Peter's warlike stores included Greek fire. Pots of this chancy
combustible were slung out on to the roofs of nearby houses. In
this way the enemy's offensive troops were transformed, at least
for a time, into a fire-brigade, and a wider field of fire for the papal
archers was gradually cleared round the southern end of the Palace.
Boucicaut retaliated and managed to set fire to a huge pile of logs
near the Tour de Trouillas which represented most of the garrison's
supply of firewood. With winter coming on, this was a dishearten-
ing thing to happen. Froissart claims that 'they lacked woode to
make fyre withall and to sethe their meate, whiche made theym
abasshed'. But in fact he exaggerates. There was enough left for
cooking. They went on grinding corn and baking bread. There was
very little else for them to eat. Peter's devoted follower Martin de
Alpartil, a junior official who came from the same half-Moorish
district in the hills of Aragon and who went through the siege himself, tells how twenty-four men toiled daily at the mill and how
this was the most tiresome fatigue of all.

The siege went on inconclusively for a month. Then three loyal
cardinals went out under a flag of truce to parley with their rebel
colleagues. The latter were so little in command of the situation that
they could not prevent Boucicaut, who was no better than a bandit,
from taking Peter's envoys prisoner and holding them to ransom for
his own private profit. One of them, Boyl, was sent back to the
Palace to fetch the money and very wisely stayed there. The other
two, Martin and Ammanati, had their soutanes clipped to knee
length and their arms bound. As night fell they were led down to
the river and pushed into a boat. They thought they were going to
be drowned, but the sacrilegious and damnable Boucicaut (as Alpartil
calls him) was still after money. The boat went downstream to the

castle of Boulbon, where they were lowered into a foul pit called La Gaugosa. Five months later, on payment, they were pulled up out of their oubliette in very poor health and set free in Avignon.

Then the besiegers tried a legitimate stratagem. The harbour-master of Villeneuve, a French royal official, knew of a large sewer which led from the latrines in the north-east corner of the Palace to a stream called the Sorguette, which in turn flowed into the Rhône. Together with one Richard, a knight and colleague in the harbour service, he collected a body of close on sixty picked men and crawled up the conduit during the hours of darkness. Passing beneath the outer wall of the Palace, they negotiated the rim of a fathomless medieval cesspit under the Tour de la Glacière and squeezed up a drain into a pantry, and then up a narrow spiral staircase until at last they emerged one by one in the kitchen. This kitchen is one of those kiln-like constructions not uncommon in the Middle Ages (there is a very fine example at Fontévrault) the main feature being a huge central chimney rising through a conical roof.

The attackers brought with them a formidable amount of gear as well as their arms. They had mallets and axes to break down doors, ropes to tie up their prisoners, sacks to collect any money they might find (the Treasury was just below Peter's quarters) and fleur-de-lys pennants for signalling to those outside. As they assembled these items on the kitchen floor and the last of the sixty struggled up blasphemously through the drain-pipe, the unusual sounds fell on the keen ears of the papal butler. Stalking majestically towards the kitchen he listened for a moment and then, in a voice accustomed to announcing more privileged guests, gave the alarm.

Trumpets resounded through the vast building. Everyone rushed to the spot. Beams and blades blocked the narrow exits from the kitchen. Peter, woken up and told what was happening, declared at once that the assault party was delivered into their hands. A couple of archers opened a manhole above the cesspit and crouched ready to shoot down any who might try to retreat along the route they had come by. Others climbed on to the conical roof above the kitchen, broke it open, and started to demolish the upper part of the chimney and tumble the masonry on to the enemy's close-packed heads. Others brought pitch, set fire to it, and began to ladle it out. At this point the harbour-master gave in. Fifty-six were taken prisoner. Lodged in the Treasury basement, though with no money in sight, they listened gloomily to the thanksgiving services which continued for the rest of that day, while their arms were distributed to callow chaplains and pen-pushers.

The pestiferous Boucicaut, who had hoped to spare himself the labour involved, now decided that he would have to undermine the walls. The mines of those days had no explosives. The besiegers would tunnel forward until they were directly beneath the foundations, where they would excavate a large gallery and withdraw, setting fire to the pit-props as they left. The first of these mines started from the cathedral and was directed against the enormous Tour de la Campane on the north-west corner. They worked on it day and night.

With all the uncalculated weight of a tall tower poised above the pit-props, mining was a risky business, even if the defenders let it proceed undisturbed. But Peter's 'sailors and pirates' knew all the latest techniques and did nothing of the sort. They kept watch for tell-tale signs above ground and established listening-posts in cellars. As soon as the approaching mine was detected a counter-mine was begun. Tunnelling out well beyond the walls, they aimed at meeting the mine and stopping its progress. In this case the defenders broke a vent through to the surface and started an underground fire. It burned sullenly for days. Alpartil, peering cautiously down from a loophole at the ugly flames licking up out of the hole in the ground, thought it resembled one of the mouths of hell.

The enemy strove to put out the fire. They approached above ground under cover of the metal doors taken from the cathedral and hurled wet matresses, soil and water into the flaming vent. At last they closed it. Fresh tunnels prodded forward towards the walls, to be met by fresh counter-mines. This time the defenders broke into the mine from their tunnel and there was a fantastic battle underground fought with combustibles and red-hot pokers. Another mine actually reached the foundations and was fired by the attackers. Now the garrison passed buckets of water and, as soon as the fire was out, worked frantically to fill in the hole beneath the masonry. Bishops and other dignitaries joined in the task. Peter's chronicler aw them staggering down to the danger-point with stones on their shoulders.

By now, he tells us, the besiegers were *stupificati et quasi desperati*. At any rate they had had enough of Boucicaut. He was dismissed in disgrace, though his successor, the Seneschal of Provence, had no better strategy to offer than to start mining against the other end of the Palace. Covered by a screen of timber constructed like a Venetian blind and lowered from the top of the wall, the garrison made a sortie and broke into the mine from above. A last tunnel burrowed blindly towards the Tour de la Gache. Presently miners and counter-miners could hear each others' pick-strokes. A long rod suddenly appeared in the counter-mine like an earth-beetle's feeler. The others had a bombard ready. There was a deafening, acrid crash and the two tunnels were one. This was the end. The rebels asked for a truce and all active hostilities above and below ground came to a stop. It was the end of November. The siege gave place to a blockade.

*

To besiege the Pope in his Palace, even after two decades of unprecedented ecclesiastical chaos, was bound to raise some awkward diplomatic problems. Nowhere more than in the Pope's own home-land, the Kingdom of Aragon. There these problems, together with King Martin's steaming bulk, filled the royal study to bursting-point. To Canon Climent, by no means an unduly imaginative man, the pressure seemed something physical. It turned back baffled from the tightly closed windows, rebounded indignantly from the debased Gothic bondieuseries lining the walls, and built up steadily against the gilded cusps on the low ceiling.

King Martin the Humane, the last of a distinguished line, had inherited an outlook that was both generous and hesitant, con-siderable energy cancelled out by pituitary imbalance, and a com-posite artificial kingdom full of latent political contradictions. It was not altogether his fault that he lived in a permanent muddle. Since his return from Avignon he had given months of intermittent thought to Peter's troubles. Finally he had devised, to his own satisfaction if to no one else's, a great gassy scheme for putting everything right, a scheme which depended almost entirely on the Duke of Burgundy's willing co-operation. He had dictated several conflicting versions of this plan to his Secretary, a canny little man who signed his own name at the end of every paragraph. And now, if what Canon Climent said was true, the instructions for the ambassadors would have to be amended yet again.

The Canon was Peter's confidential representative at Barcelona. His task was to suggest, respectfully but firmly, that the time had come for active intervention. The King of Aragon could not allow the first Aragonese pope in history to be overthrown without a handstir.

But what sort of a handstir? The King dared not risk an open breach with France. He was a constitutional monarch of sorts, and the prospect of a hostile Paris was enough to terrify his commercial-minded, unheroic advisers in the *Consell de Cent*. To do nothing would bring everlasting disgrace. To do anything would be to invite disaster.

In these circumstances the historic interview soon reached an impasse. The Canon fired his last round of ammunition. Not content with assailing Peter, he declared, the rebels had committed excesses against Spaniards in general. The latter had taken refuge with him in the Palace. They were being impiously and closely besieged, confined, persecuted and maltreated. All His Majesty's subjects in Avignon, whether they were permanent residents there or were visiting the town for any reason, had been arrested and despoiled. Some, he feared, had even been killed.

The lid blew off the kettle. The ambassadors' instructions were revised once more. The Secretary scribbled quickly in the forceful but graceless idiom which, to the lasting disgust of up-country conservatives, had replaced the more lordly tongue of Aragon proper as the language of government. The words were thrifty and unmusical, all that fourteen centuries of hard bargaining on salt-slippery quays in a Pyrenean wind had left of the language of Cicero.

> . . . *e los que son ab ell dins lo Palau son irreverentment e streta assetiats, constrets, essuehits e maltractats . . . Tots subiets e naturals del dit Senyor Rey, vulles de antich stiguen en Avinyo, vulles vagen lla per qualsevulla rao, aquells apresonant, robant e maltractant . . . metant a mort.*

The King was now simmering nicely. His envoys must make it clear that he was most surprised and disturbed. The offenders must stop it at once and pay compensation.

*De que lo dit Senyor es fort maravellat e molt turbat. Que de aquestes coses se vullen abstenir, e de les que son fetes vullen fer satisfaccio.*

The Canon saw his chance. Might the Holy Father's relatives and friends send a naval expedition to relieve him?

A small cloud of steam scudded across the royal features. First of all, it must be understood that he was not very pleased with him. The Holy Father had not yet accepted his long-standing proposals concerning the see of Valencia.

*Que lo dit Senyor no fos ben content de ell . . .*

And after saying that?

Well?

His Majesty was a most loyal son of the Church. He held certain territories as the Church's vassal. The Holy Father had always been his personal friend.

Damn the *Consell de Cent!* He would let the expedition sail.

*E en fer aço, lo dit Senyor es induit primerament per reverencia de Deu e honor de la Sancta Sgleya sua, de la qual ell es feudatari, e amor de la persona del dit Pare Sant, lo qual tots temps ha molt amat.*[28]

*

The net result of these démarches was that a privately organised naval force, on the small side for rescuing Peter but big enough to start a war scare, was sent to the mouth of the Rhône, preceded by an official diplomatic mission with instructions to protest and to conciliate. The Pope's enemies were to be scolded, he was to be urged to place his fate in their hands, while the naval expedition was to deliver him from them. One can see that Great Britain has not been the first maritime power to rely on muddling through. It is equally obvious that, in Paris, King Martin instantly won a lifelong reputation for satanic finesse and duplicity.

His ambassadors reached Avignon the day after both sides, exhausted by weeks of mining and counter-mining, had agreed to a truce. Despite the blockade the rebels had to let them through. They stayed inside the Palace for four days. Peter, well though he thought he knew his own country and its King, could hardly believe his ears when they rambled on about arbitration by the Duke of Burgundy. If there were to be any arbitration, he insisted that Louis of Orleans should undertake it instead. Meanwhile he took more comfort from the news that the naval relieving force was on its way.

From Avignon the envoys went on to the capital, followed by a deputation of rebel cardinals. The talk in court circles was still of Peter's *grant malice et inhumanité*, of that ogre who had *garni le palais apostolique d'Avignon de pirates et gens de guerre de diverses nacions, en faisant long-temps guerre mortelle de feu et de sanc*. What the ambassadors, who themselves belonged to one of the *diverses nacions*, thought of this nonsense is not fully recorded. But French public opinion was beginning to turn against the rebellion. Such moves must succeed quickly, and this one had not. As the news spread that the cardinals had no idea what to do next and had come to Paris mainly to safeguard their own incomes, they were actually hooted in the streets.

Meanwhile the warships assembled in the Bay of Rosas. King Martin had formally licensed the Pope's nephew Pedro as commander and given him strict orders not to fight anyone save the rebellious townsfolk of Avignon. The Aragonese state was not involved. Those who went were merely the Pope's kinsmen and friends with their retainers. The ships were hired for a month, and the bills for ship's biscuit, Greek fire and gunpowder lay stacked hopefully on Canon Climent's desk in Barcelona.

On 10 January the galleys, after pitching about for several days in contrary winds, succeeded in entering the river mouth and rowed up as far as Arles. The King of France had already heard of their coming and had issued strict instructions 'that without Our express licence they shall not be permitted to pass upstream to prejudice or disturb the cardinals'. The Rhône was both an international waterway and a frontier, so that the legal position was obscure. But the newcomers took care to behave correctly towards Arles and explained their intentions. Their Catalan was very close to Provençal and made a better impression locally than Charles VI's pompous proclamations couched in northern French.

Peter's secret agents had worked out a plan of attack, sending it out disguised as a page torn from an old missal, written in yellowing ink in a very obscure old-fashioned hand with an innocent letter in fresh ink on the other side. When the expedition was sighted, a code of flags hoisted on the various towers of the Palace would indicate enemy dispositions and show which section of the town walls should be attacked. From the Palace towers, high inside the town, enemy concentrations were easy to see, while from the river they were invisible.

In spite of all this careful planning the expedition failed. The Rhône was exceptionally low and the mistral blew down it like a hurricane. The big sea-going galleys could not get farther up the river than Tarascon, some fifteen miles short of their goal. On either side lay neutral or hostile territory and, more important still, on whichever bank they might land there would still remain a wide river between them and Avignon, either the Rhône itself or the Durance which comes in from the east. In short the rivers had ceased to be approach-routes and had become obstacles. They waited five weeks but conditions got no better. The enemy had ample time to make preparations and the period for which the ships were hired ran out. There was nothing for it but to turn back.

The siege and blockade had already lasted six months. The garrison, their hope of relief gone, were now up against disease and hunger. The salted meat had gone bad. The wine had been consumed too liberally on feast-days. The last of the great baleful tribe of Palace cats had been casseroled. Even their enemies the mice had not escaped. Peter himself, we are told, counted it an occasion when some sparrows caught on the roof were served at his table. All suffered from stomach troubles and weakness, and many had frost-bitten feet.

By the end of March it was clear, even to so obstinate a character as Peter, that further military resistance was impossible. In his dealings with the embassy from Aragon he had already accepted conciliation in principle. It remained to go through with it in practice. This would be most disagreeable but not necessarily final.

★

The French thought they could impose a binding agreement on the Pope by force. That only showed how little they knew the Pope. In accordance with the common practice of his day, he summoned his notaries and made a secret reservation of all his rights, invalidating in advance any unlawful concessions which he might be forced to make.

The French appeared. They were his old enemies the Normans—Gilles des Champs from the University, the Abbot of Mont-St-Michel, and a knight who had been active in inducing the townsmen to rebel. It was their moment of triumph. By this time they really thought they knew the Pope. The new agreement they required him to sign, accepting the way of cession, included a statement that he accepted it 'freely and spontaneously' and that he renounced the benefit of any reservations of rights which he might have made in advance.

If they were satisfied with this, they still did not know their Pope. The new agreement contained no promise not to make further reservations in future with retroactive effect. That is what Peter solemnly did. And a fortnight later he summoned his notaries yet again and reserved the right to vary at need the wording of all his reservations past, present and future. It was perhaps his greatest technical tour de force as a canon lawyer.

Something of this leaked out, and in June the French were back there in his study once more, threatening him with starvation and violence unless, without any reservations whatsoever. . . . By now he was quite used to it. With a sigh he gave them what they were foolish enough to want, an agreement which had been annulled in advance and would be annulled again in retrospect.

The great French historian who describes these manœuvres in detail speaks of his 'tortuous and strangely artificial conscience'. To the modern mind the legal procedures he employed more than deserve these adjectives. But it is important to realise that the deceit if there was any, left Peter's conscience quite untroubled. What worried him was something rather different.

Peter considered that he was being robbed. Four years of bitter argument and a siege lasting seven months were proof of his will to resist. Now he was, in his own phrase, in the hands of criminals. If a bandit breaks into your house, overcomes your resistance and

makes you sign a blank cheque in his favour together with a statement that you have signed of your own free will, do you feel in
honour bound not to stop the cheque? Peter definitely did not. It
may be objected that political undertakings are different. Are they?
What modern nation has considered an 'unjust' treaty, imposed upon
it in weakness or defeat, as eternally binding? What Allied statesman
in 1945 thought for a moment of keeping the Munich Agreement
and leaving the German-speaking areas of Czechoslovakia in German
hands?

'*Il est tout cler qu'il se parjure à chacun cop,*' the bandits complained
later when they found their cheque was valueless. This aspect of
the transaction did not disturb Peter in the slightest. What did
concern him most deeply was the thought that, in even pretending
to accept lay dictation, he was as it were compounding a felony.

Peter believed profoundly, as every pope must, that the Church
is independent of the State. Not only 'ought to be', but 'is'. After
another five and a half centuries most people, even most Anglicans
or Lutherans, would agree with him. A state church is an anomaly
nowadays. The idea of one, in its Gallican form, was born in Peter's
lifetime. Since then it has had a long and dispiriting innings. In
fighting it tooth and nail he commands our sympathy.

It is harder to sympathise with what he was fighting for. He had
inherited a belief in 'Christendom' in its crudest form; a divinely
established, all-embracing society, from which all rights are derived
and against which nobody has any rights, governed by a Vicar in
whom the Founder's own absolute sovereignty has been vested. One
must go as far as Malta nowadays to encounter such thinking, but
in the Middle Ages, in theory at least, it was common ground. For
Peter, a conservative canonist, it was immutable law. No one could
take anything away from the Vicar's powers. Yet in appearing to
do so he was committing *lèse-majesté*, he was infringing what our
seventeenth-century ancestors were to call 'the Crown rights of
Christ'.

'Never,' he would declare years afterwards, 'have I been so disturbed as I was about accepting that way, and I cannot believe I
could have done so vile a thing, nor one by which I offended God
so deeply.'

Alpartil, who saw him sign, says it was a mental wound to see his face, and that he came near to accepting a martyr's death instead. But his position as Pope made this impossible. The succession? And a martyred autocrat is a failure, for his martyrdom weakens or destroys autocracy. Peter no doubt thought of Boniface VIII at Anagni, we may think of our own Charles I, the French of Louis XVI.

'Moved by many compelling reasons,' Alpartil concludes, 'which were put to him by his own cardinals of the Palace, he submitted to signing the agreement.'

He capitulated so as to be able to go on fighting. But it was a bitter blow to the rights of the Holy See and to his own Spanish pride.

★

The agreement stipulated that all his men-at-arms and all but a hundred of his Curial followers were to leave the Palace. He could only thank them, pay them liberally, load them with spiritual favours and watch them stumble out through the gate into the empty, hostile sunlight. His prisoners of war, the harbour-master and his companions, were released at the same time. Being of rather low birth they unfortunately had little value as bargaining counters. In return a royal letter of safeguard was promised (though it did not come for eighteen months) with five personages to ensure the Pope's 'protection'. Rations for a hundred would be allowed into the Palace daily. Martin and Ammanati were released from Boucicaut's dungeon, though after an interview with Peter they had to leave the Palace again and take up residence in the town, subject to various petty restrictions.

Peter, by no means the first or the last pope to do so, settled down to an indefinite period of virtual imprisonment. Barriers and armed guards still surrounded the building, reducing outside contact to an arbitrary trickle of messengers and mail which ebbed and flowed as spite competed with venality. Rations fluctuated too. There were daily pinpricks, insulting demands, threatening rumours. The autumn came on and the mistral howled through the damaged roofs and broken shutters.

Once again in Peter's life it was a question of waiting until the situation changed. From days packed with incident and decisions he passed into long empty months with little or nothing new in sight. Most men of action, certainly most northerners, would have broken under the frustration. But there was an oriental streak in Peter, probably not unconnected with his Moorish blood. Once the day of capitulation was over he did not fret.

Poor Ammanati was not so impassive. He was an elderly man and his health had been undermined by five months in Boucicaut's oubliette. Now he was back in his own house or rather the pillaged shell of it, his benefices stolen, shunned by all, forbidden to approach the Palace, not even granted the honours due to a cardinal when he appeared in the street. He decided to go to Aragon, where at least they would let an old cardinal retire in peace. He escaped in disguise and reached the sea at Aigues-Mortes, that queer little salt-encrusted gridiron of a town built by St. Louis as a base for his crusades. There his Italian accent attracted attention and he was recognised by a knight in the harbour service (Alpartil calls him the Chevalier Richard of the Sewer) who had been one of those taken prisoner in the kitchen. Once more Ammanati found himself in a cell. He turned his face to the wall and was dead in less than two months.

The Chevalier Richard died not long afterwards. French sources dwell on the many charitable bequests in his will, while Alpartil records with unmixed pleasure that he died in a frenzy, *rabidus*, aware that his soul was damned, biting off his own tongue and spitting it out on the ground in small pieces.

In Paris the victors, never a homogeneous group, were already arguing about what to do with their victory. They had the way of cession accepted on paper; where did it get them? The hard core of rebels, people like Cramaud, Thury, Lagrange and the University dons, were anxious to finish the job. They proposed that Peter should be imprisoned properly somewhere on French soil. Was a nice quiet murder the next step on their agenda? Peter thought it was. The other wing, led by Malesset and backed by strong representations from Aragon, urged that now that the Holy Father had accepted their terms it was little short of a scandal to go on persecuting him. His freedom, or nearly all of it, should be restored as soon as possible.

Peter himself saw that neither of these solutions was very

probable. The King was a party to the capitulation. The royal government had taken charge. So divided and hesitant a body would scarcely favour any radical way out. The agreement he had signed was a starting-point for them all. Slowly, with the strength of weakness, he began to impose his own interpretation of its terms.

His first step was to protest that the five 'protectors' assigned to him were not of suitable rank. Only Louis of Orleans would do. Thury begged the King on his knees not to endanger all they had won by accepting. A counter-proposal was devised: if Orleans became his 'protector', would Peter undertake to follow his advice? (Orleans, it was thought, would be bound to follow the government's advice.) Here was another blank cheque. Peter refused to sign it but left the door open for negotiations. A more or less friendly negotiator appeared at the Palace in the shape of Louis of Orleans' chancellor, Pierre Beaublé, a man easy to deal with because he was frankly out for himself. In the general confusion of the times he had somehow taken possession of the bishopric of Uzès, to which he had no right whatever but which brought an acceptable addition to his income. He wanted the Pope to confirm him in possession. The Pope replied that he would see what he could do for him, but that first of all his well-beloved son must renounce all the rights he claimed and place them in the Holy Father's hands. Beaublé jibbed at this.

'What? You refuse to resign, for the sake of your soul's salvation, a see which you have occupied most improperly, even when you know that no harm will come to you if you do, and then you demand that I should renounce the sovereign see of Peter at the risk of causing a perpetual schism?'

Peter's aim was to have Orleans as his sole 'protector' without any further commitment, and above all to play for time. With remarkable foresight, considering how large his own troubles loomed, he knew that the Church in France would find the royal court a worse master than he had been.

Meanwhile his own court had dwindled sadly. Ammanati had died a martyr's death at Aigues-Mortes. Martin, finding residence in Avignon equally impossible, took refuge at Arles. Anglesola had to go to Spain; Boyl died of a fever. Fernando was the only cardinal left in the Palace. With him remained an intelligent handful, totally reliable, for the mistral had blown away the chaff. At their head was a certain Francisco de Aranda, an eccentric knight from Teruel with an untidy beard and a brilliant political mind. He became a Carthusian lay-brother and steadily refused any kind of promotion. He was one of Peter's closest friends and advisers for the rest of his life.

Outside there were others equally trusted, such as Boniface Ferrer and the two French bishops, Ravat and Lestrange. There was a nucleus of loyal dons and clergy at Toulouse. There were his friends in Aragon and his hard-pressed partisans in Italy. Peter did not forget these last; on his own blackest Christmas he got Climent to send them a shipload of wheat from Spain, where the harvest had been better than theirs. Scotland too stayed loyal though almost out of touch.

We catch a glimpse of a changed Peter in a long letter he wrote to one of his go-betweens in France. The brisk, incisive quality has slipped. He is worried and repetitive. The Latin periods roll but, like summer thunder, rumble slowly round to the point from which they started. He complains of too little advice, then of too much, and then that he must have more. Has he lost his grip, or is he temporising, or has he merely reverted to the normal circularities of Spanish correspondence?

This phase of Peter's life is by far the most generously documented. Through a vast interlocking web of letters, policy-memoranda and envoys' instructions, all highly confidential and therefore trustworthy, one can trace how he slowly and painstakingly worked to restore his fortunes.[29]

Most of these papers passed through Martin de Salva's hands. News sometimes reached the Cardinal's vantage point at Arles before it could filter through the barriers round the Palace. Bursting with loyalty and righteous indignation, Peter's senior adviser would make characteristic notes in the margin and send the document on to him. In spite of all his learning and political experience Martin remained what he always had been, an up-country Spaniard of the more humourless sort, and five months as Boucicaut's guest had not improved his temper.

The secret service was still at work, though on a reduced scale, and presently a letter from Cramaud to one of the renegade cardinals was placed in Martin's hands. The energetic Patriarch had just come

back from a trip to Germany and his letter describes, a little
airily, his impression of the state of opinion in that country.
Martin's furious marginal notes, too long to quote in full, are in
italics.

> ... And although they fully approve of the way of cession and
> of our denial of obedience (*I think this is untrue*) it does not seem
> to them a good thing to remain for too long without a pope,
> (*That is a good remark, but he twists it to a wrong conclusion*) and so
> they incline to the idea that a third one should be elected by the
> unanimous voice of all the long-standing cardinals without
> exception, a pope whom we shall then all obey. (*This I consider is
> false and a fabrication*) They add that ours has already been
> sacked (*Note the concentrated venom and ponder well*) and that a
> new pope elected in this way could dispose of him so that the
> Church would not be scandalized, and that Boniface too can be
> sacked as well. (*Note how they call him, and it isn't true*) In their
> opinion, the situation is covered by the canon law paragraph
> ... (*No it isn't! See Hugutio's Commentary* ... ) so that this pro-
> cedure will be quite valid. (. . .*!*) And in truth it cannot be denied
> that these two are pertinacious schismatics of the worst sort
> (*Note the sacrilegious, false, erroneous, presumptuous and scandalous
> language which this loathsome fellow has dared to use*) and so perhaps
> it may indeed be possible to proceed canonically to the election
> of a third without further ado. (*That would only add to the con-
> fusion*) And to wipe clean the stain which clings to us, the
> reproach that our only aim in acting as we have done has been
> to obtain a French pope, they say, let us have a good German
> one! (*God help you if that is what you want!*) ...[30]

And so the Patriarch's letter trips optimistically on while the
Cardinal's comments grow ever longer and more atrobilious, until
his last marginal note expands into a three-page memorandum on
patriarchal wickedness.

★

The blockade and imprisonment lasted for four whole years. In
the first year things looked very black indeed. Peter suffered atro-
ciously from toothache at this time, and we see him through
Alpartil's eyes rising grimly from his bed to argue with some insolent
deputation from Paris. Then as time passes the toothache goes, the

envoys' manners begin to improve, some scraps of more hopeful news mix with the bad and the points at issue are less entirely negative.

In 1399 the discussions turned on whether Louis of Orleans might become his 'protector'. In 1400, on whether he must always follow Louis' advice. In 1401, on various disagreements which had arisen between Louis and the rebel cardinals' guards around the Palace. Early in 1402, on whether a council should be held to decide his fate. In mid-1402, on whether he would co-operate to enable such a council to be held. Late in 1402, on whether the council had not better be postponed, and on whether the cardinals needed a pardon from him if they returned to his obedience.

Geographically too the revolt shrank with the years, until by the end of the period there were few whole-hearted rebels left outside Villeneuve and Paris. The Breton clergy, always an independent lot, refused to obey bishops who would not obey the Pope. Castile and Navarre became more friendly. The Carthusians elected Boniface Ferrer as their General and the whole Order returned to Peter's obedience. Toulouse and other universities in the Midi came out strongly in his favour, partly, it must be feared, to annoy the rival establishment in Paris.

Then Provence. Its ruler, Louis II of Anjou, had lost the much larger realm of Naples which had been his in Clement's time. Now he was back in Peter's immediate neighbourhood, short of funds and under considerable pressure from his Provençal subjects and his pious Aragonese wife Yolande to come to terms with the Pope whom he had rashly denied and the Heaven whose wrath he had provoked. One day he came to Avignon, walked past the scowling guards into the Palace, had a long audience with His Holiness, stayed to dinner, stayed the night in fact, and next morning obedience was formally restored in Provence. He drove a hard bargain with Heaven, whose accredited representative was in no position to haggle. Peter had to undertake to repay the enormous, long-overdue loan whereby Gregory had financed his ill-fated voyage to Rome, as well as some debts owed by Clement. But it was worth it. It was a long time since Peter had signed a document with so gratifying a heading.

*Capitula concordata inter sanctissimum in Christo patrum et dominum*
*nostrum, dominum Benedictum papam XIII, et senenissimum princi-*
*pem d. Ludovicum regem . . .*

After the royal visitor had knelt for his blessing and taken his leave,
Peter, still savouring the unaccustomed words, climbed briskly to
the top of the Tour Saint-Laurent. There, in the morning sunlight,
he stood looking southwards over the cracked pink-and-ochre tiles
of the sullen town towards the jagged line of the Alpilles. There
was friendly and obedient territory almost on his doorstep. A
great weight slipped from him. The tide was on the turn at
last.

Presently, reflecting how much there still remained to be done,
he descended slowly from his tower and settled down in his study
to read the latest report from his devoted spokesman in Paris.
Pierre Ravat was doing wonders. But this idea of a council of the
Avignon Obedience was full of snags. Martin had already made this
clear in the margin.

> They are discussing a new plan (wrote Ravat) which contains
> four proposals. First that the Pope should issue his summons to
> the council for that part which has not withdrawn from him,
> while the cardinals should do so for the other part. (*This is
> irrational*) Secondly that not all who are entitled to attend
> should actually come, but that certain persons should be chosen.
> (*To strengthen the bad side and to exclude the good ones!*) Thirdly, that
> the Pope should submit himself to the council's decisions, so that
> its work can be definite and binding. (*Not on any account! A
> thoroughly bad idea!*) Fourthly that it should be held at Avignon,
> so that it is certain that the Pope cannot leave. (*Bad too. From
> this one can judge their mentality.*)

The report went on to describe how the writer had been to see
Cardinal Malesset, leader of the moderate wing, 'an honest man
surrounded by scorpions'.

> And I was alone with him for a good four hours, and I do not
> think a man of my rank has ever spoken with a cardinal like
> that, as if we were equals. Finally I obtained from him what
> follows . . .
> On the second point he conceded that all might attend who
> wished to attend. (*Danger! Do they mean by 'all' the whole arts
> faculty of Paris and every little chaplain and slandermonger, as well
> as the townsfolk of Avignon, etc.?*) . . .

Fourthly, about the place and time (*Watch this! There is a trick somewhere!*) . . .

And so I do not see how the Holy Father can very well refuse, nor do I think that either God (*No!*) or His Holiness can find it displeasing, seeing that in this way obedience would be restored. (*Would it? There has not been a word about that so far.*)[31]

Long before Peter reached the end of Martin's remarks, which this time took up fourteen pages, the remote prospect that he might co-operate with a council of this sort had faded to nothing. He noted with approval that Martin said nothing personal about Ravat's undue readiness to accept some of Malesset's arguments. Ravat was loyal and what he was doing was most necessary. He was softening up Malesset.

As Peter had foreseen, French policy had broken down at home and abroad. Abroad it rested on the fallacy that the countries of the Roman Obedience would hasten to desert their pope as soon as France had set so shining an example. At home the experiment of an autonomous national Church detached from the papacy had only succeeded in putting a good deal of money into the wrong pockets. In actual fact the French Church had not become autonomous; it was being run, and very badly run, by the State. The King's tax inspectors were more rapacious than the Pope's, nobody bothered any more to give patronage to the wise and deserving men of the University, and semi-illiterate courtiers and their friends became bishops and abbots. There were the beginnings of a clerical mutiny, and the University was so disgusted with the results of its own policy that it once more went on strike.

All over France voices were being raised for Peter. Gerson wrote six treatises in his defence. Toulouse University composed a long letter describing the rebels' vote-manipulations and intrigues. Ravat caught the King hurrying along to mass in a lucid interval and poured a telling speech into the monarch's ears. Louis of Orleans handed him the letter from Toulouse. The thought that these crimes were being committed in his name unhinged the poor man's reason once again.

At Avignon the townsmen were jumpy. They unearthed a plot and beheaded some of Peter's secret agents, but soon the local chronicle leaves off ghoulishly totting up which city gate got which piece of whose carcass in order to describe a comet and other strange portents in the Provençal sky, things which clearly presage some great change of fortune.

Burgundy, Berry, the Patriarch, Cardinal Thury and the hard core of Norman dons fought a rearguard action. The air of Paris grew thick with unconvincing denials and decrees. Stern orders were reissued to minstrels and street singers, forbidding all mention of the Pope, the King, the Dukes or their journeys on behalf of Church Unity.

> . . . qu'ils ne facent, dyent ne chantent aucuns ditz, rymes ne chançons qui facent mention du pape, du Roy nostre seigneur, de noz diz seigneurs de France, au regard de ce qui touche le fait de l'union de l'Eglise, ne des voyages que ils ont faits pour cause de ce, sur peine de . . . deux mois au pain et à l'eau.[32]

By now the moderate cardinals were negotiating discreetly with Peter. Malesset and Saluzzo entered the Palace and even kissed his foot. He watched them come and go for some months and then, in the first days of 1403, he suddenly turned on the heat. The pair learned to their consternation that all those whose actions contributed to keeping the Pope a prisoner had, by so doing, excommunicated themselves. If he were to die, they would be debarred from electing a successor.

The chain round Peter had rusted. The time had come to break it. He decided to escape.

He explained his plan to Orleans' agent on the spot, the Chevalier de Braquemont, who readily agreed that the proposed operation came within the scope of 'protection'. A messenger went out to Martin at Arles. Don Jaime de Prades, the Aragonese ambassador, was also let into the secret.

On 12 March 1403, at three o'clock in the morning, the loose masonry which blocked a small postern doorway near the north-east corner of the Palace was very cautiously removed stone by stone. There was an elaborate system of passwords and alarm-signals, but they were hardly needed. Braquemont had seen to it that the cardinals' guards were either asleep or watching the other sides of the building. A venerable but unpapal figure stepped through the opening into the deserted space between the Palace and the cathedral. He had borrowed a Carthusian monk's habit from Boniface Ferrer, while a flowing grey beard added much, in Alpartil's eyes, to his dignified appearance. He had let it grow of late and had sworn not to cut it off until his deliverance. Beneath his habit he carried a consecrated host and a year-old letter from the King. Only his friend Francisco de Aranda, his physician Dr. Ribalta and a cubicular called Romani accompanied him.

Don Jaime, King Martin's ambassador, was waiting in the lane outside. They made a wide circle through the town, walking quietly through the fog-bound lanes until they reached the Rue de la Grande Fusterie, where Don Jaime had established his mission in one of the inns. There they were suitably entertained until daybreak. The Holy Father was in excellent spirits, his tired eyes young again and full of devilment, relishing every moment of the adventure.

As soon as the town gates were open, a small group passed out through the Porte de l'Oulle and went down to the bank of the Rhône. Some early passers-by were surprised to see a strange boat there, a long fast boat with fourteen stout oarsmen and a monk from the Abbey of Montmajour in charge. Directly the venerable Carthusian and his companions stepped on board, it cast off and turned downstream while fourteen long oars dug hard into the water. On the bank a young knight of Don Jaime's, one of several who had been standing unobtrusively under the big willow trees, unstrung his crossbow and, unable to keep silent a moment longer, addressed the puzzled bystanders.

'Go and tell the Cardinal of Albano that his Grand Chaplain has gone, and spoil his breakfast for him!'

Peter looked back at the fast receding battlements and at the great tawny block that was beginning to show itself above them. Whatever happened, he promised himself, he would never re-enter that Palace. Avignon had seen its last pope.

# CHAPTER 8

# The Way of a Conference

THE boat sped downstream to the junction with the Durance, turned, and forged steadily up that river for an hour or more. Then it drew into the far bank, where Martin was waiting with horses and a cavalry escort. A pleasant walk-and-canter through the Provençal morning, through a rich countryside of tall cypress hedges and cane wind-brakes, where every farmhouse turns a blank wall to the north whence the mistral blows and faces uncompromisingly towards the sun. Peter would do likewise. It was his sun again, blazing down on his enemies' confusion.

In half an hour they reached a village. A stony scramble up the steep hill beyond, and the party was safe within the walls of Château Renard.

It was St. Gregory's day, and in thanksgiving he dedicated a chapel in the castle to his great predecessor, whose faith had turned back the wrath of God, and who had seen the archangel sheathing his sword above the Castel Sant'Angelo as a sign that the plague was over.

His thanks given, he wrote at once to the faithful Climent in Barcelona for money, 'as quickly and as often and as much as you can', and then turned to his host King Louis of Provence. What suitable gift could he find for him? Of course, the beard he had grown in his captivity. It was just the thing. Louis would preserve it as a relic. The Norman dons had boasted that a Norman would cut it off. Peter sent for the barber and asked him where he came from. From Picardy. So the Normans were liars! He felt another ten years younger and gave the barber a hundred francs, probably the biggest tip a barber has ever received. Alpartil regretted the loss of an ornament that had clothed his master with a *gravitas* and an *auctoritas* worthy of Abraham, but popes are normally clean-shaven, and this one may be forgiven for hoping that his reign was about to enter a more normal course.

A brief letter to the King of France, polite but firm.

> Our detention did not bring about the peaceful results that some expected of it. We have set Ourselves free, and We trust the news will please you. We believe that Our departure, by divine grace, will serve the glory of God, the cause of the Church and the honour of the royal House of France.

Then he sat back and waited for the cardinals to surrender.

Several of the hardiest had died, including that sower of discord Jean de Lagrange. Alpartil writes his epitaph. 'He reached the end of his wicked days, leaving behind him a whole brood of little sons and daughters, and it is also reported that the demons who came to fetch his soul snatched away his body as well. Not undeservedly, for such was his life.' How little of all this one would guess from the placid recumbent effigy in Amiens cathedral.

Thury, on whom the rebel leadership had devolved, was living in Paris. The rest were at Villeneuve and ripe for the picking. Within the fortnight Malesset, Saluzzo, Albano and Blau duly appeared at Château Renard bearing a draft treaty of twelve long clauses. His Holiness, they proposed, would forgive all injuries, pardon the city of Avignon, confirm all concerned in their stations and emoluments, authorise all the Camerlengo's financial measures, act in concert with the cardinals and accord them favourable treatment. In return they would restore him his full liberty and their obedience, and would urge Paris to follow suit.

Peter read the document through with an effort. His reply was brief.

'Yes, I intend to act broadly on these lines. But I am not prepared to bind myself irrevocably to this course. Nor am I going to give you any sort of pledge, because it is not the custom for the Roman pontiffs to be bound by pacts of this nature.'

On this he was inflexible. He would not condone the rebellion or undertake to give the way of cession any precedence over other ways to unity. He hoped, sometime, to call a Council. Perhaps several Councils. Meanwhile he would not tolerate any further delay in restoring obedience.

They accepted his terms. There was nothing else they could do. Their policy was bankrupt. Each returned to the fold in his own fashion, Malesset with dignity, Viviers rather shamefaced as he handed back the stolen seal, Giffone grovelling in the mud before Peter's mule. Peter assured them all that he had already forgiven them and asked them to join him at dinner. From that moment, in their personal relations, he behaved as if nothing had ever happened. There was only one change. Armed guards stood silently round the walls as they sat at table. Their presence was unnerving at first. In time they got used to it.

Avignon and the Comtat were even quicker in coming to terms. The barricades round the Palace went up in flames. Tradesmen refurbished their 'By Appointment to—' notices. Flags were hung out, Peter's crescent-moon arms were seen everywhere and the town gave itself up to bonfires and rejoicings. *Viva lou Papa Benezeg!* Sightseers came to gape at the destruction done by Boucicaut's catapults, and whole processions of schoolchildren were entertained on fruit and wine at the Pope's expense. But the Pope himself did not appear. He pardoned the citizens on condition that they repaired the damage to the Palace, but he pointedly avoided the city on his triumphal progress through the district. Instead he stayed for eight weeks at Carpentras, where the little market town gave him a great welcome, *'et, pour le charmer, fit défiler devant lui un aimable cortège de jeunes filles'*.

Malesset and Saluzzo once more took the road to Paris. The University had already split on the issue; only the Norman 'nation' was still solidly hostile. Malesset, preaching before the government, praised Peter's patience in adversity and his forbearance now and urged them to bring a useless rebellion to an end. Thury and Cramaud, Burgundy and Berry were still not convinced. Then Louis of Orleans went into action. He knew the constitutional ropes. No one could effect a difficult transition more smoothly, not even Arnaud de Corbie or our own inimitable Mr. Baldwin. Summoning a highly select committee of prelates (the Archbishops of Tours and of Auch, the Bishops of Rodez and Sarlat in the Dordogne, those lights of the episcopate Pierre d'Ailly of Cambrai and Pierre Beaublé of Uzès, with one or two others) he learned from these good men that the clergy of France favoured full

restoration. As all the committee members had either belonged to
Peter's pressure-group for years, or else were as open-minded as
d'Ailly and Beaublé, the information should not have come as a
surprise. But apparently it did. He considered it his duty to inform
the King at once. They were all ushered into the presence. The
King, awakened from a troubled siesta, was so impressed that he
forgot to consult his wicked uncles and agreed to restore obedience
on the spot. With a single comprehensive gesture the Duke
placed a crucifix in his hands and signed to his notaries to start
writing.

'*J'affirme, par la saincte Croix de Nostre Seigneur, que toute ma vie je
lui garderay une obéissance inviolable.*'

Berry and Burgundy, aroused by the sound of church bells and
*Te Deums*, were inclined to argue at first. Then they thought better
of it. Orleans assured them that he would obtain far-reaching concessions from Peter in writing. He may even have believed it.
Silently they entered his undertakings in their ledgers against the
day of reckoning, and made sure that d'Ailly read them out to the
public in plain French during the great thanksgiving ceremony in
Notre-Dame.

D'Ailly, whom we last saw attending Peter as the Emperor
Wenzel's ambassador, had spent these troubled years at Cambrai,
patriotically supporting the government's actions but avoiding any
too direct involvement. Recently, seeing how the wind was blowing,
he had sought to guide public opinion with a treatise in which he
prudently abstained from deciding between the alternatives of continued withdrawal, complete restoration, or restoring spiritual
obedience and refusing taxes. In these circumstances he was relieved
to know that Gerson would preach the sermon.

'Would that a fluent tongue were given me to describe the glad
news and the new gladness!' the latter began, and his listeners in
Notre-Dame resigned themselves to the thought that his prayer
would be granted. Gladness? For Gerson, certainly, since he had
never approved of the withdrawal. For them, who had, it was at
best a feeling of doubtful and qualified relief. In the long run, M.
Valois remarks, one tires of everything, particularly of the struggle
against the spiritual power. Gerson, however, knew exactly what
to say to his audience. Rising splendidly to this moment of untruth

he described the French monarchy, whose religious policy lay in ruins before them, as 'that new Jerusalem which St. John saw coming down from heaven'.

'I shrink from clouding the universal joy with an account of the Holy Father's sufferings. How great has been the penance he has undergone during these four sad years all of you must know. Yet I can affirm with confidence that His Holiness Pope Benedict XII. has learnt much in the hard school of misfortune. Above all, he has learnt humility and gentleness. A second Anteus, he has wrung from his contact with the earth a new, irresistible strength, a strength capable of bringing triumph even over the schism. Understood in this sense, the withdrawal has not been fruitless. And now, my brethren, a new concord, a new dawn . . .'

*

'Do I have to?' Peter asked, when he was told that Berry, d'Ailly Gerson and the rest of them would be coming south in relays to pay their respects. Yes, Francisco de Aranda told him firmly, it was politically necessary and he was back in politics. Meanwhile Carpentras was insufferably hot; his sun had come out again with vengeance. He was determined not to return to Avignon. Marseille would be cooler and a better place for politics.

Berry, an orderly and pious person, came to regularise his own position and received certain privileges to do with the decoration of chapels at Bourges. D'Ailly, as His Majesty's ambassador, once more presented the royal compliments. He had nothing specific to suggest but how glorious it would be if the schism could be ended. Arnaud de Corbie wrote to ask for seven benefices for his relations, adding an eighth as an afterthought. 'And if I can do anything for you—' he ended politely. The University compiled the longest roll of supplications in its long history; there was a back-log of 39 masters in theology, 22 doctors of law, 88 medical men and 1,079 masters of arts, all of them needing patronage very badly indeed. This roll was entrusted to the reinstated Chancellor, Gerson.

On reaching Marseilles, Gerson preached before the Pope. Peter was compared with Jonah and the Palace with the whale's belly. The University came as his humble and devoted daughter. She had

ARAGON

*(Photo the author)*

THE DUKE OF BERRY AT TABLE
From the Très Riches Heures
(*Photo Giraudon, Paris*)

no advice to offer. Her only care was to return to his good graces. Did not presenting this little roll, however belatedly, constitute an act of faith? Satan might whisper counsels of vengeance in the Pope's ear, but Peter de Luna, far from heeding them, would pour down graces upon his ever-faithful University as the moon whose name he bore distilled the dew.

For what else had the University done, Gerson asked, than follow St. Paul's example when he withstood St. Peter to the face?

Gerson's performance was masterly. How carefully, for instance, did he handle this last little piece of scriptural dynamite! If he had gone no further than the next verse in Galatians ii he would have revealed St. Peter deferring to the authority of James the Lord's brother as head of the Church, which scarcely looks like the action of the first pope. And modern scholarship draws still more revolutionary conclusions from the passage. But Gerson wisely stopped in time and got what he came for. Peter merely observed that he would show the more benevolence to the University, the more it confined itself to its proper studies. He even added a little benefice for Gerson.

He had already rewarded his true friends. Climent became Bishop of Majorca. Don Jaime de Prades, the ambassador who had helped in the escape, received a princely 20,000 florins. A bull confirmed the privileges granted to all who had stood the siege. Alpartil, *semi-desperatus* after so long an absence from home, was given a year's leave. Ravat unfortunately had to wait for his archbishopric until one fell vacant. Aranda refused all preferment and stayed in his untidy lay-brother's habit. Martin de Salva's reward was to see the French humbling themselves before a victorious Peter.

That autumn everything was overshadowed by Martin's sudden death. He died on the way to Marseilles and was buried in a monastery on the river bank not far from Château Renard. Sharp-tongued, meticulous, narrow, utterly loyal, the Cardinal of Pamplona was a poor man and had little to leave but his law books, his correspondence files and a carefully written account of events up to date which he had just completed. Peter, miserably turning over the pages and pondering the canny, misanthropic corrections in the margin, knew only too well how much their author would be missed. However, the struggle must go on. He gave Ravat the document

N

to edit and it was duly published as an *Informatio Seriosa* or white paper.

Not many months afterwards Fernando followed Martin.

★

Misanthropy. That was becoming Peter's trouble too. Those who hold great spiritual power for long can seldom avoid it, which is one of the reasons why no one should hold great spiritual power. Of course he would have denied the charge indignantly. He had come through the siege remarkably well, except that his hair had whitened and his face was now deeply lined and he had lost some teeth, all of which made him look considerably older than his age. Most would have put him at over seventy rather than sixty-two. By dropping a remark here and there he gently encouraged the mistake for reasons of his own. But though his eyes had sunk back into their sockets they had not lost their softness or their life. He still had genuine charm and the perfect manners of a Spanish noble-man. He treated his beaten cardinals with enlightened generosity. Several of them, starting with Malesset, were completely won over. To Charles of France, whose poor half-mind was deeply troubled over what had been done in his name, he wrote personal words of forgiveness and comfort worthy of a father in God.

But what respect could he have for these Dukes and Chancellors? Their vanity, their irresponsibility! Deriving their pretended authority from pathetic or obscene things like Charles or Wenzel, without a workable idea in their heads, they had wasted nine solid years in trying to impose their absurd will upon the only truly legitimate authority on earth. They had come within a hair's breadth of wrecking it for ever. Now they were disconcerted or possibly tired, but not for a moment genuinely repentant. In a few years they might be at it again. And the Church's hierarchy, how had they stood up to these trials? By behaving like weathercocks. By accept-ing half-baked notions from the laity, or by putting their benefices before their duty. Malesset or Giffone, it made little difference. He despised them all.

From Paris there still flowed a never-ending stream of empty phrases and requests for favours. Even the redoubtable Duke of

Burgundy needed dispensations. Peter gave them in four long bulls. Then one misanthropic morning he sent off a fifth bull declaring the previous four null and void if there were ever any second thoughts about obedience.

He was sure they were still trying to trip him up with documents. It was his sore subject. There was a scene when the cardinals sought to establish the true text of the Château Renard agreement and have it ratified. They had nothing definite so far.

'That bit about the Council has been left out here!' Albano whispered in Malesset's ear as the much-edited text was being read out to them all by one of the Pope's notaries.

Peter noticed that something was amiss.

'What's that you are saying, Albano? What are you saying? Albano is hiding something up his sleeve!'

'Holy Father, the article referring to a Council is missing at this point. You will remember it was promised at Château Renard.'

Peter looked unhappy.

'This will mean a lot more trouble for me than for you.'

'Holy Father, I only mention it for the sake of your reputation.'

Peter went white with anger and turned round to the four notaries behind his chair.

'All right, all right! Put in the article about the Council!'[33]

But nearly a year later the text was still in dispute, and Peter had gone to the length of gaoling one of the cardinals' notaries.

Louis of Orleans was easier to satisfy. They met at Tarascon. After all that Louis had said in Paris, he had to bring back some fresh papal undertaking. What it said was unimportant. Could not Peter realise that, so long as all is thought to be going well, people simply do not read these things? It took several weeks before Peter was able to grasp this idea, so elementary to a politician, so incomprehensible to a jurist. Then he rose to the occasion with the bull *Scrutator mentium*. Splendidly ironic title! What document was likely to open a window into Peter's mind? Louis was right, of course. It gave nothing, yet even the University was satisfied. No one ever read it.

However, there was one competent observer at the papal court. Gerson was spending a month or two there, long enough to notice the misanthropy and to disapprove of it. On New Year's Day,

1404, he preached before them all at Tarascon. A very different sermon from his last one. A tiresome sermon containing meddlesome advice. The Curia should not monopolise benefices. There must be no attempt to coerce Rome; rather than that, His Holiness should make sacrifices. Fortunately Louis of Orleans fell asleep. Peter did not. One sentence of Gerson's, as he led up from the Circumcision to the benefits to be expected from a General Council, rankled particularly.

'Every deeply rooted and passionate attachment, whether it be to honours or riches or pleasures, turns a man into something possessed by a demon.'

So that was what they thought of him? That he was attached only to his own dignity? That he had done nothing more than beat them all at their own game? How silly of them not to see that if dignity was all he wanted, he could have accepted the way of cession from the start and sunk back into respectable, indeed venerated retirement years ago. No, he had work to do, and there was nobody else in sight who could attempt it. He alone could close the schism in the proper way, by making his adversary in Rome come to terms. It was time to put his plans into operation.

★

He had shown great skill in negotiating from weakness. Now he intended to negotiate from strength. There is a catch in this, as cold warriors are still discovering from time to time. Peter's plans were no less ambiguous. His own name for them was the *via reductionis intrusi*. Experience would show what was the right proportion of arms to arguments needed to reduce the usurper.

As a jumping-off place, Marseilles had great advantages. It was out of reach of French land forces, but readily accessible to ships from Aragon. The Abbey of St. Victor was fortified, stood close to the harbour and was big enough to hold Peter's court, or rather his advanced operational headquarters. Rear headquarters were still at Avignon.

He held a conference. The cardinals were unanimous; he should send a mission to Rome to prepare the ground for a meeting with Boniface. Peter could not resist the temptation to remark how much they would all have been spared if only they had supported this policy earlier.

There had been no contact with Rome since Fernando's mission eight years back. Now more months elapsed while a safe-conduct was arranged. But at last Pierre Ravat entered the gates of dusty, venerable, turbulent, insanitary Rome, where things were still in such an everlasting muddle that Boniface had not been able to derive the slightest profit from Peter's misfortunes.

In all these eight years the Roman Obedience produced no ideas whatever. It survived by its own momentum and by a gratifying lack of imagination on the part of its supporters. At one moment Peter and Boniface were actually being besieged simultaneously, but in Boniface's briefer ordeal in the Castle Sant'Angelo only local issues were at stake and nobody outside Rome cared what happened. These things were part of the immemorial life of the city. The Colonna were at it again.

As the pilgrims began to pour in for the Jubilee of 1400 the Romans, scenting a good year for business, came to terms with Boniface. Thirty-one scapegoats were arrested and the youngest was made to hang the other thirty, including his own father and brother. In this way decency and order were restored for the Jubilee year at least, apart from the presence of bands of howling flagellants in dirty white who flogged one another hysterically as they followed crosses which sweated counterfeit blood. They came from 'Scotia'. They robbed orchards and behaved promiscuously. Doubtless they were Irish. Boniface's officials had little time to worry about them. They stood all day at the threshold of St. Peter's with long rakes to gather in the small change.

The confusion within the gates bred growing indifference outside. The English had deposed Richard II, and the Germans, Wenzel; neither nation had time to spare for Rome's troubles. The northern half of Italy was fully and delightfully absorbed in trade, art and city-state politics. The south had come under an ambitious upstart, Ladislas, who had designs on the Papal State. And Rome had turned itself into an ecclesiastical stock exchange.

Probably no pope before or since has practised simony on the scale of Boniface IX. The details must be read in the pages of modern Catholic historians such as Hughes or Seppelt. Pardons were sold without the slightest provision for penitence or for making good wrongs done to others. Benefices, while not yet vacant, were sold in advance to the highest bidder and cheerfully sold again to anyone who cared to offer more. There were two Jubilees in ten years, both of them frankly commercial. In this connection Boniface invented indulgences *ad instar*; instead of making your pilgrimage, you paid the papal collector what the journey would have cost plus a commission and got your spiritual reward like that. Or, if you were a cleric, you could buy a dispensation to hold six incompatible benefices at once. This was a better bargain than the expectancies, for Boniface was liable to revoke them all without warning and start afresh with a new issue.

Most of the money was spent on petty wars in central Italy, though Boniface had the usual tribe of Neapolitan relatives and, specifically, a mother who was 'of all women the most avaricious'.

These financial operations put a great strain on the Roman Curia and on our old friend Dietrich in particular. No doubt Pierre Ravat must have met him trudging along the Vatican corridors, a more mature and considerably more weary Dietrich, still struggling conscientiously to hold back the lapping waves of administrative chaos. His subordinates lived in terror of him and bent their heads over a waspish handbook on Vatican procedure 'By Dietrich von Nieheim, least of all the abbreviators'. While Peter was starving in his beleaguered Palace there had been a phase, all too brief, when Dietrich called himself 'the elect of Verden', for Boniface granted him the see and even let him go to north Germany to take possession of it. We are not told in his memoirs what it cost. But the Archbishop of Bremen and the Duke of Brunswick, who otherwise seldom agreed on anything, unaccountably joined forces to keep poor Dietrich out, and presently Boniface gave the see to somebody else. Back in Rome once more, Dietrich worked as devotedly as ever for a pope who had cheated him and a system he deplored. He would have felt lost without his *Schicksalsgemeinschaft*, his fate-companionship. At least he had been out of Rome during the year when the Jubilee coincided with the plague and visiting prelates died so fast that Boniface was able to resell the same bishopric several times in a single week.

Boniface, though under fifty, suffered from gout and the stone.

It was a valid excuse for not leaving Rome and meeting Peter. Ravat proposed a cardinals' conference. Boniface refused. Or arbitration. Boniface refused again. Or that the two popes should order their cardinals not to elect a successor if either of them should die. Boniface refused this too. He would give no reasons and was becoming irritated.

'Why does not your master resign? Why hasn't he resigned, seeing that he promised to do so and put himself in the power of the laity? Let him resign if he wants to or is bound to, and nothing will be lost. But we, who hold our power from God, do not wish to resign.'

Ravat objected to his tone. Boniface grew angry, shouting that Peter was a heretic and ought to be imprisoned for life. Ravat replied that at any rate Peter could not be accused of simony.

At this the Roman pontiff's temperature rose steeply and went on rising after the interview was over. In fact Ravat's observation proved fatal. Two days later Boniface was dead.

His last words, when a cardinal asked him how he felt, were: 'If I had more money, I should be well enough.'

Disregarding the safe-conduct, Boniface's nephew promptly arrested Ravat and all his suite. The nephew demanded a ransom; Florence advanced it and sent the bill to Peter; Peter refunded it and borrowed the sum from the clergy of Languedoc. For the first critical ten days, when Ravat might have achieved much in private conversation with the Roman cardinals, he was behind bars in the Castel Sant'Angelo. No doubt that was the idea.

By the time he was released again the cardinals had made their minds up. They asked him whether Peter would now resign automatically, and on hearing that he would not they bundled Ravat out of Rome, entered into conclave and chose a third Neapolitan pope, Innocent VII.

This result produced few heart-searchings within the Roman Obedience but a whole fresh crop in France. Another opportunity had been missed, though it was not quite clear how Peter was to blame. To this was added the indignation which people feel at being taxed. On returning to power Peter had found an empty treasury. It had to be refilled, and the Camerlengo, back in harness like everyone else, had bent his energies to recovering arrears of papal taxes from people who had been paying them to the Crown instead. On top of this a special tithe was imposed with the King's consent to pay for Peter's next project.

In Aragon, a much poorer country, the response was quite different. King Martin advanced 200,000 florins, other loans and offerings poured in, and the *Consell de Cent* promised two galleys.

For Peter was going to push forward into Italy. He had always believed in a conference with his rival. Now at last it seemed that his own side might allow him to proceed with his plan. If he were to move closer and, better still, if the Italian states began to desert the Roman cause, his rival's dislike of a meeting would melt under the pressure of facts. This was a policy which might produce results, but it would be expensive. Peter must have a private fleet, some military backing, and substantial funds for what might loosely be called prestige advertising in Italy. Hence all that activity by the Camerlengo.

By singular good fortune the door into Italy was open. Genoa, exhausted by factional strife, had put itself under French protection. Two strong men now controlled its destinies—Jean Boucicaut, Marshal of France, as governor, and on the spiritual plane Cardinal Ludovico Fieschi. Why should not theology follow the flag? The suggestion was in perfect harmony with the Marshal's own ideas. He was an elderly hero with a strong facial resemblance to Alice's White Knight, as pious as his brother Geoffrey (who had besieged Peter) was not.

A commission went to Genoa to prepare the way. It included Martin's young nephew Miguel, a young man high in Peter's favour who had just been made the third Cardinal of Pamplona. Peter was good with intelligent young men and always had several of them prominent in his service. They adapted themselves better to his energy and his egotism than did older men, and he enjoyed watching their keenness and helping them in their careers.

The Genoese and their clergy were exhorted to take a decision equally pleasing to the Almighty, to Charles VI and to Marshal Boucicaut. They only hesitated for as long as it took to reassure Cardinal Fieschi, who feared that the loss of his Roman emoluments would mean destitution. The immediate spectre exorcised by a mortgage on the Priory of Bollène, the salt-tax of Avignon city and

the apostolic dues of Carpentras, and his long-term anxieties alle-
viated by a pension of 12,000 gold francs and sundry well-found
benefices, the Cardinal was able to enter Peter's College with a good
conscience, while the prelates, clergy, magnates and people of the
whole Genoese coast hastened to follow so illustrious an example.

Peter's hopes went far beyond Genoa. The Count of Savoy,
whose territories at that time reached the sea at Nice, had always
been a supporter, and he had much influence in north-west Italy.
A cardinal's hat rewarded his chancellor, Chalant. In Milan the
Visconti were friendly, being linked with Louis of Orleans. Pisa and
Florence showed signs of wavering. Aragon's sea power was bringing Corsica and Sardinia into the fold. The partisans were active
again round Montefiascone. In Rome itself the Colonna were
potential allies. In fact there were few powerful figures in Italy
still firmly on the Roman side apart from Ladislas of Naples, and
since his dominions had changed their papal allegiance five times
already, it was not unreasonable to hope that they might change
once more.

The wave of success washed up some unlikely flotsam. Peter found
himself recognised in Cyprus, in the Canary Islands and in a place
called Caffa in the Crimea. He set up a new bishopric in the Isle
of Lanzarote, far beyond the Pillars of Hercules. The Byzantine
Emperor wrote politely. Owen Glendower brought over the
Welsh, and in 1407 a bull of Peter's established a Welsh university.
(It disappeared into the mists of Snowdon with Glendower himself,
and nothing more was heard of that good cause until Gladstone
took up again where Peter had left off.) In the Pyrenees the Count
of Foix came over and imprisoned the Roman bishop of Bayonne,
the same luckless Menendo who had been caught by Captain
Bernaldez in the year the schism began. Peter chuckled over this for
days and considered it an excellent omen.

It only remained to assemble the ships and soldiers. Peter was
impatient with his supporters. Could they not see the opportunity?
He made his secretary Clemanges fling shovelfuls of Latin exhortation to all points of the compass. The Knights Hospitallers had ships
in plenty. The Bishop of Tortosa must send twenty men-at-arms or
an armed pinnace. Why had not those two galleys sailed from
Barcelona yet? Had Paris given its subjects leave to enlist in his

forces? Was the Duke of Bourbon coming to help him in these military matters?

The French ambassador, watching this human dynamo at work, wrote home sourly that the Holy Father seemed intent on entering Italy as a Caesar rather than an Aaron. With 132 men-at-arms and 44 crossbowmen? The image of Peter as a war-lord grew faster than his military strength. The fact was, the French had never forgiven him for defending himself during the siege.

The French ambassador had more to write about when he learned that Peter was holding secret military conversations with the two young men who both claimed to be King of Sicily. They were Louis of Anjou, the ruler of Provence who had welcomed him at Château Renard, and Martin of Aragon's warlike son Martin the Younger, who was actually in possession of the island. Peter proposed quite simply that the two should bring their stale quarrel to an end and join forces to escort him to Rome. To them it seemed an attractive idea. But the elder statesmen in Paris and Barcelona were deeply shocked. The diplomatic game in the western Mediterranean had been played for well over a century with Aragonese versus Angevin chessmen. The rules did not allow the chessmen themselves to make common cause against a third side.

King Martin sent an embassy to Peter to express his simmering disapproval. Why had he not been consulted? He in particular, he bubbled, *qui com amich, cosi, vassall e fill de obedencia del dit Sant Pare raonablement devia esser consultat*. It would cost too much money. It would weaken the defences of Sicily. It would cause great confusion. Did Peter realise—and here the royal cauldron boiled over—how much the House of Aragon had done for him already? *Quants affanys, tribulacions, dampnatges e menyscaps ha sostenguts la Casa d'Arago per la Sua Santedat?* The envoys could expand on this theme at some length, he added irritably in their written instructions; they knew all about it. And then they could press him for a nice long list of spiritual and political favours.

*

Peter set sail for Genoa. The galleys from Barcelona had come, bringing two Spanish cardinals and the faithful Alpartil, proudly back from leave 'with my own well-armed followers'. A storm struck the fleet and drove it into Villefranche. Peter remembered his voyage along this same coast with Gregory and took it all in his stride. They were on the move again, that was all that mattered.

He had seven cardinals with him. Nine others stayed behind at Avignon, making frivolous excuses. That had happened to Gregory too.

The weather cleared up and the six galleys made a triumphal progress along an unspoilt Riviera. Monaco, Albenga, Savona. Speeches, keys on embroidered cushions, banquets in Dominican friaries. On 16 May Genoa was in sight with gaily decorated boats dancing three miles out through the afternoon sunlight to meet them. On the quayside, Cardinal Fieschi at his most devotional. The Marshal in full armour and three hundred notables. Another three hundred personages all in red. D'Ailly smiling ambiguously. Even Brother Vincent again, once more drawn into the current of history. The Archbishop with an infinity of clergy. Keys. A procession to the cathedral. Bunting, bells, benedictions. Two addresses of welcome with the inevitable Latin puns on the Pope's name and the city's. A speech of thanks from Peter. A series of banquets, prolonged to the borderline of apoplexy. Promotion to the rank of cardinal bishop for three of the College who were with him, which would teach the others not to stay behind.

From these celebrations only one group was excluded. The Pope's armed escort had to stay on board ship. It was tactfully explained that, had so many fine men landed, the Genoese husbands would have lost their domestic peace of mind.

Brother Vincent preached ecstatically to vast crowds and miraculously overcame the obstacles of language. D'Ailly preached to more sophisticated gatherings with many *doubles entendres*. Peter reconsecrated fifty prelates, giving each a golden ring with a precious stone. St. Colette knelt before him and received generous facilities to start her mission. Peter was deeply moved; she would do the sort of work which he, with all his power-politics and preoccupations, had not been worthy to attempt. Then back to his own plane. The Golden Rose for Marshal Boucicaut. Delegates from Montferrat, Pisa and Livorno. His most brilliant young men sent forth to convert Florence.

His sun stood at its zenith.

Then, with the fierce heat of high summer, everything died, as it always does in the south. Money was running out again. Pisa and Florence were at loggerheads and forgot about him, absorbed in their quarrel. An epidemic in Genoa. Cardinal Serra struck down, and the trusted cubicular Romani who had escaped with him from the Palace. No troops from France. The Duke of Bourbon still delayed. Everywhere they were dragging their feet.

In mid-August, at the deepest point of the torpor and frustration, the news came that Innocent VII was having nephew-trouble. The Vatican and the Roman city council had found a new bone of contention. Which of them owned the Milvian Bridge? They solved their problem by breaking the middle arch so that the bridge was unusable. There was a general sigh of relief at this statesmanlike act, and twelve city councillors came to pay their respects to Innocent. As they left again the nephew fell upon them with an armed band, dragged them into the Santo Spirito Hospital, stripped them naked, killed eleven of them and threw their bodies out of the window. The twelfth was spared because he was a cardinal's cousin. The great bell on the Capitol spread the news. The people rose. By next morning Innocent, his nephew and the whole Curia were in headlong flight along the shadeless road to Viterbo, except for a few like Dietrich who stayed to be plundered in their own houses. Of the others nearly thirty fell dead of heat-stroke by the roadside and several more died after they reached Viterbo from drinking iced wine. In Rome Innocent's arms were hacked down or smeared with filth, while the surviving councillors swore solemnly that they would never obey him again.

The news reached Peter in less than a fortnight; his Intelligence always worked well. But how to use it? His resources were slender and in spite of appearances he stood almost alone. His court at Genoa was all showmanship. His best advisers were dead or dying around him, and those still left at his side lacked either experience or else unqualified loyalty. Could he possibly make a dash for it? Set sail for Rome immediately and do a deal with the city councillors before their mood changed? The temptation to try was agonising. Yet it was too risky. One way or another he was almost certain to become their prisoner. He needed the full backing of France behind him.

He wrote a desperate appeal to Charles, or rather Clemanges wrote it in the sort of language that was considered appropriate. It fell on deaf ears. The French were ready to use force against their own Pope on occasion, but never for him. Just then they were too busy anyway, for the impetuous young Duke of Burgandy, within a few months of succeeding to the old Duke and his policies, had brought the country to the brink of civil war. In fact Louis of Anjou was on his way to help Peter when urgent messages from Paris made him turn back.

Meanwhile the epidemic raged in Genoa. Peter withdrew forty miles along the coast to the castle of Finale, where he spent the winter pacing the draughty halls, letting his beard grow again as a sign of sorrow and reviewing his prospects. It all came down to one thing. The plan he favoured meant putting his trust in princes. And in them is no salvation.

★

The outlook was bleak once more. Innocent, at Viterbo, turned down fresh proposals for a meeting. Even when driven out of Rome he would not take the smallest step towards unity. Dietrich and some cardinals murmured and St. Bernardino scolded, but outside these restricted circles there was almost total indifference. The Italians at large had already evolved their self-protective attitude towards organised religion. One conforms. The Church is not a fit subject for public concern and controversy. The pope should always be an Italian. More arcane details are best left to the priests.

There was too much public opinion on the one side and too little on the other.

In these circumstances Peter, true to character, moved still farther back to Nice and just waited. For over twelve months he stayed poised between Avignon and Italy. There was nothing else he could do. But he was ageing and he felt uneasily that time was no longer on his side.

1406 was an unhappy year. Young Miguel de Salva died of the epidemic, which lingered on, while his other new cardinal, Chalant, proved ineffective as a nuncio in Paris. There was also a curious attempt to work the Pope's downfall by black magic. It was an international plot, he learned, with ramifications stretching up the Rhône valley and into Germany. Two of the would-be magicians confessed. Peter took necromancy very seriously; he appointed a special court to try them. It heard of a secret coven in the hills and studied an exhibit, a black box containing magic formulae denouncing the Pope and Cardinal Fieschi in illiterate Latin, many little drawings of crescent moons, a wax statuette of a child pierced through by nails and other nastiness. To Peter the episode remained mysterious and disquieting, yet another evil thing cooked up by his enemies. Was it only an over-elaborate confidence trick?[34]

There were worse things to worry him. The mood in France was changing again and his friends there, Bishops Lestrange and Ravat, were running into trouble. Finally one evening Peter's latest young man arrived breathless and dishevelled from Paris. The Toulouse Letter had caught up with Guigon Flandrin.

Guigon was the youngest of a whole dynasty of Flandrins, all of them eminent papal jurists. As a junior don at Toulouse he had composed an irreverent exposé of the great rival University and its feud against the Pope. The letter had played a large part in the move to restore obedience and had left the Paris doctors covered with ridicule. They did not forgive him. After waiting their time for four years, they suddenly brought a prosecution for *lèse-majesté*. Their leading counsel was a certain Maître Cauchon. He was out to make a great career for himself, and this was his first political trial. He brandished the letter before the court. Was it not most disrespectful to call the formal official policy *'ténébreuse et fumeuse'*? Were royal decisions no more than a cloud of smoke? And this infamous document even dared to refer to the professors as cuckoos, *'ce qui est moult mauvese et détestable injure, attendue la nature du cucul'*.

The letter was condemned. Cauchon had his eye on a benefice of Guigon's. His application to overrule Guigon's immunity as a cleric was due to come up before the Parlement. Guigon was sure it had succeeded. He had not waited to see. *Lèse-majesté* carried the death penalty. He escaped from his lodgings the night before and rode hell-for-leather southwards.

Peter and Francisco de Aranda heard Guigon's story in dismay. They saw at once that it marked another turning-point in relations with France.

And Maître Cauchon? He was a coming man. He took over Guigon's benefice and climbed rung after rung of the juristic-ecclesiastical ladder until he ended fittingly as the senior of Joan of Arc's judges.

Only Louis of Orleans could save the situation, and he had been losing ground of late. His campaign against the English in Gascony had been an expensive fiasco. Burgundy accused him of levying oppressive taxes and squandering the proceeds. His 'ribaldries' were highly unpopular. The Queen was his partner in all these indiscretions and it was rumoured that he had become her lover. In view of these setbacks and distractions at home, Louis' Italian dreams had faded, and with them had gone his need for Peter. It was time he cut down his commitments. He knew just how to write such a letter.

> There is also the danger that if you delay any further, the serious measures which certain people are already preparing against you will be put into effect. With all my efforts I have scarcely been able to delay them. Unless you hasten to translate your holy intentions into deeds, I fear my shoulders will refuse to bear a weight which grows constantly heavier and that someone else, not you, will win the glory of this great achievement. I know that this is what many are aiming at. Forgive me for saying openly what I think. Did I not know how holy your intentions are, I would never have undertaken to uphold your cause. And now it is essential that all should be made to see that I have been right about you . . . [35]

Peter smouldered. The condescension of it! But he was wise enough to keep his feelings to himself. By his mere presence in Paris Louis was a brake on the University fanatics. And so in fact he remained for another nine months, until the night came when, returning carelessly through the streets after a vist to the Queen, he met Burgundy's hired bravoes and they hacked him down. With his death Peter lost his last influential ally in France.

★

For the fourth time in twelve years the French clergy met in
Paris to decide whether they should obey their Pope. The University
led the attack. Gerson and d'Ailly gently deprecated committing the
same mistake twice and urged a General Council. They claimed that
Peter was ready for one and that the faculty of theology supported
their view against other and less competent departments.

An extraordinary debate followed, fifteenth-century French at its
frothiest (for they all spoke in the vernacular), a debate full of unconvincing analogies and weird metaphors, about the cardinals as
planets moving of their own volition, captains being thrown over-
board to save the ship, neighbours falling down wells and not being
rescued, night-birds who hide their beaks in their feathers at the
sun's rising and King Uzziah being smitten with leprosy when he
laid hands on the High Priest. For this last unhappy comparison the
versatile Dean Fillastre had to tender an apology.

The Archbishop of Tours tried to bring the debate down to
earth. He began by reminding the University of its long roll of
requests made to Peter, and read out the humble letter written on
that occasion. Why all this chopping and changing? How could a
body representing only a fraction of the Avignon Obedience and a
still smaller fraction of the universal Church sit in judgment on the
Pope? And was this Pope the sort of man who would yield to them?
'I do not think so,' the Archbishop went on. 'He comes from the
country where the good mules come from. Once they have taken a
particular road, you can flay the skin off their backs sooner than you
can make them turn back!'

After that there were more farmyard metaphors. The Abbot of
Mont-St-Michel inveighed against papal taxes, which were the real
grievance behind all this oratory.

'A true shepherd should feed his flock, not shear it.'

'In my part of the country,' replied Dean Fillastre, 'We shear our
sheep at least once a year. Otherwise they have thorns sticking in
their fleeces.'

And Cramaud thought the two rival popes were a pair of foxes.

The level of discussion was a symptom of the sickness which had
overtaken the French Church. On Peter's side perhaps the most telling
point was one of the Dean's; this Pope had put an end to simony,
and no longer lived by selling benefices to the highest bidder, and

LOUIS OF ORLEANS
A contemporary statue from a monument to Cardinal Lagrange
(*By courtesy of the Conservateur, Museum Calvet, Avignon*)

PEÑÍSCOLA,
TODAY.
(Photo T.A.F.,
Barcelona)

their response was to deny him the taxes which were his only legitimate source of income. On the other side, the only new idea was a strange one of Jean Petit's; a third, temporary pope should preside over a Council which would decide whether to elect a fourth pope.

The upshot, after Cramaud had acted as teller, was a handsome majority for renewed partial withdrawal. As a royal decree had already suspended the collection of papal taxes, all that the synod could do was to confirm this step. Which was all it was meant to do.

At this moment news reached Paris of Innocent's death. He died in fact just before the synod began. Once more Peter's Intelligence brought him the news quickly, in about a fortnight. As he saw no particular reason to pass it on with equal speed to the synod, they only heard five weeks later.

Once they knew, letters of windy exhortation flew in every direction, but by that time the cardinals in Rome had chosen a fresh pope.

Gregory XII, of the Correr family of Venice, was mild and very old, an ascetic in looks and by reputation, tall, bent, thin as a ghost, a piece of ancient alabaster. By this time the Roman cardinals were becoming just a little ashamed of the schism too, and before electing Gregory they had bound themselves by the strictest compact yet devised, one that made him in their eyes less a sovereign pope than a stop-gap charged to bring unity by his abdication. Elected and enthroned, the old man proclaimed again his zeal for this role. He renewed his promises irrevocably; he would meet Peter and negotiate with him. He showed a touching eagerness to set out for the meeting. If need be, he declared repeatedly in his quavering Venetian voice, he would take a fishing boat or go on foot.

This was indeed something new out of Rome, and Peter saw to it that Paris received the news in record time. While Gerson acclaimed yet another dawn from his pulpit, Gregory and Peter exchanged letters.

> Gregory, bishop, servant of the servants of God, to Peter de Luna, whom some in this unhappy schism call Benedict XIII, greeting and the wish for peace and unity. He that humbleth himself shall be exalted. Striving obediently in so far as we may after this most wholesome counsel we have determined, setting aside all contention, to address you in charity and to exhort you to the reunion of the Church, and further we invite you to discuss the matter with us. . . . For the more valid, certain and

o

well-founded are our own rights, the more praiseworthy we deem it to relinquish them. . . . Therefore let us both arise, let us come together in a single desire for unity, let us cure the Church of that sickness which has so long afflicted her! To this task we urge you, to this we invite you; for we are ready to yield up our own true rights to the papacy if and when you renounce your pretended rights or die, provided that those who on your side comport themselves as cardinals are willing to join with our venerable brothers the cardinals of the Holy Roman Church and so ensure the canonical election of a sole Roman pontiff. And in order that these results may follow the more speedily, we are sending envoys to arrange with you a fitting place to conclude them, and in the meantime we shall abstain from creating any new cardinals. . . .

Given at Rome, at St. Peter's.

Benedict, bishop, servant of the servants of God, to Angelo Correr, whom certain adherents in this pernicious schism call by the name of Gregory, greeting and the wish for peace and true unity, and the grace to accomplish it. We have received your letter containing certain observations concerning the attainment of that unity in Holy Church for which we have repeatedly striven. . . . Having studied your letter, we give thanks that in the fullness of time it has been granted us to find a man such as we have been seeking ever since we were raised to the supreme apostolate. . . . For hitherto, as we do not doubt you are aware, we and our followers have laboured to move your two immediate predecessors without receiving any satisfactory answer. . . . Oh fortunate man, if indeed the Lord has reserved you for this, and if you omit nothing in performing it! To this we invite you with devout encouragement, for this you will find us ready, to see this is our most fervent wish and always has been, that by divine guidance and favour the union so desired by all may come through the means of our humility.

Yet we cannot pass over in silence what your letter would seem to imply, namely the suggestion that we have ever refused or hindered the way of a conference. . . .

Therefore we assure you that we are ready, together with our venerable brothers the cardinals of the Holy Roman Church, to meet you or your pretended cardinals or any successor of yours in a safe and fitting place. . . . And there we are prepared, for the peace and salvation of souls and the reunion of Christendom, to yield and renounce our most genuine rights to the papacy clearly, freely and simply, if you will at the same time renounce your pretended rights. . . .

We will gladly see your envoys, and will also abstain from creating new cardinals. . . .

Make haste therefore, put aside delay, join forces with us and, seeing how short is human life, do not postpone any further so worthy an act but embrace at once the path of salvation and peace, so that at the Last Judgment all that great multitude who will follow us in this union may be received with us into the tabernacles of the blessed.

Given at Marseilles, at St. Victor's.[36]

Copies of these two letters were widely distributed. To hopeful churchmen their language marked a notable advance on what had gone before. Humanists settled down to enjoy a continued exchange between two such distinguished Latin scholars as Clemanges and Leonardo Bruni, the papal secretaries on either side. Higher critics perceived that while Gregory had done little more than sign Bruni's letter, Clemanges had only been suffered to add the final paragraph to Peter's.

In Paris the latter had a mixed reception. Peter's enemies deplored his reservations and his preference for conferring with Gregory instead of resigning outright. For the last time Louis of Orleans balanced the scales. The outcome was a huge royal embassy, travelling south to give the Pope his last chance.

The mission had thirty-six members. Almost every prominent publicist, whether for the Pope or against him, had a place in it. Cramaud was counterbalanced by the Archbishop of Tours; d'Ailly was there to calm the four other bishops; among the five abbots, the moderate St. Denis kept an eye on the extremist Mont-St-Michel; of the ten theological dons Gerson, though heavily outnumbered, might hope to restrain the Plaouls and the Petits; while in the jurists' ranks the quick-witted Dean Fillastre was more than a match for Pierre Cauchon.

Their instructions were as clear as the French language and intellect could make them. They were to visit both popes and induce them to resign, if possible without meeting. If Peter would not promise this unequivocally in writing, they were to present France's withdrawal from his obedience. If his cardinals gave any trouble, they were to be threatened with loss of the right to join in choosing a new pope.

As seen from Paris this programme looked irresistible. Gerson and his moderate friends tried to close their eyes to its high-handedness. They reflected that a desperate remedy was called for and that legality would follow success.

A few days short of Peter's court two small clouds appeared on the horizon. One was the Treaty of Marseilles; they learned that the two popes had just concluded a formal agreement for a summit meeting at Savona on the Genoese Riviera. This had not been fore-seen in Paris. It was clearly a triumph for Peter. He would get his long hoped-for conference after all, and within his own territory. Their instructions to prevent it were already, apparently, out of date.

In their perplexity they sent for Cardinal Thury, the least pro-Peter of Peter's cardinals, to meet them at Aix-en-Provence and explain what had happened. He came, bringing with him the other small cloud (though it was not immediately recognised as such), namely the envoy from Rome who had negotiated the treaty.

Gregory naturally had several nephews. This one, Antonio, was an intelligent young Venetian whose merits had somehow been overlooked until his uncle's elevation. Then, appointed bishop of a small Venetian colony in Greece, he was promoted four weeks later to the more considerable diocese of Bologna as well as being made head of the papal treasury. Despite these new cares he found the time to act as nuncio to Peter, and he was now on his way to Paris, having heard much of the King's generosity and hospitality from his new friend Cardinal Thury and being loath to deny the monarch a chance to display it.

Thury, in fact, was the other main architect of the treaty. When the talks nearly broke down at an early stage (Peter having embarked on an interminable monologue in support of his own legitimacy) the Cardinal tactfully took over. Presently Peter sent along Francisco de Aranda. The resulting treaty was a document of twenty-three articles, laying down the precise number of galleys, soldiers, pre-lates, lawyers, theologians and servants who might accompany each pontiff. Savona, a place cut in half by a stream with a bridge and having two castles, one dominating each half of the town, was the perfect setting, as Peter had noticed in his voyages along that coast. All imaginable safeguards were incorporated and the entire popula-tion would be sworn in to observe them. Severe penalties were laid down for the smallest act of provocation, even for thoughtlessly using the expressions antipope and anticardinal.

As they sat in the inn at Aix listening to Thury, the French envoys saw that this legal masterpiece had cut the ground away from under their feet. Thury, whom they trusted, was confident that the meeting would bring about union. This was Peter's own way, he declared, and he meant to go through with it. The Archbishop of Tours, author of the remark about the good mules, nodded in agreement. And Antonio, in Italianate French eked out with sub-episcopal Latin, explained at some length that his uncle was moved less by his solemn vows than by his love for all Christendom, by a supernatural zeal which he felt daily growing stronger within his breast. What did he think of Peter then? they asked cautiously. Ah, the perspicacious young Venetian said, one could see that he was one of those proud, noble characters who must be handled very carefully. Any attempt to intimidate him would be fatal. If they withdrew obedience from him, moreover, his uncle would not resign. How could he if the two popes were no longer on an equal footing?

Next morning the mission climbed on to their thirty-six mules and started on the last lap to Marseilles, fatally unsure of what they meant to do when they got there.

They would meet a man who knew exactly what he wanted. It was what he had always wanted. He was convinced that if the two of them could meet behind closed doors he would emerge as sole Pope and the aged Venetian as his senior cardinal. In ability and character he towered above all these Roman claimants. He was a negotiator of genius, he knew his canon law backwards, he could speak as an eye-witness of how the schism had begun, he could talk anyone else into silence, he was utterly dedicated and determined. He had right on his side and right would prevail. He would have beaten down Boniface; how could he fail to overcome a dithering old gentleman like Gregory?

There was only one proviso. He must go into the conference unencumbered. He could make no fresh promises.

★

It was the performance of his life.

The Camerlengo met them outside Marseilles. Admirable lodgings had been arranged for them all. That evening they were received in the Abbey.

Once again they lined up to kiss their host's foot. They could not help glancing at the halberdiers, who to Alpartil's delight had been specially reinforced. But the Curia's attitude was scrupulously correct, and they found Peter himself relaxed and altogether charming. He had an exceptional memory for faces. He greeted each enemy and half-friend by name, asking after his health and activities and obviously enjoying the encounter. They could not help responding.

At the audience next day Cramaud's demands were less trenchant than his hearers on either side expected. Peter took his cue. He replied in considerable detail. He went on for hours. At last he finished. The French thanked him and withdrew. On comparing notes they found that while all of them could bear witness to the conciliatory tone of his remarks, each had been relying on his neighbour to interpret their meaning.

Seeing that they were on a slippery slope, the Archbishop of Tours pressed for something in writing at the next meeting. Peter spoke quietly and firmly. He had explained everything yesterday, he said, and very clearly too. There was going to be a conference, as he had proposed from the start. If people had listened to him then, they would have had unity thirteen years ago. He had nothing to add to his letter to Gregory. He had made his own offer in clearer terms than his, but the most precisely worded declarations were useless when confidence had been lost. He could not give them unity with his hands tied behind his back. They must trust him.

There was an emotional short-circuit. It was too much for Cramaud. He was a volatile and sentimental crook at heart. He stared at Peter and at himself with new eyes. Whatever their differences, this dignified and indomitable old man was Christ's Vicar. He fell on his knees.

'If I have spoken evil of my Father, to the danger of my soul's salvation, I implore him to have pity on me now!'

Others did the same. There were tears, self-accusations and excuses. Afterwards, none of them could explain how it happened.

Peter dismissed them all with his blessing and invited them to dine with him on Whit Sunday.

Cramaud excused himself when the time came. He knew he had gone too far and had made a fool of himself. The others enjoyed their dinner. Pierre Plaoul had a friendly scholastic argument with Peter, maintaining that a sinner could be pardoned against his will. Both had the problem of rehabilitating the Roman anticardinals in mind, and both were too well-mannered to say so. When Plaoul had been brought to remember his manners, the mission was lost.

They retired baffled to Aix and discussed among themselves whether to publish the royal decree withdrawing obedience. Gerson dashed off some *Reasons for Postponing Withdrawal* which they decided to accept. Two of them stayed to watch Peter, three returned to Paris to explain their conduct to a secretly relieved government and a University which branded them as traitors, and the rest went on to Rome.

There the roles were reversed. The mission now knew what it wanted. For the first and only time in all these years the French had the same immediate aim as Peter. Gregory must come to Savona. But this time they found that the Pope did not know his own mind and that others were supplying the deficiency.

Gregory too was a sentimentalist. He was devoted to Catherine's memory and was never without one of her teeth. He was also devoted to Church unity, to his family and to sugar. Unfortunately the priorities fluctuated from day to day and the last two were a powerful combination. His six nephews took care that he never lacked sugar or good advice. In this way Marco was appointed perpetual governor of Viterbo and Montefiascone, while scarcely inferior posts were found for Francesco and the others. The only limit to this good work was when Paolo, on being made the ruler of Ancona, found the position firmly occupied by the previous pope's nephew, the one who had murdered the eleven councillors. Such problems might be ironed out if only Gregory had more time. He therefore appointed a commission of twenty-four legal experts, with Dietrich among them, to determine whether he was still bound to go to Savona. He was genuinely pained when they reported that he was.

Gregory was subject to other pressures too. The parvenu King of Naples, Ladislas, preferred a weak half-pope as a neighbour. He sent a shady friar with instructions to stick close to Gregory and stop any nonsense about resigning. He also threatened to take over Rome if Gregory left.

The French mission arrived on the scene just as the hot season was starting. They exchanged compliments with Gregory, and Cramaud lent him 4,000 francs after the nephews had explained that their poor old uncle literally lacked the wherewithal to reach Savona.

On 8 July Cramaud and his colleagues were startled to hear that he was not obliged to go there, though of course he would. On the 13th Gregory wrote asking to be excused because he had no ships. On the 18th he explained that as a Venetian he distrusted Genoese vessels; would the King of France provide others and pay for them? Next day he could not accept such a gift from a ruler outside his own Obedience; he accepted Genoese ships but not Genoese sailors. On the 22nd he would only come by land, and Marshal Boucicaut must be replaced. On the 28th, not even by land. On the 31st he would come by sea after all, but only in French ships. On 4 August he would not go any farther than Pisa.

D'Ailly and other men of goodwill laboured through the Roman summer. They offered a garrison to defend Rome against Ladislas. They offered a hundred Genoese hostages and fifty from Savona, castles as pawns, funds for the voyage, six armed galleys for six months free of charge, even the captains' wives and children as hostages. They too would stay as hostages.

Cardinals and ambassadors trod on each others' heels as they implored Gregory to do his duty. Flushed out of one senile refuge after another, the weak old reprobate finally turned at bay.

'How do you imagine I can feel safe on French soil? If you treated your own Pope like that, how will you treat me?'

'Most dread Lord, His Most Christian Majesty has pledged his solemn word that no harm will come to you.'

'Has he? There are so many great princes in that kingdom that the word of one is no surety against the anger of the others.'

A mission from Peter arrived too. It included that discreet individual Simon Salvador who had been to Rome before. They demanded the treaty's fulfilment six times in three weeks and then left again, protesting that they had no authority to modify it.

\*

As a result of all this Peter's stock rose once more. Charles wrote him a friendly letter and even Cramaud, on his way home, went to see him on the Ile-St-Honorat off Cannes and gave him an entertaining account of Gregory's manœuvres. They sat together in the best room of the monastery, amicably enough, with a flagon on the table beside them. It was 2 September. The weather had broken and it was a stormy night outside.

And so Gregory wanted stricter safeguards?

'Safeguards!' Cramaud exploded. 'We offered him guarantees that would have satisfied the Sultan of Babylon!'

And they had been holding him up as an example to Peter only four months ago. Peter made the obvious point and the Patriarch had the grace to look ashamed of himself.

Cramaud had only lost four months and 4,000 francs, but Peter stood to lose much more. As he assured Cramaud, he would continue his journey to Savona, but he feared it would prove an empty gesture. Nor would he be given much credit for it in Paris, in view of the University's obsessions.

They were talking openly. Cramaud wondered how he could raise a question which was beginning to worry him and his friends. It was the suspicion that the two Popes were acting in some sort of collusion. At Rome the French had noticed Peter's confidential envoy, Simon Salvador, coming and going very busily. Sometimes he would be received in private audience while they sat about in anterooms. There was a story that he was seen going to the nephew Antonio in the middle of the night and, more sinister still, that Antonio's hunchback visited him in return. Simon Salvador had been to see Boniface and Innocent too.

And what would be the purpose of such collusion, if it really was taking place? That was hard to say. Presumably a secret agreement that each should remain Pope in his own sphere.

There was a simple answer to all these rumours. Unless unity came very soon, both Popes were likely to be repudiated and left without any Obedience at all. It would happen to Peter first, of course, as he had France in his. So what wicked thoughts could he be putting into those innocent Italian heads? In the interests of unity he had always done his best to keep on speaking terms with Rome, and in consequence Simon Salvador knew his way about the Vatican by now. That was all there was to it.

No, there was something else. Ten years ago they had agreed at his suggestion not to go on hurling public anathemas at each other every Good Friday. The censures remained in force, but the annual ceremony seemed rather tasteless. So there had been a secret agreement of sorts. It was never published, but both sides kept it.

Peter disliked excommunications. People may sometimes excommunicate themselves, he thought, but the clergy should be much more chary of doing it, whatever the provocation. It was an eccentric opinion he had long held and acted on.

Their conversation was interrupted by the arrival of an antibishop from Gregory's court. Peter insisted that Cramaud should stay. The Italian prelate appeared, his clothes wet and dishevelled and his face pale green. Protocol prescribed a grave demeanour with a slight inclination of the head. The unhappy man attempted it and floundered. His eyes protruded and his mouth opened and shut voicelessly. Pope and Patriarch shared the thought that he looked exactly like a large fish which has just been landed.

'Most dread Lord!' he managed to gasp at last.

Peter made him sit down and drink a glass from the flagon. When he was a little steadier he asked him who he was.

'Most dread Lord, I am the unworthy Bishop of Cherson.'

Cherson? Where was that?

In the Crimea.

Cherson was not another name for Caffa, by any chance? Peter had appointed his own bishop to Caffa.

No, Caffa was another place, Genoese. Cherson belonged to Venice.

And the Bishop of Cherson had an important message?

Yes. His Holiness Pope Gregory could not come to Savona. He asked that the meeting-place should be changed to somewhere closer to Rome.

Did he give any reason?

The envoy tried to speak, but a new wave of sea-sickness prevented him. He could only helplessly shake his head. At last he gulped a few words. Gregory begged him to accept somewhere within his own Obedience. He did not feel safe in Peter's. That was the end of the message.

'Then listen. From what I know of your master Angelo Correr's character, I cannot suppose that such a man would be capable of breaking his word. The terms of the treaty were fully discussed at the time. One cannot reopen the discussion just before the date fixed for their fulfilment. Savona is absolutely safe. We are both old men. God has given us a chance to gain glory. Let us hasten to profit by it. If we delay, death will come and the glory will fall to another. That is all. Please take that message to your master immediately. I shall expect him at Savona.'

The Bishop staggered out to resume his voyage. Peter turned to Cramaud. Collusion![37]

★

After the French had left, Gregory, badgered beyond endurance by his cardinals, crawled northwards out of Rome one morning. On reaching Viterbo, fifty miles up the road, he showed every sign of staying there indefinitely.

His cardinals hit on a desperate remedy. If he would move on towards Peter, they would countersign grants of portions of the Papal State to his nephews and their heirs in perpetuity, thus buying off their opposition. The purist in Dietrich disapproved, but as the responsible princes of the Church 'neither blushed nor feared to offend God' by the arrangement, he shrugged his shoulders and turned his practised hand to drafting the necessary document.

> . . . And since Our beloved sons the noble personages Marco, Francesco and Paolo have so notably aided Us, sparing neither devotion and solicitude nor toil and hardships, and have exposed themselves continually to dangers and expenses, and taking it into account that their status has been changed by reason of Our elevation to the supreme apostolate, to such an extent that they cannot revert to their former condition without shame and contempt, We . . .

In this manner Forli, Orvieto, Corneto and some other smiling townships passed out of the dead hand of the Church.

Checking a tendency to go off at a tangent towards Perugia, the cardinals steered their master firmly up the road to Siena. Until very recently it was a desolate stretch of country. As the cavalcade toiled slowly over the bluffs of putty-coloured clay towards the graceful lily-tower in the far distance, an unhappy figure, barely recognisable as a bishop, came out of the lunar landscape to meet them. To onlookers it was a picture by Sassetta; to the bishop, the end of an appalling journey. There was a message to be delivered, perhaps a word of recognition for his services in return, just conceivably a refund of the five hundred florins he had spent out of his own pocket. But the Pope glared venomously out of his litter and refused to say a word. The nephews' thoroughbreds covered him with fine clay dust as they minced past. 'And so,' Dietrich tells us, 'with his sorrows piled upon him, he sickened for a little space and died.'

Gregory had lingered twenty days at Viterbo; he spent nearly twenty weeks at Siena. The town was full of embassies and their disingenuous advice. Venice, for instance, was jealous of a meeting on Genoese soil. The German princes feared French influence. Ladislas bullied. The Florentines wanted the conference in their own territory for commercial reasons. The French were much the worst, and Gregory wrote to the King complaining of 'those beastly ambassadors'. The English were the best, for they were indifferent to his movements; all they cared about was that the Archbishop of York should be demoted to Salisbury and Salisbury promoted to York, and being practical men they were ready to pay handsomely.

The ornate marble pulpit in the Duomo resounded with seventeen unconvincing reasons, devised by Ladislas' friar, why the Pope should go no farther. Down in the scallop-shaped piazza a lone voice shouted, 'To Savona!' and its owner was promptly imprisoned for his pains.

Peter was right in what he told Cramaud. His bull from Savona, complaining that Gregory had not come, fell on deaf ears. He had kept Clemanges working remorselessly on it for ten days, with fresh legal arguments to be incorporated at any cost to the style and with amended drafts being re-amended in the grey of the morning, as though the telling phrases would really drive their way into French brain-pans through the bony casing of prejudice. It was useless. Not even his own cardinals stirred. All save a handful were living graciously at Avignon.

He sent fresh envoys to Siena. Gregory had once suggested Pietrasanta as a possible meeting-place. If he would go there, Peter would move up to Portovenere on the extreme edge of Genoese territory and his own Obedience. The two places were in sight of each other. After that one more step and they would meet.

Time was running out. So was cash. Peter could hardly meet his legitimate expenses, which were 15,000 francs a month while he travelled about like this. Gregory was almost as hard put to it to meet his illegitimate ones, though there were sometimes windfalls. When a prelate died at the papal court his goods were forfeit. Antonio the nephew-treasurer was so diligent in enquiring after the health of the aged Cardinal of Pécs, who had come all the way from Hungary to see unity achieved before he died, that the old man took the road north again in mid-winter.

'I tell you, you will not get me or my property!'

Peter had few visitors to leave their possessions as *spolia* if they died at his court. He borrowed 40,000 gold pieces from Marshal Boucicaut, who had become a staunch ally and stood by him when the rest of official France was wavering. In return Peter mortgaged Châteauneuf-du-Pape and three other castles near Avignon. He also granted a pardon to the Marshal's black-sheep brother Geoffrey who had besieged him. But the bull of pardon was no mere cash transaction. Indeed it is to be feared that Peter took some pleasure in composing its penitential clauses. The repentant Geoffrey Boucicaut was bidden to spend the next twelve months continually visiting every sacred building in Avignon, appearing daily in his vest and drawers to recite the *Miserere* on his knees before the Palace gate, endowing ten chaplaincies, fasting frequently on bread and water, making the pilgrimage to Santiago, and finally leaving for Jerusalem, whence he would not return without special permission from the Holy See.

These matters were arranged as Peter passed through Genoa on the way to Portovenere. The voyage ended in a storm which broke his mast. He landed at Portovenere on 3 January 1408. With him were some cardinals, his staff of secretaries and personal advisers, a skeleton Curia, Don Jaime de Prades the admiral of his fleet, two hundred and twenty soldiers and one bombard. It was the end of the road.

★

At the turn of the year Gregory too began to move again. Warily and infinitely slowly, like some ancient but still belligerent crab, he crawled a little nearer to his rival. At Lucca, still forty miles short, he stopped and dug his toes in. Ambassadors in relays poked at him and urged him forward. Why not at least to Pietrasanta, as he had promised? Or could they not go to Pisa and Livorno respectively, where they would only be eleven miles apart? Or better still to Carrara and Avenza, only three miles apart? A dozen other combinations were suggested. All these pairs of places were in Gregory's territory. Peter said he would accept any place that could be reached by his galleys. What more could he offer, short of walking into a trap? But Gregory turned down every suggestion and met each concession with a fresh demand.

'One pope like some water-beast has a horror of dry land, while the other like a land-animal refuses to approach the sea.' So wrote the exasperated Leonardo Bruni to a friend. Yet in fact Peter showed himself ready to go a good deal farther than Gregory, who would not even venture to the seaboard of his own Obedience. A good test of an historian's bias is to see how he handles these negotiations; to apportion blame equally is to show prejudice.

Already, at Portovenere, Peter was perched on the furthest rocky tip of his own domain. The cliff-bound promontory points like an accusing finger at the lush places of the other Obedience. High up stands the comfortless castle in which Peter established his court and his bodyguard. Below that a church, then resounding with unaccustomed ceremonial. Next a tight-packed triangle of fishermen's houses where the junior officials lodged in a permanent haze of fish-fries and thin bubbling wine. Then the quayside, an attractive pattern of shuttered windows and pink and green verticals, and finally the little Port of Venus, where Catalan rebounded from Genoese. Walls and towers protect the village on one side and cliffs on the other, running down to a prong of rock on which a tiger-striped Genoese church has supplanted the goddess's temple and flaunts its impermanent victory. Unless it rained, Peter and his cardinals took their evening stroll along this small headland, their scarlet cloaks flapping and the barefoot children wide-eyed at such magnificence.

There was no road out of Portovenere then. One came and went again by sea. But whither?

Don Jaime de Prades had his own idea. He was a soldier-statesman and believed in action. In 1403 he had cut the Gordian knot that bound Peter to the Palace. Now he proposed to sail to the mouth of the Tiber, break Ladislas' blockade, join forces with the republican citizens and with Gregory's disaffected governor and instal Peter as true Pope in the Vatican. The Romans were already in touch with Peter and had characteristically tried to borrow money from him. They wanted a pope who would look after them. The bold stroke would shatter what little confidence was left in Gregory's camp, reduce him to a wandering pretender and force him to come to terms.

By now the situation was so desperate that Peter gave Don Jaime's scheme serious thought. At first he rejected it, but when Gregory's dishonesty became crystal clear he approved. So did at least two of his cardinals, Thury and Albano. Boucicaut joined in enthusiastically and lent four galleys. Portovenere began to look like a naval base. A shortage of oarsmen? The monks of some nearby monasteries were conscripted and found themselves on the galley benches.

Events in France were likewise moving to a climax. With Louis of Orleans murdered, power passed temporarily to the Duke of Berry. The murderer, Burgundy, was in the wings. No one could doubt that he would very soon be in the centre of the stage again. His tame don Petit was reading out an academic defence of the murder. In January a royal decree was drawn up; if the two popes had not achieved unity by the end of May, France would desert hers and become neutral. In the usual French manner the ultimatum was not sent to Peter at once; he received the text through his own Intelligence service. There were strange cross-currents in Paris.

Finally, in mid-April, the royal ultimatum was formally delivered at Portovenere, and Peter saw himself given forty more days in which to achieve the impossible.

Should he play for time, or should he bring matters to a head? The former course was in every way more prudent. But he was beyond mere prudence now. The French were impossible. And without their firm backing further progress was impossible. Gregory had heard that France was on the brink of disowning Peter, and was waiting for the rift to solve his problems. The only chance, and a slim one at that, was that King Charles might respond to shock treatment.

Peter never did things by halves. His reply to Paris addressed the King politely but in language that had not been heard for over a century. It was clearly not his own fault, he wrote, that unity was still delayed, but in spite of that his revenue had been withheld and his appointments not recognised for a year. And now neutrality was threatened. Was this the loyalty pledged only a few years ago? No, it was a step contrary to the respect due to Christ's Vicar, contrary to the King's own interests and honour, contrary to the divine will which alone could decide when the schism would end. The King should stop listening to evil advice and should revoke his decree; if not, he would incur the penalties set forth in a bull drafted exactly a year ago but hitherto held back. He enclosed a copy.

> Benedict, etc, in perpetual memory of the increase of wickedness among mankind.
>
> It has come to our knowledge that certain children of perdition, who, ambitious of rising higher than becomes them, may thence dangerously fall . . . exert all their powers to prevent us from executing our most salutary design, despising the bonds of Holy Church and pretending an ardent desire for its union while they most wickedly withdraw themselves from its obedience. . . .
>
> We have patiently suffered these things in the hope . . . yet they persevere with great boldness and presumption. . . .
>
> Therefore we, having duly considered the seriousness of the matter, do pronounce sentence of excommunication against all who knowingly shall obstruct the union of Holy Church or shall impede us. . . . And we likewise include in this our sentence all those who may perversely affirm that they are not bound to obey our mandates, whatsoever may be their rank, whether cardinal,

patriarch, prelate or of imperial or kingly dignity . . . And
should they dare attempt it, let them know that they will incur
the indignation of an all-powerful God and of His blessed
apostles St. Peter and St. Paul.[38]

His secretaries had gone over the wording repeatedly, Guigon
with an eye to legal niceties and Clemanges to those of style. But
the content was Peter's, and that still disturbed him. Peter, like most
men, had been granted a few thin shafts of pure light from outside
the long tunnel of his life. One of these had disclosed to him that
intended treachery, however base, is no good ground for excommunication. Why was he shutting his eyes to that light now?

Well, he thought unhappily, what else could he do? The light
jarred with the law and practice of many centuries and with what
everyone expected. In his age treason, not cruelty, was the ultimate
crime. And if Malesset had responded to the threat, perhaps the
King would. One cannot see to work properly by a single shaft of
light, however high-slanting. Much better call for lamps and candles
and work in their rational man-made glow.

A pair of Spanish couriers set off for Paris with the fateful documents. Now he could only wait for the reaction. It would be make
or break.

Meanwhile Don Jaime and the Marshal were anxious for the
Roman expedition to start. The fleet put to sea. The inevitable gale
struck, and a day or two later the ships were back at Portovenere.
While the damage was being repaired, news came that Ladislas had
forestalled them and occupied Rome.

As soon as the news reached Lucca, Gregory declared that abdication in any form was something damnable and diabolical, never to
be mentioned in his presence again. He broke off negotiations with
Peter. The nephews, believing that all their troubles were over,
illuminated their houses and gave a dance. Gregory forbade his
cardinals to leave Lucca and announced that he was going to make
four new ones. These were Antonio, another nephew, Ladislas'
friar and a fourth equally deserving person.

At this the clock struck twelve and the patience of Christendom
ran out. The first to act were Gregory's cardinals. Nine out of
twelve of them dodged the nephews, fled to Pisa and disowned
their Pope.

P

They wrote at once to Peter, asking him to come to Livorno. He should have done so, whatever the risk. Instead he sent four of his own cardinals to meet them. With Malesset, Thury, Blau and Chalant went four of his closest supporters, including Ravat.

When they met, an Italian proposed that they should all join in summoning a General Council, disregarding both Popes. At first Peter's group indignantly rejected this. Blau declared that he would never attend a Council unless his own Pope had summoned it and was present himself. But a Council seemed the right way forward. Simon Salvador returned to Portovenere with the news so far, and Peter sent them an encouraging message. In private conversation the two groups of cardinals began to find they had much in common.

Then Cramaud appeared at Livorno, bringing the news of how Paris had reacted to Peter's bull. The Pope who had dared to reprimand a King of France had been utterly repudiated. In the royal gardens by the Seine all had joined in hacking the document to pieces with penknives. Church leaders who supported Peter were in prison, the Abbot of St. Denis, a bishop and a dean among them. A warrant was out for d'Ailly. He and the Archbishop of Reims had gone into hiding. A terrible fate awaited Clemanges, who was thought to have drafted the offending bull. The couriers who had delivered it were being hotly pursued and would be the subject of peculiar indignities when caught. Orders had been sent to Marshal Boucicaut to arrest Peter himself.

Chalant and the four non-cardinals left hastily at daybreak lest Cramaud should order their arrest. They sailed back to Portovenere and urged Peter to leave French-controlled soil at once. This was also the advice of the three cardinals who stayed on at Livorno. They wished him to accept a joint General Council.

He called a meeting of all his advisers present at Portovenere. They said the same. 'Certain godfearing persons', a euphemism for his secret service, confirmed that the Marshal had indeed received orders to arrest him and could not delay their execution much longer.

Peter wrote a last letter to put the record straight.

> To Angelo Correr, who in this pernicious schism calls himself Gregory, wishes for peace and unity and the grace to achieve them.

If it does not vex you to acknowledge the truth, particularly when it is so well known, you will be unable to deny what you proclaimed to the world in your original letter. . . .

But you, man, if you have a spark of decency in you, think of what remains to be done for the cause of union and make up your mind for God's and pity's sake to do your duty. . . . You will find us always ready to perform what we have offered and, if you act correctly now, to forget your previous short-comings and stubbornness. We call God and the publicity attending these dealings to be our witness that it has not been, is not and will not be our fault if true unity in His Church is long in coming.

Given at Portovenere in the diocese of Genoa, on the Ides of June in the fourteenth year of our reign.[39]

To stay any longer would be foolhardy and would get the Marshal into trouble. Peter embarked with his suite and four of his cardinals and set his course westwards for Aragon. He was under no illusions. The tide had turned against him once more. By using excommunication as a political weapon, he had made certain that it would.

# CHAPTER 9

# The Way of a Council

I T was a bad year, with storms in the Gulf of Genoa even in mid-June. The galleys hugged the land. Don Jaime intended to give Genoa itself a wide berth; elsewhere, in the smaller places, he did not foresee any trouble. But the Ligurians are malicious and bad news travels miraculously fast along that fickle coast. Benedict XIII was finished. The French authorities had thrown him over. They would still be there after he had passed. And so all the delightful little places where he had scattered blessings and golden florins by the handful were closed to him.

When the foremost galley nosed into Portofino, the fishermen demonstratively loaded a couple of rusty bombards. On past Genoa, therefore, through a wild night of winds and lashing rain. Next morning Noli too denied them entrance, but grudgingly let them anchor off a monastery outside the town, while the Curia recovered from sea-sickness and the crew dried their rain-sodden clothes in the sun.

At Villefranche in Savoyard territory things were better. They spent three or four days in harbour while Peter held a consistory with his four remaining cardinals. He made some promotions and sent off some letters. His spirits rose. It was good to stop feeling a fugitive. It was a still greater relief to have finished with France. As for his cardinals at Pisa, he had written to say he trusted them not to do anything against him. He could leave it to their consciences. They knew the truth, and they had tried resisting it before and had seen what happened. Meanwhile there would be a Council. Not at Pisa though; anything which might happen there could only be a bogus one, a *conciliabulum*. The true Council would meet, in obedience to his summons, at Perpignan.

Next morning they re-embarked. A light haze obscured the sun. Peter set sail from Villefranche and from reality.

★

A Council. The idea had been mooted for thirty years but as yet it had never escaped from the scholar's study. Suddenly the word was in every mouth, in pulpits, at street corners, in kings' council chambers. With it went great confusion of thought.

The Church has inherited both Popes and Councils. Their authority like their origin is distinct, and perhaps in the last analysis their claims cannot easily be reconciled. As a matter of history Councils, in the very early centuries, were at the height of their power when the papacy was still in embryo. Bishops of Rome neither summoned these great creed-defining Councils nor presided over them. Later on they started doing such things in the West, and canon law consolidated the Pope's position *vis-à-vis* a Council in the sense that Peter understood it and the modern Roman Church understands it. To use a Council against a Pope would be a revolutionary step. Peter had law and tradition on his side. The only weakness in his case is that conservatism in religion, as in politics, is the defence of recent traditions, not of primitive ones.

The conciliar party meant to commit treason anyway. Yet ecclesiastical ideas, even treasonable ones, are invariably behind the times. The conciliar movement proposed a form of Church government on the lines of the medieval King-and-Parliament just as the Middle Ages were passing away and monarchies were becoming absolute all over Europe.

The conciliar theorists had to prove, within the framework of medieval thought, that a Council can judge a Pope and depose him. As the most relevant canon law text, *Dist.* 40, *c.* 6 of the *Decretum*, says precisely the opposite, this task called for no little virtuosity. Every thinker outside the bonds of loyalty to Peter or Gregory addressed himself to it. Heady optimism reigned in Paris, glum caution at Bologna. The Bible and the Fathers were scoured for anti-papal arguments. A surprising number were found. There were arguments from early Church history, from the writings of St.

Cyprian, from how Constantine, Theodoric and Otto the Great had handled the popes of their day. The great Italian canonist Zabarella produced the theory that the papal office was 'quasi-vacant'. Perhaps he was right, though it seemed strange that neither he nor anyone else had noticed that the papacy was 'quasi-vacant' during the past three decades.

Gerson could not bring himself to start pretending that he had been living for most of his life in a papal vacuum. The title of his latest tract, *On the Pope's Removability from the Church*, shows that he did not follow Zabarella. The Pope was still very much there and, being an obstacle to unity, would have to be removed. How? The end justified the means. It was as simple as that. Gerson repeated the thesis, combined with variously permuted appeals to ancient history, divine and natural law, equity and necessity, in no fewer than six long treatises written in as many months. Above all he felt the need to convince himself.

Both he and d'Ailly were considerably shaken. Theirs was the dilemma of cautious liberals in an illiberal society. They were far from being hostile or indifferent to Peter. D'Ailly's feelings were the more personal, for he had known him longer and better. Both were loyal up to a point, fond of him in a way, and exasperated too. They had committed themselves fairly far in his defence. In their view that had now become impossible. He had failed, and Christendom (or at any rate about two-thirds of it) was going to act in unison and wipe the slate clean. This fresh approach was international and democratic. It represented public opinion and they were publicists, well aware that public opinion alone decides at what point firmness becomes obstinacy.

To Gerson Peter was an intellectual problem. He was angry with himself for not having found the correct solution sooner. By the time he reached his fourth treatise, he had worked himself up to asserting that one might even kill a lawfully elected pope if he was intransigent.

D'Ailly trod more softly. When the King's warrant was issued against him, he started to talk himself out of trouble. His *Propositions* were a clever bridge, allowing him to cross over to the conciliar party without repudiating the past. There was not a word of blame for Peter. Still less did he talk of violence and killing. All were bound to help the Church in her hour of need. It was an emergency. They must proceed resolutely but with caution.

Peter could guess which way Gerson and d'Ailly would jump. As he could do nothing to influence them, he ignored them. The essential thing was to go on talking success and to reach Perpignan.

The ships lay just outside Marseilles for several days, held up by contrary winds, while Don Jaime wondered what would happen if the winds held and a hostile force rowed out from the city. At last the weather changed overnight. With a tremendous nor'easter behind them they drove straight across the Gulf of Lions. At one in the morning, seventeen days out from Portovenere, they ran at the steep coast and slipped between the rocks into the smooth waters of Port Vendres, another landlocked harbour beloved of the same goddess. More to the point they were in Aragon, which at that time extended well north of the Pyrenees. They could rest and reorganise.

When the sea was calmer they moved round the headland to the amenities of Collioure. Peter and his suite were made welcome in the castle and walked slowly along the beach, past the bright blue boats shaped like slices of melon, to give thanks in the parish church which juts out picturesquely at the mouth of the harbour. With plain square faces, self-reliant manners and emphatic Catalan voices all around him, Peter felt more than ever grateful for the homespun solidity of his own north-countrymen. King Martin sent warm messages and put the royal castle of Perpignan at his disposal. The shipowners were glad to see their galleys back again. Bills were presented and somehow paid. Climent worked feverishly. Unimaginative bishops came to ask the Holy Father's advice about small points of friction with their parish clergy. There was a general post of local promotions. The Curia, greatly depleted but with its files triumphantly intact, sorted itself out and set to work again. A team of propagandist friars went forth to sell Peter's version of events to Aragon.

Perpignan made ready for the Council. The town has always had a certain panache, and in Peter's time its liveliness was volcanic. It was noted for excess—for theatrical weddings and funerals, gigantic processions, bacchanalian dancing, a Stahkanovite tempo at work, frantic religious devotions and sexual energy on a scale that was the

envy and the scandal of the whole Midi. There was three times the
normal quota of courtesans. More than that, almost the whole
population at that time was openly adulterous, something unheard
of in Latin countries, and if ever the offence was punished it was
only to afford the spectacle of a naked couple being paraded through
the streets. Naturally this was no deterrent.[40]

And now an Œcumenical Council. Geography had dictated the
choice. At least the Council would not be a dull one. The town took
matters in hand with its accustomed energy. Vast quantities of golden
bunting were procured, and both wantonness and its public repres-
sion were sensibly put into cold storage. A devout populace knelt
as Peter made his entry.

Everywhere there was talk of Councils. Peter's was due to open
on 15 November; he had got in first. Gregory announced his intention to hold one next Whitsun somewhere north of Venice. The
cardinals would hold theirs at Pisa in March. There was even a
fifth synod in the series at Paris, which confirmed the break and
reorganised Church appointments for the benefit of people like
Cauchon. Few save interested parties attended it. The sight of Peter's
unfortunate couriers being trundled in tumbrils through the streets
to the pillory was all the confirmation most Parisians needed.
Addressing the crowd before Notre-Dame, a doctor of theology
bawled out that he would sooner kiss the anus of the filthiest beast
of burden than the Holy Father's mouth.

Up in his room in Perpignan castle Peter made Guigon find a
certain letter. It was dated 26 February 1405, three and a half years
back, and the writer was Isabelle, Queen of France.

> . . . et promectons en bonne foy et en parole de royne et jurons à
> nostre dit père aux saintes evangiles de Dieu par nous touchiéz . . . que
> tant comme il vivra nous lui serons bons, vraiz et loyaulx amiz et
> devots fille et filz espirituelz, et garderons, conserverons et deffendrons
> sa personne, son honneur, son estat, ses prerogatives et autres droiz
> quelxconques . . .

He put the letter down on the table. A lot could happen in three
years.

More excommunications. They were unavoidable now. His
Spaniards would lose heart if he did nothing. Formal proceedings
were opened against the University—'if it is possible to call it that'—

and against thirteen Church leaders including Cramaud, Petit and Plaoul. In due course a bull set forth their condemnation. *Si arbor fructum non producit . . .*

It was a miserable autumn. The King of Navarre stayed four days in the castle as Peter's guest, went on to France and promptly defected too. Don Jaime and the Cardinal of Gerona died suddenly. There were only three cardinals left with him now, Flandrin, Fieschi and Chalant. Peter accordingly made five new ones just before his Council opened. Two of them were Frenchmen, those proven loyalists Pierre Ravat and Jean d'Armagnac.

A fortnight later Armagnac too was dead.

Peter and his seven cardinals at Pisa exchanged pressing invitations to each others' Councils. Each side refused the other's invitation. There matters stood when Peter's opened on 15 November 1408.

★

From the first moment the Council of Perpignan was a personal triumph for its sponsor. Rising above every adversity, above the demonstrable failure of his policy for union, above the loss of roughly half his Obedience, two-thirds of his cardinals, the most efficient part of his civil service and nearly all his money, above betrayal by some of his most trusted friends and the unexpected deaths of others, above the unmistakable smell of final defeat— rising above all these circumstances the old Pope, by sheer force of character, took charge of the proceedings from the moment they began and bent all who attended to his will. It was a masterly achievement, though some of the credit must go to the fairness and steadiness of his countrymen.

At seven in the morning every bell in the town rang out and went on ringing for the next hour and a half. The head of the procession emerged from the castle gate. The Pope's mounted standard-bearer, the sub-deacon with the cross, the white mule carrying the sacrament, the pontifical penitentiary and the keeper of the regalia. Thirty-nine proctors of abbeys, thirty-three of cathedral chapters and six of bishops. The unmitred abbots, followed by eighty mitred ones. The Prior of the Grande Chartreuse, Boniface Ferrer. The Franciscan and Dominican Generals. Thirty bishops, eight archbishops, three patriarchs and seven cardinals. And after them all, walking with a firm step beneath a baldacchino borne by four lay notables, His Holiness Benedict XIII.

Nobles, knights, councillors and papal crossbowmen made up the rest of the procession, with the almoner on his horse coming last of all and scattering handfuls of small change in the traditional manner.

The great majority were Spanish, yet the south of France was not badly represented and there were some from as far away as Savoy, Lorraine and Sicily. Simon de Mandeville, Archdeacon of Glasgow, was there to represent Scotland. Some had passed through France in disguise. There were the delegates of four universities and of five military orders, envoys from Aragon, Castile and the Count of Armagnac. Over three hundred attended altogether.

They all entered the church of Sainte Marie la Réal. There, omitting no single detail of the customary ceremonies, Peter opened his Council.

He had decided to lay before the assembly the balance-sheet of his whole reign. A full historical account, he announced, would be read out by Cardinal Chalant 'and, we trust, diligently followed by you all'.

> The truth, as it touches the common welfare, will be established in the course of this public enquiry, so that being made known to more it may find more ready to defend it.

Such were the straightforward opening words. It was Martin de Salva's last work, brought up to date by Ravat and edited by Peter himself. To let the recital sink in it was cut up into seven sections. Chalant read one each day. In the latter portion of the narrative Cramaud was accused of underhand intrigues with Gregory and Gregory was accused of having sold Rome secretly to Ladislas of Naples for 15,000 ducats. In other respect the undisputed facts were allowed to speak for themselves. In the tenth session Peter spoke again, asking for the Council's verdict on his actions and for advice on what to do next.

At this point the Council went into committee and the proceedings, already a little ponderous, became private and slower still. Behind the scenes there were serious dissensions. Chalant came out in favour of a proxy being sent to Pisa with full powers to abdicate if Gregory did so too. Peter, if he accepted this at all, was determined to add the words 'juridically and effectively' to this last condition. Chalant protested at the latent ambiguity. Peter presided at every meeting. He talked and talked. The Fathers, unprepared for a long Council, began to go home.

The inner committee, still arguing, dropped from sixty to thirty, then by further stages to eighteen, and finally to ten. At last, on 1 February 1409, the remaining Fathers reassembled to publish their findings.

The Archbishop of Saragossa stood to speak. His voice rang fresh and clear through the church.

'Having carefully considered all that Your Holiness has undertaken and performed, regardless of the toil, the danger or the cost, and considering furthermore the injustices, oppressions, interferences and obstacles which have been heaped upon you by the presumption of certain persons, as well as the vacillations, cavillings, evasions and chicanery of the present antipope and his predecessors . . . for all which things done and suffered Your Holiness has earned both merit before God and enduring praise among men, this sacred Council after mature deliberation on these events with a pure heart and sincere purpose believes, holds and maintains that you are a true Catholic Christian and Christ's rightful Vicar.'

Their advice as to his future course would be handed in on paper.

Peter thanked them and the public session closed. He had been vindicated.

He received the committee in private and read their advice. It was to follow the way of cession, to send envoys to Italy and to arrange that if he died he should have no successor.

He finished reading. He threw back his head like a bird of prey.

'I shall do none of these things,' he stated indignantly. 'Besides, I know perfectly well that you are not all of you in agreement.'

'Holy Father,' they answered, 'there is only one of us who dissents.'

'Then he has more sense than the rest of you!'

There was an uncomfortable pause.

'If I am forced to abandon my rights,' he went on, 'the Church will lose its legitimate head on earth for all time. It will lose the true succession from St. Peter and the power of the keys. There will be no means of recovering them either, unless we are vouchsafed a second Incarnation.'

They were thunderstruck. They looked at him to see if he really meant it. He did.

★

Twelve days passed. Finally he consented to send envoys to Pisa. The Council of Perpignan was wound up, or rather prorogued, with the customary *Te Deum*. It had shown itself honest and disconcertingly independent. That was to be expected from a mainly Spanish gathering. Peter was not dissatisfied. It had been brought to a close before Pisa began and before he had had to commit himself irrevocably.

Fieschi and Chalant thought otherwise. They made up their minds to leave the sinking ship. Fieschi had few friends and kept his plans to himself, but Chalant spoke guardedly to Boniface Ferrer.

'What good can anyone do at Pisa?' Ferrer asked. 'All they can do there is to make another antipope.'

'What does that matter?' replied Chalant, voicing the thoughts of many. 'What does it matter, so long as they make one? Let him be an antipope, or the Devil himself if you like. He will improve with keeping!'

The envoys to Pisa were handpicked. Fieschi and Chalant were not among them. They took the long route by land. If their slow progress was deliberate, the French helped by imprisoning them for several weeks as they passed through Languedoc. By the time they reached Pisa the Council there was nearly over.

It was an impressive, indeed a magnificent assembly, splendidly housed in the soaring black-and-white nave of the cathedral and supported by all the powers of Europe save those backward, cragbound countries which stood by Peter—Spain, Scotland, Savoy, Sicily, Sardinia and Cyprus—and the handful of eccentric potentates who still acknowledged Gregory. The Council was attended by twenty-two cardinals, four patriarchs, ten archbishops (and thirteen others by proxy), seventy bishops (and another hundred by proxy), eighty-seven mitred abbots, sixty priors, the generals of the four great orders, a hundred deputies from chapters, delegates from

thirteen universities, three hundred dons, the Grand Master of
Rhodes, the Prior-General of the Holy Sepulchre and the Grand
Procurator of the Teutonic Knights. Behind it stood the intelligent
hopes of all liberals, the massed theological learning of France,
Germany, Italy and England, the ambassadors of seventeen reigning
monarchs, the strong arm of Cardinal Cossa of Bologna and the
will of Christendom for unity. The president was Malesset.

There was only one thing lacking, legitimacy. It was not a
Council. Nearly a quarter of the Church boycotted it, neither Pope
recognised it, and Rome does not count it a Council today. Besides,
it failed.

So dismal a verdict would have seemed utterly improbable to
any who sat there. For one thing, it was so completely unanimous.
If Peter's Council had dragged, this one ran on oiled wheels.
Nobody argued. No one came to contradict, save one mad Englishman who was thrown out and some Germans from the ex-King
Rupert who only stayed a day and left twenty-four theoretical
objections affixed to the cathedral door. Inside, each revolutionary
proposal was greeted with a monotonous murmur of '*Placet!*' The
only prelate who might have argued, Peter's staunch supporter the
Archbishop of Reims, was killed in a chance tavern brawl as he
passed through northern Italy. The rest had quite made up their
minds concerning what the Holy Ghost was to move them to do.

The two Popes were summoned five times from the open west
door. When the stentorian words had reverberated into the farthest
corner of the Campo Santo for the fifth and last time, they were
declared contumacious. It only remained to depose them.

The ultra-scrupulous still hesitated before this step. They had
read, poor men, all Gerson's recent tracts, but they had also read
his earlier ones. If only the two Popes could be shown to be tainted
with heresy! A select committee set about collecting what evidence
it could. Much of it came from a certain archpriest of Poitiers who
had been sent as a spy to Perpignan and had been kicked out. Now
he took his revenge. Long before Peter became Pope, the committee was shocked to learn, he had been keeping two demons in a
wee box. He had searched far and wide for books on magic. One
was found under his pillow when he left Nice. Being only an
indifferent magician himself, he had professional ones brought out

of prison so that he might interrogate them on points of technique. (All this sounds like a garbled echo of the sorcerers' conspiracy of 1406.) His court, it seems, was swarming with necromancers. Francisco de Aranda was a clairvoyant, able to announce the elder Duke of Burgundy's death as soon as he died at the other end of Europe. And then at Portovenere there had been seen a mysterious individual with a long black beard, perhaps none other than the 'Great Hermit' who had already summoned up two powerful demons to do Peter's bidding, the God of the Winds and the Revealer of Hidden Treasure. If a third, the Prince of Sedition, could be induced to join forces with these two, Peter would be in the Vatican before anyone could say abracadabra.[41]

There revelations were considered and wisely held in reserve. Without citing them directly, the dread sentence was formulated and laconically approved. On 5 June Cramaud read it out.

> It is decreed that Peter de Luna and Angelo Correr, hitherto called Benedict XIII and Gregory XII, have been and are notorious schismatics, nourishing, defending, approving and pertinaciously maintaining this long-standing schism, that they are also notorious heretics and have departed from the faith, and that they are guilty of the notorious and horrible crimes of breaking their oaths and vows, by this their incorrigible conduct and contumacy notoriously scandalising Holy Church. . . . And furthermore the Council by this definitive sentence deprives, casts down and deposes Peter and Angelo, each and both of them, forbidding them to bear themselves as sovereign pontiffs and declaring further that the Roman see is vacant . . .

Gerson and d'Ailly had repeatedly warned the Council against filling the vacancy too soon, but now, with the two Popes burnt in effigy and all Pisa in a state of the wildest euphoria, these warnings were forgotten. Nor were Peter's envoys who arrived at this moment able to get a word in edgeways. The mob shouted them down and Cardinal Cossa threatened to burn them alive. They left again precipitately, while Fieschi and Chalant, who had repudiated Peter and escaped from Perpignan, took their seats breathlessly in the rebel conclave. Next day the seventy-year-old Cardinal of Milan, a deserter from Gregory, became Alexander V.

By now the hot weather had reached as far north as Pisa. The work of reforming the Church was shelved for three years. The

Council dissolved in an unprecedented scramble for benefices, which Alexander bestowed with the greatest freedom. Cramaud got Reims; he had had his eye on it ever since the Archbishop was murdered.

When the dust settled, it was perceived that there were now three Popes.

★

Gregory held his Council last, at Cividale on the north-eastern frontier of Italy. Hardly anyone attended it and for months on end absolutely nothing happened. Occasionally the old man held another session and from the Alpine foothills, like summer thunder, came a far-away mutter of excommunications. '*Et declaramos eos inobedientes, apostas, schismaticos, blasphemos, perjuros, conspirationis necnon hariolandi falsi et laesae majestatis criminibus irretitos . . .*' The sound spent itself across the hot plain and was inaudible even in Venice.

Presently that city, from whose territory these comminations were being launched, changed sides and recognised Pisa. Armed guards arrived to watch the exits from Cividale. As the summer broke and the first heavy rains of autumn fell, Antonio packed his uncle's regalia and other valuables methodically into old sacks and loaded them on to a string of mules. Gregory, dressed as an itinerant tradesman, led them out through the downpour past the incurious guards and was soon aboard a cargo boat bound for Naples. The guards caught his chaplain instead, a decoy dressed in a red cloak. On discovering their mistake they beat him up; he chinked, and they found him lined with gold pieces. A guard wearing the red cloak rode tipsily back into the town scattering bogus benedictions. So ended the Council of Cividale.

Gregory lingered on for some years, travelling from realm to realm with Catherine's tooth in his pocket. One minor despot after another deserted him until only the lord of Rimini was left. He could never reassemble anything like a Curia. For even Dietrich had left and was writing his memoirs, three vast vitriolic volumes whose aim was to prove that he had always belonged to the Resistance.

★

The Church which defines schism as separation from the Pope
had deposed the Pope for schism. It need hardly be said that Peter
was not impressed. Even the Latin they had used was below standard.
Notorious, notorious, notorious, notoriously! Wherever Clemanges
had got to, he was evidently not at Pisa.

Poor Clemanges! He had taken refuge in an undistinguished
monastery near Sens. In Paris they were after his blood. He denied
having drawn up the bull which threatened the King with excommunication. It was not in his style, he insisted. Nor was a list
of names of Paris dons hostile to Peter, which had also come to
light. Finding such questions distasteful, he wisely stayed within the
walls of his obscure convent. Its name was Valprofonde.

Such retirement was utterly foreign to François de Conzié. He
was, of course, serving the Pisan Pope. Who else could be Camerlengo? He was the true professional, indispensable as ever. If the
Devil himself should take over, as Peter feared he soon might,
Conzié would be there to keep his books straight.

For his part Peter was travelling slowly through Catalonia with
long rests in the better-appointed abbeys. The pace of Spain suited
him admirably now. He had left Perpignan behind him. It was a
place of unprofitable controversies and was now in the grip of
some epidemic. He was going to see his well-beloved son King
Martin.

Their relations were still excellent. From time to time they had
furious disputes over church appointments, a subject in which the
Pope's interest was fully matched by the King's, but these flare-ups
only welded a strong friendship the firmer. Martin too was un-
daunted by Pisa. His son was campaigning in Sardinia, and great
things might come of it.

Instead, just at that moment, the news came of the young man's
death. It cast a long political shadow on Aragon and on Peter.
Everybody insisted that the widower King must marry again at
once and beget another heir. A suitable young lady was selected
for him with breakneck speed and they were married within the
month.

The wedding over, Peter turned to his own affairs with one of his
great bursts of energy. He entered Barcelona in state, fulminated the
bull *Exsurgat Deus* against those who were 'boldly glorying in their

damnable presumption and rebellion against Us and the Roman Church', started once more the bad old practice of hurling fresh thunderbolts at the same people every Good Friday, prorogued the Council of Perpignan (which had never been finally dissolved) five times in Barcelona and eighteen times in all, found Spanish benefices for his loyal henchmen, cast his line back across the Pyrenees into the troubled waters of south-western France and wrote two books.

The first of these is a canonist treatise. The second one, *The New Sub-Schism*, is still rather heavy going by modern standards but positively light reading by his. In a work of this nature the taste of the day required tortuous rhetoric, far-fetched Biblical analogies and bad puns. The opening sentence of a hundred and ten words contains all three. Later on Peter himself creeps in, bringing genuine indignation and a pleasant touch of irony. He gets huge enjoyment from his tilt at the cardinals, servile and arrogant by turns, electing him, besieging him, grovelling at his feet, neglecting their duty in their Villeneuve palaces and finally deserting him again to join the enemies of a lifetime and take part with them in a farcical new election. They call him a heretic. When, do they think, did he become one? Was he a heretic in 1394 when they made him Pope? Or in 1403, when they returned to his obedience? Or could he have been one last winter, when they were sending him polite invitations, correctly addressed, to their so-called Council at Pisa? And what novel doctrines has he propounded latterly? Or ever?

He lived outside Barcelona on the lower slopes of Tibidabo, in Martin's cheerful summer palace of Bellesguart. He was active from morning to night, but it was all on a reduced scale. He could make his ever-faithful Climent Bishop of Barcelona, but Scotland and Cyprus were too remote to control; he confirmed occasional appointments there and that was all. Foix, Armagnac, Savoy and the islands were debatable. He was really the Pope of Aragon and Castile.

And of Avignon! He was making no more concessions to anybody. All who considered themselves on his side would have to help hold the line. They must hold Avignon for him. A strategist would have written off the outpost as untenable. A politician might have said good riddance. Peter, by now, was neither. Avignon would be held to the last man.

Q

This was his youngest nephew Rodrigo, the only professional soldier in the family. Furnished with a modest force of Catalans and Alpartil as his political adviser, Rodrigo prepared soberly for action. A nephew of Peter's had to work for his living.

History repeated itself with some minor variations. The royal herald strutted once more along the bridge, but this time Rodrigo threw the man's banner into the Rhône and broke his trumpet over his head. Then a thousand French troops arrived, and Thury as the antipope's legate. The town changed sides and the second siege began.

Holding the Rocher des Doms as well as the Palace, and thus having a frontage on the river, the garrison was able to make some sorties by boat to lift cattle from the island. A more ambitious raid on Villeneuve produced only a donkey and the Cardinal of Saluzzo's gardener. Thury died and Conzié succeeded him as legate. The great bombard of Aix, a temperamental piece several times bigger than Mons Meg, arrived behind thirty-six struggling horses, and soon its deep voice was added to the daily uproar. Again the besieged held their own against artillery, mines and four assaults. Again a relieving force failed to get up the river. Again, after seventeen months, hunger conquered, and two hundred emaciated Catalans marched out with their weapons held proudly on their shoulders. Again the town footed the bill.

By that time the long-brewing civil war had broken out in France and the Burgundians were conducting massacres in the streets of Paris. Gerson had been campaigning bravely against Burgundy's tame don, Petit, and his tract defending Louis of Orleans' murderers. Finding himself in great danger, he spent some weeks in the roof of Notre-Dame. His friend d'Ailly had adjusted himself better; his main concern was to keep the income he derived most irregularly from the see of Limoges.

★

The royal palace in Barcelona was in something of a flutter. Martin had been married again for eight months. If he went on like this there would never be an heir. The Queen's ladies-in-waiting put their pretty heads together and decided that something must be done. According to the chronicler Monfar they found an old Castilian cookery book. A drake, pot-roasted very slowly with certain extremely rare herbs for days on end, would render His Majesty *más apto para la generación*. They found the herbs with some difficulty and prepared the dish. Martin ate it. Within forty-eight hours the court was in mourning.

Aragon was left without a king. Behind the rivalries of the various claimants stood a fateful question. Was the progressive province, Catalonia, to go on dominating the country as it had done in Martin's reign, or was power to swing back to the arid uplands of Aragon proper? Or even further, towards union with Castile? With this was linked a social conflict, merchants and ship-owners versus conservative nobles, a linguistic conflict, Catalan versus Spanish, and a political one, provincial parliaments versus the trend to absolute monarchy. There were also the wishes of the third province, Valencia, to be taken into account.

Four of the six claimants had serious support in the country. The leading pair were already on the verge of civil war. A young relative of Peter's, a partisan of the Count of Urgel, murdered a prominent figure on the other side.

Peter took the situation in hand. By passing sentence at once on his relative he proved his impartiality. He was able, even in that disastrous century, to impose a civilised solution. It was one of the great acts of his life. Nine arbitrators, three from each province, were chosen and met at Caspe. No less than five of them came from Peter's own entourage, including Vincent and Aranda. They gave their verdict in favour of Ferdinand of Antequera, heir to the throne of Castile. Peter hoped for a united Spain.

The decision has never been popular with Catalan nationalists, but it is understandable. The new King with his green eyes, reddish hair and Castilian manners made a great impression when he came to kneel before the Pope at Tortosa and swear fealty for his overseas dominions. Peter thought he had broadened his base. Two years later he knew better.

\*

The Pope elected at Pisa, Alexander V, was a good man if slightly ineffectual. His faults were those of generosity and other-worldliness.

He never got within a hundred miles of Rome, and within a year he was dead.

The Pisan cardinals met at Bologna and elected somebody very different, the strong man of Bologna, the martial Balthazar, Cardinal Cossa.

What Peter said is not recorded. His memory went back to the piratical Captain Bernaldez with whom he had once taken ship. Young Cossa had been a rival in the same line of business off the coast of Naples. Later on he had gone to study law at Bologna. They had certainly picked an all-round man.

So Balthazar Cossa became John XXIII. For a great and good man to take his name and number, even after an interval of five centuries, was a sign of the most stout-hearted independence, for by the time that d'Ailly and Dietrich had finished with the first John XXIII his reputation was lower than any pope's since Marozia's sons and lovers. In actual fact Cossa was no worse than many other leading churchmen of the early Renaissance. It was his cardinals who were to blame. If the papacy is to be reformed, one should provide a reforming pope.

John moved to Rome and Dietrich, by now a very senior official, took him in hand. It was not easy to know where to begin. Perhaps, Dietrich thought to himself, he ought to start with John's habit of sleeping in the daytime and staying up very late at night, which could only be an accompanying phenomenon of hair-raising successes with the other sex. Dietrich put his ideas down on paper. He wrote industriously through the Roman afternoons, and soon the aide-memoire *On a Suitable Routine for the Roman Pontiff* appeared in John's in-tray.

John was already a worried man. He perused the schoolmasterly advice in deep despair, decided that almost all of it was impracticable in his case, and resolved at least to give up dictating to his secretaries during mass. He appointed d'Ailly a cardinal, an infallible recipe for ensuring that progressive churchman's disloyalty. D'Ailly, he understood, wished to reform the calendar. Next year however, when a Council was held in Rome, d'Ailly was no longer interested in the calendar. He was out to reform the Church in head and members, starting naturally with the head. John had a large block of unprogressive Italian bishops behind him and was able to stave off any such measures. But it was not a happy gathering. An owl flew in and perched high above the Pope's head, gazing down at the proceedings with unwinking cynicism. A French cardinal made the obvious remark about its being the wrong bird. Peter would have risen to the occasion with some classical tag about Athene and wisdom, but John's education had been different and his Latin was simple.

'*Hoc est malum signum!*' he managed at last.

It was. D'Ailly's crowning achievements were close at hand. As France was so unsettled the reforming Cardinal went to Germany and converted the energetic new Emperor Sigismund to his ideas. Then Ladislas lent a hand by attacking Rome 'in order to protect it'. On the first day the Romans swore to eat the flesh of their own children rather than submit to the invader. On the second, they put up the feeblest resistance at the gates. On the third day they hung out flags for Ladislas while John fled northwards. The Pisan Pope was now at the Emperor's mercy. Sigismund's price was a loan of 50,000 florins and a fresh Council at Constance.

When Ladislas, very soon afterwards, was poisoned by his mistress, John thought better of these arrangements. He still had a few friends in France; Who does not sin seven times a day? asked Cramaud plaintively. But it was too late. D'Ailly and the others hounded him over the Alps and into Sigismund's territory. Already he had no illusions.

'Aha! There is the trap for foxes!' he exclaimed, as he looked down on the lake-ringed town where the Council was meeting.

D'Ailly was already there with a suite of forty-four persons. Hostilities began at once. D'Ailly maintained, logically enough of course, that John owed his present position to the new doctrine that a Council is above a pope. That doctrine had triumphed at Pisa and must triumph again. John must go.

For several weeks John and his swarm of little Italian bishops still had a majority. They tried to get through the agenda quickly and close the Council. Before they could do so Sigismund, the new Constantine, arrived dramatically on Christmas Eve. The scales began to tip, for the Emperor had been reading d'Ailly's tracts. The Council slowly filled up with hard-hearted prelates from the north. Lastly there appeared an eloquent horde of French professors who claimed and somehow obtained a voice in the deliberations. John's doom was sealed.

As a first step the Council accepted a tactically brilliant proposal of d'Ailly's that voting should be by 'nations', as it was in that fount of true learning the University of Paris. There were four 'nations' in Europe: French, German, Italian and English. In Paris this was regarded as part of the eternal scheme of things, and transferred to Constance it had obvious advantages. France, with less than a hundred dioceses, and England with twenty-five, each had the same voting power as Italy with close on three hundred. This piece of political genius robbed John of his majority.

The next step was to insist that all three Popes must be treated on an equal footing. John objected that this made nonsense of the previous Council of Pisa. D'Ailly replied gravely that a Council was not infallible. Only the Church as a whole could make that claim. He had written something to that effect as early as 1380, he pointed out severely.

What a pity he did not make it clearer in the tracts he wrote just before Pisa! John might have quoted from them to some purpose. But advanced double-think was beyond his intellectual powers. He preferred to escape from Constance during the confusion of Shrove Tuesday, disguised as a groom. After a few months of wandering he was caught, brought back to Constance, and put on trial. The case against him was prepared by the archpriest from Poitiers who had given evidence about Peter's sorcery at Pisa.

'The most scandalous charges were suppressed,' Gibbon assures us. 'The Vicar of Christ was only accused of piracy, murder, rape, sodomy and incest.'

He was deposed with his own consent, and then imprisoned for nearly four years without it.

Shortly afterwards Gregory, whose Obedience was confined by now to the immediate surroundings of Rimini, took a more dignified way out and abdicated by proxy. In accepting his resignation the Council, as a polite gesture, allowed itself to be re-convoked in his name for what that was worth. Naturally no one present apart from his representatives thought for a moment that he was the legitimate pope.

The Council of Constance has been regarded in a variety of lights.

Logistically it beat all records. It lasted for three and a half years and was attended by more prelates and clergy than ever, as well as by Sigismund's enormous suite, minor royalties and ambassadors in profusion and an uncomputable multitude of hangers-on. A huge fair established itself outside the town. The figures for entertainers (1,700) and for prostitutes (700) may be slightly exaggerated; in this connection clerical historians dwell on the large number of laymen attending the Council. It had useful secondary effects, transforming the modest economy of Constance, giving an impetus to the German theatre and enabling the humanist Poggio to discover priceless manuscripts in the monastic libraries of the district.

It is also usually claimed that it ended the schism.

Whether it did so validly, and to what extent it was a true General Council, are points which remain rather more doubtful. The official view nowadays is that it was valid in parts. If, overcoming one's natural surprise, one is bold enough to ask which parts, one will receive various answers, depending on whether one consults Salembier or Hefele or Baudrillart. Modern orthodoxy has to avoid admitting that the decree *Sacrosancta* (which declared that a Council's authority is above a pope's) was one of the valid parts. The same applies to the decree *Frequens*, intended to ensure frequent Councils to regulate the Church in the future. As the great majority of those present regarded these two decrees as the Council's supreme achievement, the first of them worthy (as Gerson said) of being carved on the façade of every parish church in Christendom, it is clear that to interpret Constance correctly calls for even greater resourcefulness than was shown by those who guided its decisions.

The easiest way to arrive at the conclusion that Constance was valid in parts while Pisa was invalid altogether is to start with the belief that Gregory was the sole true pope. Peter, needless to say, did not share this notion. To him Constance was if anything more lawless and revolutionary than Pisa. Pisa had been a free assembly of bishops, however irregular; Constance was an imperially controlled congress of publicists with a special rigged voting system unique in Church history. It represented everything he had been fighting these past twenty years.

★

Peter was still fighting, though each year a little less effectively. He had chimerical hopes of various French dukes, of Louis of Anjou, of Ladislas, even of Cardinal Blau. Simon Salvador was his Vicar-General north of the Pyrenees. His secret agents came and went and he studied their reports indefatigably. His stock in Sicily, he learned, had never been higher. The French government was secretly on his side and would declare for him when the time was ripe. In the hills near Avignon the indomitable Madame de Serres, widow of one of his Gascon partisans in Tuscany, was still defying the Pisan legate in her fortress of Malaucène. Perhaps the tide was on the turn.

At the regular meetings with his closest advisers more and more time was taken up with such castles in the air. As he explained in overwhelming detail how yet another self-seeking politician was secretly burning with zeal for his cause, his companions looked at each other and wilted. They were loyal, or they would not have been there, but they had heard it before.

At last Brother Vincent voiced their discontent. The Church was devoting all its energies to fighting for its own interpretation of its own position. It should be saving souls instead.

Clericalism. Putting the institution before the work it was meant to do. That was the trouble, and it had been the trouble for more than Peter's lifetime. Vincent had put his finger on it at last.

Peter could never accept this. He argued back. Then abruptly, in the Spanish manner, Brother Vincent would disclaim interest. 'It is nothing.'

Peter, however, had taken Vincent's point. He turned it over in his mind, admitted to himself just a little of its cogency and saw more willingly that it was not without practical possibilities. Why not show himself as the only Pope of the three who could do something useful?

His scope was limited, but he did his best. He promoted the Congress of Tortosa, an assembly of Christian theologians and Jewish rabbis, intended to convert the latter by reasoned argument, not by pressure. It lasted for sixty-seven sessions. A more profitable field was universities. He completely reformed Salamanca, issuing new statutes and taking endless trouble with them; he added improvements on six separate occasions. He did the work so well that when his conciliar rival came to re-publish Salamanca's statutes a decade later he was reduced to cribbing Peter's exact words without acknowledgement. Peter also tried to found a university in his own home town, Calatayud. It came to nothing, but he succeeded at St. Andrews. Scottish students who opposed the Pisan pope had been finding life difficult in Paris. One Henry de Ogilvy obtained the bull at Peniscola and carried it north to another windswept castle on a colder shore. The arms of Scotland's oldest university still bear Peter's crescent moon.

After various moves he had established his small court at Peniscola. The castle was a gift from the Knights of Montesa. It was in a part of the country where he was popular, far from cities with their ructions and epidemics, much easier to defend than Avignon and with good communications by land and sea. Rodrigo looked to the defences while his uncle started to make the neglected building habitable. Much had been rescued from Avignon, the Curia's files, some furniture, and best of all the library and the tapestries. Peter welcomed these with childlike delight, seeing the warm russet of Illueca on his walls again. There was his old favourite *The Voyage of Brut*, the same tubby ships, the same talkative kings and over-zealous trumpeters, the same tall-hatted ladies reduced to silence by the same heraldic waves. Come to think of it, he had done some voyaging himself.

He looked round well satisfied. His last stand would be made in civilised surroundings.

In the summer of 1414 Ferdinand invited him to a conference at Morella, up in the hills inland from Peniscola. The King had already received confidential envoys from Sigismund, and Peter went prepared for trouble.

He had aged much this last year or two, and would have aged still more but for the sensible diet he kept to, mostly fruit with a glass of wine or some herbal concoction of his doctor's and on feast days one of the meagre partridges of the country, so skinny that they reminded him of the sparrows which had been his fare at Avignon. But at need he could cover fifteen miles a day and more on his mule through the rich olive groves and stony gorges of the Maestrazgo, provided he had a day's rest fairly often.

Morella, like so many of Peter's places, is still a delight to see. It is a dramatic landscape, but the colours are softer and the lines more graceful than is usual in Spain. The conical hill, the steep-packed town between the castle and the lower ramparts, the swoop and plunge of the terraced olive groves remind one of some Tuscan hill-town. Ferdinand and Peter chose it because it was cool in summer.

The King and his Castilian grandees—there were few Catalans now—stationed themselves a stone's throw outside the gate and waited for the papal cortège to toil slowly up the last hill. It was a modest party that came up from Peniscola. The old bearded Pope, his five penurious and undistinguished cardinals, a dozen advisers and secretaries, his ex-Jewish doctor, Rodrigo with a handful of guards. They had stopped at a farmhouse down below and had a final brush-up; the result was respectable rather than showy.

Whatever his thoughts, Ferdinand was a gentleman. He rose from his knees to hold a pole of the baldacchino, and when the mayor took over his pole at the gate the King led Peter's mule. After mass the papal party went to their simple quarters in the monastery just below the castle. There were banquets and politenesses. They had to borrow the royal dinner service when returning Ferdinand's hospitality, as theirs was of pewter, but they saved face by serving a Castilian meal with Castilian wines specially imported.

The conference lasted for fifty days. There is a local legend that the flies were troublesome, that Peter cursed them, and that Morella has been free from flies ever since. The legend may best be accepted in parts, like the Council of Constance.

Ferdinand's plan was unoriginal. It was the way of cession. Peter should go to Constance and resign there, trusting to Sigismund's safe-conduct. In view of the very long journey and of what happened to John XXIII and to Hus, Peter's blank refusal does not seem utterly unreasonable. Brother Vincent supported Ferdinand and preached an unfortunate sermon comparing the Luna Pope's life with the phases of the moon. Brother Vincent was becoming rather tiresome.

Finally Peter agreed to meet Sigismund half-way.

*

They met at Perpignan. Sigismund hastened there from Constance with a brilliant retinue four thousand strong, as soon as the business with Hus had been concluded.

'It would have been far better,' observes Professor Salembier sternly, 'if this false doctor and rebellious priest had never been born.' But the Czech reformer had been born, his doctrines had set Bohemia on fire, and he had come to Constance to discuss them and had been handed an imperial safe-conduct on his arrival. Something, therefore had to be done about him. The Fathers of the Council, who had seen many innovations of late, felt that a friendly discussion with Hus would be one too many. It would look better if they burned him. Sigismund's safe-conduct was set aside on grounds which seem good to the Professor. D'Ailly conducted the trial, or rather 'the public examination of conscience undergone by a guilty man', and expressed his horror at a doctrine which might be used to dethrone kings. Hus was burned at the stake and his ashes were thrown into the Rhine. One would hate to have to rely on a safe-conduct from Professor Salembier.

Sigismund left Constance immediately after this edifying episode and reached Perpignan in nine weeks, fair going in view of the joyous entries he had to make on the way and his zeal in performing them. Sigismund was a force to be reckoned with. A quick mind, boundless ambition, political experience gained in a hard school, little piety but a strong dislike of heresy, seven languages, a good shot, a fine physique, a forked beard and an eye for the ladies. Those who met him for the first time were almost invariably bowled over. After he had passed on his way they noticed the truly prodigious trail of discarded enterprises, pledges, women and debts. Sigismund lived so full a life that any kind of accountancy in these matters was out of the question. Next week he might be plausible or disappointing, lavish or bankrupt, and there was no way of telling.

Peter reached Perpignan before him, and was with difficulty restrained from declaring the Emperor contumacious when he failed to arrive on time. He too was in excellent form. His hopes now revolved around Joanna II of Naples, Ladislas' redoubtable sister and successor, a lady whose private life made Joanna I's seem homely in comparison. By promoting a marriage between her and Ferdinand's second son Peter planned to open a door into Italy. After that there would be only one more door to unlock. His envoys to Joanna, once they had made it clear that the marriage could not be a happy one if the spouses acknowledged two separate popes, had instructions to get in touch with those who held the keys to this last door. These persons were the Prefect of Rome, the Castellan of Soriano and the Cardinal Legate. Such men undoubtedly had their price.

'And then,' Peter wrote happily, 'if these matters can be arranged, the Holy Father will forthwith set out for Rome and, if it pleases God so to dispose, he will enter the city, where he ardently desires to end his days in glory under the shield of the true faith.'[42]

But that still lay ahead, and sad to say the negotiations with Joanna were dragging. At the moment he was only entering Perpignan. This time the castle was reserved for Sigismund and the papal contingent took up residence in the Franciscan friary.

No cardinals were allowed to accompany Sigismund, but other statesmen converged on Perpignan in shoals. Ferdinand with his Castilian entourage, a sick man resolved to take no chances with the Emperor. His Queen and Martin's widow, the Queen Dowager. The Counts of Armagnac and Foix, Provence, Savoy and Lorraine. The Archbishops of Reims and Tours with seventy-five French clerics, all of them equally prejudiced against Peter and the German Emperor. The Bishop of Worcester, out of his depth. The Grand Chancellor of Hungary, confident but unintelligible. A plenipotentiary from Navarre. And Brother Vincent with an untidy crowd of enthusiasts addicted to self-flagellation and flouting authority, frowned on by the others like nuclear disarmers would be at a similar high-level conference today.

The first formal session went well and the Emperor was full of optimism. Ferdinand was seriously ill, but after they had sent for the Moorish dancing-woman of Mizlata and she had treated him successfully with a combination of squill, celery, parsley, asparagus, mandrake, henbane, cloves, cinnamon, hartshorn, viper's flesh, dragon's blood and slugs, he felt well enough to take part in the critical private meetings.

There the difficulties became apparent. For the first time Peter was the sole *de facto* Pope. It only remained for four-fifths of Christendom to accept him. This, he suggested, ought not to be impossible.

It was? He was amazed to hear it. In that case he could only offer to resign on three conditions. They were quite easy to meet. Pisa must be formally annulled, all must recognise him as true Pope before he resigned, and his successor must be canonically elected. This last condition, he explained patiently, meant that as the status of all cardinals who had been appointed during the schism was open to doubt, only those created before it began would have the right to vote. In actual fact, he added half apologetically, there was only one of them left alive, himself.

At a formal session a few days later the seventy-three-year-old Pope developed this and allied themes with the greatest fluency and clarity for seven hours.

Sigismund demanded his unconditional surrender. The private meetings continued remorselessly. By this time Peter had learnt of the dissensions at Constance and of the widening rift between Sigismund and the French. He shifted his ground slightly and then re-occupied it. He propounded a bewildering variety of schemes for electing the new pope. He would even consent to nominating fewer electors than the others did, always provided that . . .

Eight weeks passed. Sigismund woke up with a start to hear Peter holding forth about a fresh condition. The Council must be moved from Constance to the south of France. This was the one thing that the Emperor could not possibly accept, for it would take the Council out of his control. Just for that reason the French delegation urged him strongly to accept it.

The Emperor now knew that his journey had been most unwise. He had no power to make all these concessions. His control over the Council had its limits. That these should be revealed in public was humiliating. He prepared to leave. Peter was still talking.

'According to you, neither I nor any rival of mine can be sure that we are or have been popes. In that case the same applies to all the cardinals except me, and I am the only person qualified to elect a new pope. Within a single day, if you wish it, I will elect one. I will even promise that I will not elect myself.'

Sigismund shook his head furiously and rose to his feet. Peter spoke again.

'Now I see that all you want is my personal disgrace.'

*

Brother Vincent fell ill, lay at death's door, refused to see Peter's doctor, recovered miraculously and dragged himself up into his pulpit. His text was from Ezekiel.

'O ye dry bones, hear the word of the Lord!'

He went to Peter and repeated the gist of his sermon. They could not go on like this. The time had come to give way for the good of the Church, for the sake of all the souls in Christendom.

They argued together for the last time. Had not Vincent said once that no schism could end with the lawful Pope's surrender? Was it not their duty to stand fast until such time as God should heal the schism in His own way? 'Other men's quarrels may be settled by men, but those of the Roman See are, without question, reserved for His own judgment.' Peter quoted from Gratian, as he had always done. For him the great canonist's lapidary sentence clinched the matter. No forced abdication could be a valid one.

It need not be like that, replied Brother Vincent. He could do it from a sense of duty, or better still for love. For love of his enemies, or rather for love of all who were faithful Christians, though they might disagree with his claims. In any case, for love.

For the first time it seems, in all these thirty years of ecclesiastical cold war, someone spoke with a voice greater than his own. Someone mentioned the part of Christianity which matters, looking back beyond what men have made of it, beyond the formalism, the rules, the accretions and the dressing up. Why not sooner? That is the condemnation of a whole age, and of ours too.

We may believe that the message touched Peter; it touches everyone. But his mind was too deeply embedded in the other sort of Christianity and he had lived through too much. He was inflexible. If they disagreed with his claims, they were not faithful Christians. He could not give them what was bad for them.

\*

The conference broke up. The French, rebuked by Sigismund, withdrew indignantly. The Agincourt campaign was in progress and France was in no position to quarrel with the Emperor. Alarming rumours spread through the town. Two nobles fought a duel. Sigismund left suddenly without saying goodbye to anyone.

Messengers from Ferdinand tore up the road after him to say that Aragon would abandon Peter unless he gave way. At this Sigismund halted, waiting at Narbonne.

Peter saw treason in the high-born Castilian faces around him. His agents, those 'trustworthy and godfearing persons' who figure so often in his official records, warned him to leave before it was too late. It was Portovenere over again. He called a consistory at day-break, transferred Climent to Saragossa and made some other sound defensive moves on the episcopal chessboard, and announced his own immediate departure. By half-past eight he and his followers were on the road to Collioure, where his galleys lay waiting. It was the uncertain weather of late autumn. A squall ripped down from the Pyrenees and lashed the sea outside the harbour. They went on board and waited for it to subside. If it did not, things would be difficult.

Ferdinand's messengers arrived on the beach and boarded the ship. They begged Peter to return to Perpignan.

He looked hard at them. He was standing on the poop, very erect, like an old cormorant.

'My greetings to His Majesty. Tell him I can do nothing more. He will do as he pleases. And be good enough to add these words: You have sent me, who made you what you are, into the wilderness. *Me qui te feci missisti in desertum*.'[43]

They left. He knelt down on the deck and prayed. Then he stood waiting. The squall dropped abruptly and the sun came out. The crude, everyday light poured down on to the deck. The whole ship's company took it as a sign and crossed themselves. He took it as a sign too, but in another sense. He turned his back on the too bright sunlight and went below, while the galleys weighed anchor, edged out past the church at the harbour mouth and set course for Peniscola.

# CHAPTER 10

## *Peñiscola*

PETER stepped on to the quay, mounted a mule with an effort and toiled laboriously up through the gaping villagers, over the fish-scales and the cobbles and the muddy straw, until he reached the gate of his castle. All other gates were closed to him. In his heart he knew he would never leave this place again.

Behind his back his Obedience began to disintegrate. The first step was the Narbonne Agreement. Left to themselves, the assembled statesmen lost little time in coming to terms. The Spanish kingdoms would renounce their Pope and join the Council of Constance as a fifth 'nation'.

Some bishops from Aragon protested unheeded, and on the other side of the fence the Paris doctors saw a luminous vision fade away, the scheme of Church government by four and only four 'nations', a scheme for which they had found the most extravagant metaphysical warrant. Had not four rivers, for a start, watered the Garden of Eden? The Spanish diplomats did not deny it, but insisted inconsequently on separate nationhood at Constance, and on this point at least Sigismund felt he might safely give way.

The Spaniards had a more distressing task in front of them. Once more Brother Vincent was deputed to break the news. In front of Perpignan castle a vast crowd listened to his words. Peter, he told them, was indeed the true Vicar and always had been, but as an obstacle to unity he had lost the right to their obedience. He and all who had followed him must swallow their bitter medicine. The good of the Church came first.

This said, he read Gerson's fulsome letter of thanks without enthusiasm, declined the invitation to Constance and turned his back on his own past and his own country, padding away north-wards out of Church politics as fast as his donkey could carry him. In backward, wind-daunted Brittany he found new work to do. Three years later he died at Vannes and was buried there, a saint already to the simple folk he had helped and canonised by worldly ones in Rome and in less than a generation, in fact at almost the same time as Catherine.

Sigismund knew the pure joy of a great statesman who has only just been saved from a fiasco. When Ferdinand ratified the treaty he had his letter read out to him at table no less than six times. Soon the arbiter of Europe was flashing northwards too, outpacing Vincent on his donkey but pausing for twenty-three days at Avignon to admire the illuminations, borrow or extort money from everyone in sight and scatter his favours and jewellery among the ladies. He lodged in Peter's old *livrée*.

In March he was in Paris. The government, though almost bankrupt after Agincourt, loaded him with presents and fêted him and a thousand of his knights for eight weeks, hoping that he would save them from Henry V in his *Act V* mood. The Emperor instantly underwent one of his changes. He put nothing in the offertory box at Notre-Dame, gave the choirboys one *écu* to share between the lot of them and tipped the keeper of the royal relics half a franc. The canons of Notre-Dame were so indignant that they entered these particulars in their official record. In political conversations he was equally unforthcoming. Emerging from these with relief, he gave a banquet of unparalleled splendour, leaving the bill to be paid by the Duke of Berry. Then he went to England and signed a treaty directed against France.

An open-handed period in London and Canterbury left him destitute again, so that on landing in the Low Countries he had to pawn the Garter, Henry's parting gift, in order to pay his way back to Constance.

It was time he took charge of the Council once more. Gerson was still campaigning against Burgundian tyrannicide, while a greatly changed d'Ailly was trying to abolish the system of 'nations' and go back to the old manner of voting, besides fighting a vigorous rearguard action to uphold the rights of cardinals. With John gone, d'Ailly found himself in an exposed position. His ill-bred opponents

R

were asking why he held fourteen benefices at once. He was becoming daily more conservative.

\*

Nobody in Spain enjoyed repudiating the Spanish Pope. The
process was far more haphazard than it had been on previous
occasions in France, for whereas the French are a nation, a Spanish
state is a reluctant round-up of individualists. The withdrawal
proceeded so slowly and encountered so much opposition that
Peter was not without hopes of bringing it to a complete standstill.

His bulls, confidential letters and secret instructions darkened the
stationery of Peniscola and the counsels of those who read them.
We find Climent, as nuncio to the Queen Regent of Castile, en-
tangling that poor lady with a diabolical chain of logic. If Peter was
not the legitimate Pope, neither was his predecessor Clement who
had granted a tricky dispensation for her marriage, and in that case
her own son could not be legitimate either and the throne of all
Spain belonged to Ferdinand, which explained Ferdinand's attitude
to Peter, did it not?

Again, we find Barcelona thrown into the wildest confusion by
Peter's interdict. The new Bishop published it and then fled to
Peniscola. Opinion was deeply divided, with most of the clergy
on Peter's side and most of the laity against him, for even at that
early date Barcelona was the most anti-clerical city in southern
Europe.

Through these distractions the royal commissar, Felipe de Malla,
steered a steady course, suppressing direct rebellion and well aware
that he would then encounter the time-honoured Spanish attitude
to the state and its demands—'we obey your order, but we do not
carry it out'—and that a sensible commissar in Spain should expect
no more. He made innumerable public speeches, prodded the civil
governor, browbeat the hundred councillors, arrested some people
and ignored others, spoke firmly to the papal tax-collectors and
more gently to the aged Cardinal Ravat, having due regard to the
'decrepit old age' of Peter's senior supporter in the city. But these
ancient churchmen are sometimes less decrepit than they look. A
year later Ravat, although he had gone quite blind, was presiding

vigorously over a meeting of the Catalan bishops and strengthening their resolve not to send delegates to Constance.

After a time Peniscola was cut off, with royal guards and watch-fires on the sand-spit to check the outflow of bulls, and Peter's supporters throughout the country gradually simmered down. *Se obedece, pero no se cumple.* The powerless Pope and his very small court were left in peace. It would be blackguardly to do more, and besides who could tell whether Benedict XIII might not come in useful as a counter in Aragon's adventurous foreign policy? Ferdin-and's son Alfonso, who succeeded to the throne at this time, was already thinking along these lines. Peter was kept in cold storage.

His Obedience in a formal sense was now reduced to Peniscola, the County of Armagnac just north of the Pyrenees, and Scotland. Various honey-tongued envoys from Constance, with Cardinal Chalant among them, landed at Leith, but the Regent Albany found them unconvincing and his arrangements with his own Pope quite satisfactory. He glared in the general direction of Constance and decided that they were 'all out of step except our Jock', or rather our Peter. Many Spaniards felt the same way. Benedict, they said, was 'in his XIII', and the phrase *està en sus trece* passed into their language and is still in use to express a dour admiration for utterly single-minded cussedness. In districts as well regulated as southern England, of course, the sentiment is unknown, and such idioms lose something in translation.

Of course Peter knew days when he was less than single-minded. Sometimes a black depression came over him and stayed with him obstinately for weeks until his own greater obstinacy conquered it. When Ferdinand's guards arrived and camped on the sand-spit and there was talk of desertions in his minute Curia, he thought quite seriously of giving up. He even spoke of it to his cardinals. Some, he could see, would welcome such a step. Not that they were real cardinals anyway like Pamplona or Lagrange or Malesset. They were just his creatures, small men who had made a mistake and were looking for a sensible way out. To go now would be so much easier for everybody, and saintly people such as Vincent thought it was the right way. He did not, but he was an old man and very tired.

On such days he would sometimes walk down to the waterfront. Life at Peniscola was informal save on ceremonial occasions, when he insisted on every detail being exactly right. He would look at his two galleys lying idle and useless alongside the quay, and then, turning his back on them, he would step down on to a stretch of rusty beach and pace very slowly along the line of small flotsam and queer papery seaweed which the slack wash of this inland sea had brought to rest.

And then he would notice the old fisherman, perhaps much the same age as himself, about seventy-five. The man sat there in the slanting sun, his thin old arms the dull tone of some African wood, a section of net stretched out conveniently between his pitch-stained big toes. Peter knew the story. It never varied. There had been many fish in the net, and then it had caught on a rock and torn and all the fish had escaped. And the old fisherman? He was patiently mending the holes in his net.

Back up the hill to the great polygonal fortress. A fresh spurt of energy. A letter to Alfonso of Aragon to keep him guessing. And on the next dark night a fishing boat from Peniscola would land two well-spoken but reticent men some miles farther down the coast on the first stage of their journey to Italy. One would go to Queen Joanna and her latest consort in Naples, the other to the Prefect of Rome. Old bargaining positions were resumed with the unflagging optimism of peasants at a weekly market. How much would the Prefect be asking, now, for Civitavecchia? Ah yes, a really beautiful little harbour, most suitable in every way for His Holiness, and a bare dozen leagues from the Vatican itself. . . .

*

Clemanges, now rehabilitated, pleaded with the Fathers of the Council to save themselves time and trouble by recognising the sole surviving claimant and the only person alive who could remember how the schism had begun. Why not re-elect him? To declare him ineligible was to set bounds to the working of the Holy Spirit.

This excellent advice was rejected. There were further delays. At last, a year after the Narbonne Agreement, two Benedictine monks from Constance presented themselves at the gate of Peniscola. Admitted by a highly suspicious Rodrigo, who still commanded his uncle's bodyguard, and having been searched most thoroughly for hidden arms, they were granted audience next day.

Three high south windows let in the morning sun. The splendid tapestries from Avignon covered the walls, three cardinals sat next the throne, and on the ancient hawk-like head was the venerable tiara taken from Rome at the start of all these troubles, at a time when the two black-robed monks were only small children. They were impressed in spite of themselves.

'Here come the crows of the Council!'

Peter's sally was utterly unexpected. Afterwards, when his story grew in the telling, the senior monk claimed to have made a quick repartee about crows and carrion. At the time he kept any such ready wit to himself. This old antipope was not dead yet and Rodrigo stood close behind him.

Instead he began to read out the Council's citation, while his companion kept a wary eye on the face beneath the tiara and noticed with relief that its owner was making a great effort to endure the insufferable Councilese phrases with patience. Only now and then did an indignant 'That's a lie!' punctuate the recital. But at last the word 'heretic' proved too much. There was a crash as a tough bony fist came down on the arm of the throne.

'I, a heretic! I am the Pope. The heretics are at Constance. But for them the schism would have ended years ago. The Church is not at Constance, not even if all the world believes it is. The Church is here in this castle and nowhere else. *Hic est arca Nohe!*'[44]

Noah's Ark or St. Helena? asks Fr. Doizé unkindly. Modern relativity would say both.

Constance knew nothing of these alternatives and discounted the sentence passed at Pisa as well. Everything had to be done all over again, even down to the loud-voiced summonses from cathedral porches. The Council's investigating commissions and sub-commissions bumbled happily along their allotted path. This time there was no silly talk of witchcraft. Nothing could be found against Peter except his refusal to abdicate at others' bidding. Gerson, in his latest treatise, said it was enough. On 26 July 1417 another sentence of deposition was published, neither better nor worse than Pisa's eight years back, though this time Sigismund's trumpeters blaring through the streets of Constance gave it some added political force.

Once again a Council stood before a choice of priorities. Reform the Church, or elect a new pope? Once again the second proved more attractive. With the election of Martin V, a clever Roman of quietly autocratic views, the conciliar movement betrayed itself and began to go downhill. The kings drove some hard financial bargains with Martin and were happy to leave all else to fate. The prelates, so long as most of the available money stayed in their own dioceses, were not much interested in wider problems or in Councils to solve them. The movement failed quite simply because it contained too many people like d'Ailly. A great opportunity was neglected. Exactly a century later there came a harsher and more purposeful Reformation.

The Council was wound up, leaving future theologians to split hairs about how much of it was really œcumenical, and the good burghers of Constance to find somebody willing to purchase astonishing quantities of part-worn sheets prominently marked with eagles. For Sigismund, unable as always to meet his bill, had left them the entire imperial store of linen in part payment, and their wives, knowing what had gone on between those sheets, flatly refused to make use of them in the home.

★

The next year saw Scotland accept Martin. The European-minded but ungrateful university of St. Andrews took the lead in this move. It also saw two last attempts to solve Peter's difficulties for him.

One was the visit of Aragon's church leaders to Peniscola. Peter's old friends all implored him to give peace to the Church. They showed, as the Archbishop of Tarragona wrote to the King, 'as much affection, good will and humanity as any true sons and loyal servants in the whole world could show to their Father and benefactor'. Their words were in vain. A sad procession left the castle and re-crossed the sand-spit. They went 'with great sorrow and many lamentations and tears, seeing so great a man commit so great an error'. The remaining cardinals left with them.

One leading prelate refused to join in this formal act of desertion. It was of course Climent, Archbishop of Saragossa. For this the authorities transferred him back to Barcelona. His monument is the nave of the cathedral there, which he completed, and where a pair of scared-looking angels guard his simple tomb.

The other attempt was made by Martin V's legate, an Italian cardinal named Adimari. On arriving in Aragon he came up against the passive resistance of Climent and the more equivocal attitude of King Alfonso, who was playing an involved political game and saw no reason to give away one of the best cards up his sleeve. The legate was equally determined to dispose of Peter.

Peter ate little but fruit and confectionery. One July day he finished lunch with three or four of his special small gateaux, lightly baked wafers enclosing a honey filling. He lay down for his siesta. An hour later he woke up with all the symptoms of poisoning by arsenic. He was promptly and most violently sick, which saved him; in fact he had been given too large a dose. He was very close to death for nine days. As he slowly and most painfully recovered two of his minor attendants left the castle suddenly. They were traced, arrested and brought back by Rodrigo, whereupon they confessed to their own and the legate's crime.

After four months of convalescence Peter was well enough to issue a bull on the episode. He addressed it to the *Consell de Cent* and to public opinion in general. *Acerbis infesta* has some sixty lines of biting polemic. It is as good a piece of Latin as anything Clemanges ever wrote, and it makes full use of the more fatuous phrases of adulation which had been heaped upon the proceedings and the pope of Constance. Here, says Peter, is the fruit which Sigismund's headlong husbandry has brought forth. Here is the sublime achievement of so great a concourse of men joined together in Christian unity. Here is the new beauty, the seemliness restored to God's house, the devotion inspired by their religious example. See by what manner of death, by what sort of holy wafer, by what paths they hope to reach the Apostolic Chair. Look at them all, he says, just look at them.

There is no need to suppose that the Roman Pope himself was directly responsible, or even that his legate had read Gerson's and Dietrich's bombinations justifying any crime that would give the Church its formal unity. The legate acted according to his own lights, which were those of the more colourful Italian dukedoms.

Spain was rather old-fashioned, and Peter's friends made the country too hot for him. He went back to Mantua to explain the failure of a mission as best he could.[45]

Peter was now a very old man and the events of his life were over. He was still not without an Obedience of sorts, for the Count of Armagnac adhered to him more or less openly. The veteran Simon Salvador was his Vicar-General in those parts. And Alfonso of Aragon was by no means hostile. In Spain, France, Scotland and elsewhere there were many people of all degrees who knew him to be the true Pope and worth more than all the other popes of the period put together. Cautiously they kept in touch.

Hope still flickered. There were strange happenings in the world outside. Once the Duke of Gloucester asked him for a dispensation. There were Frenchmen who attributed the disasters which had overtaken their country to the faithlessness towards the Pope of Avignon. Guigon, still working for Peter, had a secret meeting with the Dauphin. Martin V, forgetting his origins, denied the right to appeal from a pope to a Council, and Gerson furiously exposed the inconsistency. If what Martin said were true, he would not be Pope. In fact those who had elected Martin were already beginning to have their doubts. Peter had seen it all happen before.

Martin had to wait two years before he could enter Rome. Then he found a city laid waste by bandits and disease, the Lateran a shell, cattle corralled in the roofless basilica of San Paolo and wolves digging up improvised graves in the Vatican gardens. His tenure was uncertain. When the warships of Aragon were seen on the Peniscola skyline, sailing against Naples, Peter allowed himself a last day-dream. Would they not take the rightful Pope to Rome?

The mood passed, and looking out eastwards over the sea one clear evening he knew it could never happen. He would end his days within these walls. His secretaries, when they wrote to Climent and others, had taken to ending their letters with the words *script. in arca Nohe* or *script. in domo Dei ubi est vera ecclesia*. That was as it should be. The future remained inscrutable.

He thought of the thirty-seven cardinals who had served under him. All but three were dead, though many had been younger men. He had outlived friends and enemies and five rival popes. The last of these, Balthazar Cossa or John XXIII, had been buried at

Florence not long ago. His Medici bankers had given him a fine tomb. Aranda, who knew everything and had his spies in Italy, told him about it. It was on the wall of the baptistery at Florence, with a canopy by one of their new-fangled artists called Michelozzo and an effigy by another one called Donatello.

And what wording had they put on it? That must have presented a little problem.

They kept the epitaph very simple. '*Quondam Papa*'—'Sometime Pope'. Even that caused annoyance in certain quarters. Yet the words certainly stay there, if only because it would spoil a work of art to alter them. But '*Quondam Papa*'! How would some sacristan explain that queer inscription to parties of pious foreigners five centuries later, when they were all, thank heaven, forgotten?

But it would not be a bad idea to leave just one inscription behind, Peter ruminated. Perhaps with a coat of arms and so forth. It would have to be somewhere safe, where no schismatic little busybody could have it defaced. Why not the University of Salamanca? After all, he had taken a lot of trouble over their statutes. And universities like to show their independence.

Presently he thought of something better, something that none of his rivals could have done, being the men they were. In a sudden flash he saw that this new idea was very important. This was why he had been spared from death by poison. Being powerless, he could do something completely disinterested. If it helped somebody, somewhere, sometime, it would be immeasurably worth while.

He settled down again to work in his study, high in the seaward tower, seven paces by five and slightly irregular in shape, having a big pointed arch across the middle of the room and two narrow windows pierced through the thick walls. His secretary fetched reference books from the library on the floor below and helped to find the right passages, and Peter dictated. He wrote his book first in Latin and then, to reach wider, in his own language, Castilian with an Aragonese flavour.

> And so as in ancient times Boethius, that noble and faithful governor, was sent out into perpetual exile and cruel bondage when he would not fawn upon the tyranny of King Theodoric, so we, cast forth from our own chair and dwelling-place by the

malice of rebels against the Apostolic faith and the Church's
right obedience, and suffering more gladly than justly this
manner of exile, have thought fit to compose this work. . . .

The *Libro de las Consolaciones de la Vida Humana* is Peter's last
word, as medieval as its author. The product of a lifetime's experience and moral questioning, it is cast in a form which to us seems too
dependent, for it contains little but quotations and brief comment-
ary. The Fathers, Job, Seneca. If it owes much to them it owes next
to nothing to *el noble é costante barón Boécio*. There is no Platonism.
No alarming late-classical matron personifies Philosophy, and what
philosophy there is, is of the homely sort and entirely Christian.
A few of the chapter-headings hint at the writer's own misfortunes,
such as the fourth, 'If a man is deprived in this world of vain honours
or of vainglory, or suffers belittlement and humiliation before others
or before himself', or the fifth, 'For the loss of any power, dignity
or dominion, whether ecclesiastical or secular'. But autobiography
is absent. Bad luck has not bred self-pity or self-justification. Peter
is not writing this book for himself in trouble, but for others.

★

He wrote the last lines and walked on the wide terrace in the
January sun. It is a wonderful season in that coastal part of Spain,
the calms of January, when the winds drop and the almond blossom
comes and a clear light floods the air. Aranda, Rodrigo and his
doctor shared it with him. It was 1423.

Did he realise that his life had been spent for a mirage? That unity
on his own terms was impossible then and still is now? That religion,
like art, will always burst through the rules which men try to make
for it? That prescriptive right is a myth and a fiction, and that the
only legitimacy worth having is that conferred by general consent?
That the canonist mentality is more harmful than the benefice-
hunter's, because power distorts the institution while wealth merely
corrupts the men who serve it? That the more the Church resembles
a state, the further it will depart from the spirit of its Founder? That
for these reasons and others the medieval papacy was an aberration
in Christian history? That even had he been right in thinking of the
visible Church as an absolute monarchy, he had made it that much

harder for others to believe it too? That a Vicar of Christ must do more than stand on his rights?

Of course he realised none of these things. He would have smelled the heresy in every one of them. He died as he had lived, a late-medieval canon lawyer, professionally confident in the most far-fetched claims for his throne and in his own right to occupy it. He saw no other remedy for the schism than for men to acknowledge the lawful Pope. He had held out for this solution for forty-five years, taking on the whole of Europe, fighting honourably against simony in high places and State control of religion, using every weapon at his disposal, despising every easy way out for himself or others, never giving in. He had earned his rest.

Something of the Middle Ages died with him. A new approach to truth was gaining ground. In his own university, Montpellier, they were starting to dissect human bodies, and not many years later the Donation of Constantine was proved a forgery.

Naturally he did not let the succession fail. As his life drew to its close he appointed four of his circle cardinals and made them promise to elect another pope. So Gil Sanchez Muñoz became Clement VIII. He was a Curia canonist who, long ago, had helped Cardinal de Luna on his mission to Spain. But with Peter gone the attempt to prolong the struggle was soon seen to be a mistake. The schism came to a dignified end in 1429, when the shadowy Pope of Peniscola lifted the censures from his rival and resigned, and his College elected Martin as sole Pope.

Clement VIII was insignificant as a factor in power-politics but far from negligible in the realm of ideas. With his voluntary cession, both the original lines of popes had transferred their rights to Martin, who now had an undisputed title independent of Constance and its anomalies. The whole conciliar movement could safely be repudiated. It was. No modern Catholic textbook has a good word to say for it.

Martin paid his debt like a gentleman. Gil Sanchez Muñoz ended his days as a bishop and lies magnificently in Palma cathedral. Peter lay in a simple tomb at Illueca until it was desecrated by French soldiers in the Peninsular War.

In Languedoc there was another pretender elected by a single dissident cardinal, leading a fugitive existence in the gorges of the

Viaour, and the schism took longer to peter our, ending as such things usually do in the staunch fanaticism of simple folk. As late as 1467 a schismatic blacksmith was burnt at the stake at Rodez.

Long before then the solely puzzled Count of Armagnac, who had been supporting these people, appealed very sensibly to Joan of Arc for a ruling. His letter reached her at the height of her victories, just as she was setting out for Paris. She had only been six when the Council of Constance ended, her voices had said nothing of Gil Sanchez Muñoz or of 'Benedict XIV' and her warhorse was at the door. She sent the Count a brief letter, telling him he must wait for a definite answer.

> ... *Car je suis, pour le present, trop empeschiée au fait de la guerre. Mais, quant vous sarez que je seray à Paris, envoiez ung message pardevers moy, et je vous feray savoir tout au vray auquel vous devrez croire ... par le conseil de mon droiturier et souverain seigneur, le Roy de tout le monde.*

There the matter rests. Even Peter could hardly be dissatisfied.

In the meantime Salamanca has put up a generous inscription in its cloister and St. Andrews has a cast of his skull. Saragossa, thanks to Climent, received and still keeps his glowing red tapestries. Alpartil spent his old age there in the shadow of the great lantern of Lo Seo, a Mudéjar-Gothic structure built on Peter's orders and bearing his arms as Pope. In these surroundings he composed an affectionate and not unreliable chronicle.

Today the pundits are becoming a little more chary of calling Peter an antipope. The fisherfolk of Peniscola remember him best, of course. They still live in some awe of their Papa Luna and point over the sea-cliff to a hole down near the water's edge from which, whenever he thinks of the miserable eighteenth-century Roman who dared to steal his title-number, the fierce old Pope puffs up a tall column of controversial foam.

# Notes

1. *Seidlmayer, p. 206,* gives documentary evidence (a dispensation *super defectu etatis*) that Peter was born in 1342, not in 1328 as is usually stated. The mistake started with Guillaume Boisratier's story that in 1394 Peter told him he was sixty-six. If Boisratier's memory was not at fault (he told the story fourteen years later) Peter must have exaggerated his age for his own reasons. Cf. *Alpartil, p. 362 (footnote).*

2. These entries in the *Camera's* accounts are given in full in *Kirsch.*

3. The following description is based largely on *Gregorovius,* with some details from Bishop Ameilh's poem in *Muratori, R.I.S. III (pt. 2), p. 705.*

4. *Baluze, III, p. 595.*

5. The evidence for Geneva's activities before the conclave is unsatisfactory. He spent much time canvassing and it seems he had some ingenious scheme in mind. Some hostile witnesses declare that he favoured Prignano, and one of them, Marino, gives his actual words as quoted. Yet is it likely that a man such as Geneva should genuinely have wanted an Italian of humble origin as pope? By combining Marino's testimony with what we know of Geneva, we arrive at a more probable interpretation, which also explains his immoderate laughter later on. Marino and his like were outsiders, guessing. Another such witness says it was Geneva's enemies in the College who favoured Prignano. The exact truth will never be known.

6. These words and others quoted as spoken by various people during the conclave are found in the original sources, with slight variations. See *Gayet* and *Baluze* in particular. *Valois* and others have reconstructed the conclave in considerable detail.

7. The Urbanist Menendo, Bishop of Cordoba, puts a resolute and well-turned speech of encouragement into Peter's mouth at this moment. Unfortunately it inspires no more confidence than the same Menendo's assertion that the cardinals were 'tranquil' when the mob burst in.

8. The conversation which follows is taken verbatim from Eymeric's deposition. *Gayet, I, pièces justicatives lre. série, pp. 118 seq.*

9. For the conversations quoted in this section, see *Baluze, II, p. 581* ('*Quid facit ille fatuus?*'); *p. 600* (Glandève); and *p. 707* (Fernando's account of Peter's 'morning after'). For the reasons for rejecting the conflicting (Urbanist) story that Peter sent messages to Prignano early that morning, assuring him he was pope, see *Gayet, II, pp. 4–5.* The story is full of contradictions; for instance Peter cannot have employed five different persons to carry two almost simultaneous messages.

10. Gaudelin's account, including his conversation with Urban, in *Gayet, II, pp. 174 seq.*

11. Fernando's testimony gives his own and Peter's words. *Baluze, II, p. 709.*

12. '*Quare ego stabo hic cum domino nostro, quia ipse nichil facit de hiis que peto? Certe, inquit, non servirem Deo, si non faceret michi bonum!*' *Baluze, II, p. 710.* A lot depends on what Peter's exact words were and on how Alfonso's version of them is translated! Alfonso respected his motives for going to Anagni—see end of chapter.

13. *Baluze, II, p. 700.*

14. *Gayet, II, p. 217.*

15. For Peter's 'piracy' and Captain Bernaldez, see *Valois, I, p. 215.*

16. *Baluze, IV, pp. 262 seq.*

17. *Gayet, II, piéces justicatives 2e, série, pp. 148 seq.* Cf. Seidlmayer, *p. 226.*

18. This section is based on *Dietrich of Niem, De Scismate, I, xxviii–lxi.* The longer quotations describing the cardinals' interrogation are from *xlv, li* and *lii.* Cf. *Valois, Jacob* and *Heimpel.*

19. For Peter's *Livrée de la Jugie* (or *de Poitiers*) see Mollat's footnote to *Baluze, II, p. 367*; P. Pansier in *Annales d'Avignon, III, pp. 233 seq.* and J. Giraud, *Évocation du Vieil Avignon* (1958).

20. *Valois, II, pp. 321 seq.*, quoting Lancaster's words as given in the *Chronicle of Saint-Denys.*

21. Unless one counts Damasus in the 4th century, who probably thought of himself as a Roman.

22. *Ehrle, Neue Materialien, ALKG VI, pp. 148 seq.*

23. During the next decade Peter showed a curious reluctance to use excommunication as a political weapon against what he regarded as treason. This reluctance cannot have sprung from his canonist background. It is so out of keeping with general practice and his own conception of his rights that it must have had some very specific point of origin. His

private examination of the 'Judas' issue, when he quashed the case against Vincent, seems to fit the bill. In the *Libro de las Consolaciones, xi,* written at the end of his life, he mentions the subject of excommunication and says that it should be imposed and accepted as a medicine, and in no other way.

24. The cardinals' interrogation in *Ehrle, Aus den Acten des Afterconcils von Perpignan, ALKG V, pp. 412 seq.,* in *Puig, pp. 42-3,* and in a slightly different version in *Baluze,* under each cardinal's name.

25. Peter's words to Albano in *Alpartil, p. 360 (footnote).* His words to Guillaume Boisratier in *Puig, p. 48, Alpartil, p. 362,* and *Valois.* Cf. Note 1 above.

26. Text in *Ehrle, Neue Materialien, ALKG VI, pp. 162 seq.*

27. *Boysset's Chronicle ad ann. 1396, in ALKG VII.*

28. *Puig, pp. 79 seq. and appendix xviii.*

29. *Ehrle, Neue Materialien, ALKG VII; Puig, chapter vii and appendices;* summarised in *Valois, III, chapter iii.*

30. *Ehrle, Neue Materialien, ALKG VII, p. 154.*

31. *ibid. pp. 255 seq.*

32. *Valois, III, p. 80.*

33. Albano repeated this conversation in his evidence at Pisa six years later. *Valois, III, p. 357.*

34. P. *Luc, Un complot contre Benoit XIII.*

35. *Valois, III, pp. 497–8.*

36. Text of the two letters in *Dietrich of Niem, De Scismate, III, iv and v.*

37. On 'collusion' see *Valois, III, p. 121 and pp. 536–8,* and *Puig, pp. 157–9.* Neither authority believes in it. For Cramaud and the Bishop of Cherson with Peter at the Ile-St-Honorat and Peter's words to the latter, see *Valois, III, 549.*

38. Text in *Monstrelet's Chronicles, I. ch. xl, pp. 82 seq.*

39. Text (considerably longer in fact) in *Dietrich of Niem, de Scismate, III, xxxv.* See Dietrich's earlier chapters for details concerning Gregory, e.g. *xix–xx* for grant of towns to the nephews, *xxi* for encounter with the bishop near Siena, *xxiii* for the Cardinal of Pécs.

40. Pierre Vidal, *Perpignan.* For details of the Council, see *Puig, pp. 175–87,* and *Ehrle, Aus den Acten des Afterconcils von Perpignan, ALKG V and VII.*

41. *Puig, pp. 212–14; Valois, IV, pp. 92 seq.*

42. For Peter's chimerical hopes and secret negotiations in Italy, see *Valois, IV, pp. 334 seq.* and *Puig, pp. 310–11.*

43. *Puig, pp. 297–9.*

44. *Creighton, II, p. 82; Puig, p. 323.*

45. Details of the poisoning and text of *Acerbis infesta* in *Puig, pp. 348 seq.*

# Bibliography

ALPARTIL, Martin de. *Cronica actitatorum temporibus d. Benedicti pape XIII* (ed. F. Ehrle, Görres-Gesellschaft, Paderborn, 1906)

BALUZE, S. *Vitae Paparum Avenionensium* (ed. G. Mollat, Paris, 1927)

CASAS, A. *El Papa Luna* (Barcelona, 1944)

DOIZÉ, J. *Le dernier pape d'Avignon*, in *Études* vols. 94 and 95 (1903)

DOMINICI, G. *Pedro de Luna secondo nuovi documenti*, in *Civiltà Cattolica* anno 74, vol. 4 (1923)

EHRLE, F. *Aus den Acten des Afterconcils von Perpignan, Die kirchenrechtlichen Schriften Peters von Luna, Neue Materialien zur Geschichte Peters von Luna*, in *ALKG*, vols. 5, 6, 7 (Paderborn, 1892)

KIRSCH, J. P. *Die Rückkehr der Päpste Urban V und Gregor XI* (Paderborn, 1898)

LUC, P. *Un complot contre Benoit XIII*, in *Mélanges d'archéologie et d'histoire*, vol. 55 (1938)

LUNA, Manuel. *Don Pedro de Luna ante la historia y el derecho* (Madrid, 1923)

LUNA, Pedro de. *Libro de las Consolaciones*, in *Biblioteca de autores españoles*, vol. 51, ed. P. Gayengos (Madrid, 1860)

PILLEMENT, G. *Pedro de Luna, le dernier pape d'Avignon* (Paris, 1955)

PUIG Y PUIG, S. *Pedro de Luna, último papa de Aviñón* (Barcelona, 1920)

SAINT-DENYS, *Chronique de* (ed. M. L. Bellaguet, Paris, 1841)

SEIDLMAYER, M. *Peter de Luna und die Entstehung des Schismas*, in *Gesammelte Aufsätze zur Kulturgeschichte Spaniens* (Münster, 1933)

VALOIS, N. *La France et le Grand Schisme d'Occident* (Paris, 1902)

Of these Alpartil, Ehrle, Puig and Valois are the most useful.

S

For the background in general:

CAMBRIDGE MEDIEVAL HISTORY, vols. 7 and 8.

CREIGHTON, M. *History of the Papacy*, vol. 1 (1897)

ELLIOTT BINNS, L. *Decline and Fall of the Medieval Papacy* (Methuen, 1934)

HUGHES, P. *A History of the Church*, vol. 3 (Sheed and Ward, 1955)

JACOB, E. F. *Essays in the Conciliar Epoch* (Manchester University, 1952)

JORDAN, G. J. *The Inner History of the Great Schism* (Williams and Norgate, 1930)

LUNT, W. E. *Papal Revenues in the Middle Ages* (Columbia University, 1934)

MOLLAT, G. *The Popes at Avignon* (Nelson, 1963)

OKEY, T. *Avignon* (Dent, 1926)

REID, W. S. *Scotland and the Church Councils of the 15th Century*, in the *Catholic Historical Review*, vol. 29 (1943)

SALEMBIER, L. *The Great Schism of the West* (Kegan Paul, 1907)

SEPPELT, F. X. *Geschichte der Päpste*, vol. 4 (Munich, 1957)

WALEY, D. *Later Medieval Europe* (Longmans Green, 1964)

WATKIN, E. I. *The Church in Council* (Sheed and Ward, 1960)

WAUGH, W. T. *History of Europe 1378–1494* (Methuen, 1949)

For the Urbanist case:

ULLMANN, W. *Origins of the Great Schism* (Burnes Oates, 1948)

For the Clementine case:

GAYET, L. *Le Grand Schisme—les Origines* (Paris, 1889)

For events in the Roman Obedience:

DIETRICH OF NIEM. *De Scismate*, ed. G. Erler (Leipzig, 1890)

GREGOROVIUS. *History of the City of Rome in the Middle Ages*, vols. 5 and 6.

HEIMPEL, H. *Dietrich von Niem* (Münster, 1932)

For other personalities:

DARWIN, F. D. S. *Louis d'Orléans* (John Murray, 1936)

GARDNER, E. *St. Catherine of Siena* (Dent, 1907)

GIGLI, G. *Le Opere di S. Caterina* (Rome, 1721)—her letters.

JORGENSEN, J. *St. Catherine of Siena* (Longmans, Green, 1938)

KITTS, E. J. *In the Days of the Councils—the life and times of Baldassare Cossa* (Constable, 1908)

MORRALL, J. B. *Gerson and the Great Schism* (Manchester University, 1960)

SCHWAB, J. B. *Johannes Gerson* (Würzburg, 1858)

SERRA, J. R. *El Cardenal Zalba* (Martin de Salva), in *Hispania*, vol. 4 (1944)

## Chronological Table

| | | The Popes | | |
|---|---|---|---|---|
| | | *At Avignon* | *At Rome* | *Conciliar* |
| 1375 | Dec. — Peter made a cardinal | Gregory XI (1370–78) | | |
| 1376 | Sep. to — Move to Rome | | | |
| 1377 | Jan. | | | |
| 1378 | April — Conclave in Rome | | Urban VI (1378–89) | |
| | Sep. — Schism begins | Clement VII (1378–94) | | |
| 1379–90 | Peter's mission in Spain | | | |
| 1383–85 | Urban at Nocera | | | |
| 1393–94 | Peter's mission in France | | Boniface IX (1389–1404) | |
| 1394 | Sep. 28th — Peter elected Pope | Benedict XIII (1394–1423) | | |
| 1395 | Feb. — First Paris synod | | | |
| | May–July — The Dukes' mission | | | |
| 1396 | Aug. — Fernando's mission to Rome | | | |
| | Aug. — Second Paris synod | | | |
| 1398 | May–June — Third Paris synod | | | |
| | July — France withdraws obedience | | | |
| | Sep.–Nov. — The Siege | | | |

| | | |
|---|---|---|
| 1403 | March | Peter escapes from Avignon |
| | May | France restores obedience |
| 1405 | May–Oct. | Peter in Genoa |
| 1406 | Nov. | Fourth Paris synod |
| 1407 | April | Treaty of Marseilles |
| | Nov. | Duke of Orleans murdered |
| 1408 | Jan.–June | Peter to Portovenere |
| | May | Gregory's cardinals rebel |
| | May | France breaks with Peter |
| | Nov. to | |
| 1409 | Feb. | Council of Perpignan |
| | March–June | Council of Pisa |
| | June | Peter 'deposed' |
| 1412 | | Compromise of Caspe |
| 1414 | | Peter settles at Peñíscola |
| 1414–17 | | Council of Constance |
| 1415 | Oct.–Nov. | Sigismund meets Peter |
| | Dec. | Narbonne Agreement |
| 1417 | July | Peter 'deposed' again |
| 1418 | July | Peter poisoned |
| 1423 | May 23rd | Peter's death |
| 1429 | July | Clement VIII resigns |

Innocent VII (1404–6)
Gregory XII (1406–15)

Alexander V (1409–10)
John XXIII (1410–15)

Martin V (1417–31)

Clement VIII (1423–29)

# INDEX

# Index

Adimari, Alamanno, Cardinal, 263–4

Adria, 'Kingdom' of, 95, 116, 141

Agincourt, 254, 257

Aigrefeuille, Guillaume d', Cardinal, 58, 59, 60, 94, 143

Aigues-Mortes, 179, 180

Ailly, Pierre d', Cardinal: early career, 129–31; mission to Peter, 132–4; bishop, 139, 147; Wenzel's envoy, 156; and restoration of obedience, 190–2; moderate, 203, 208, 211, 216; breach with Peter, 226, 230–1, 238; adaptable, 242; cardinal, 244; at Constance, 245–6, 251, 257–8, 262

Aix-en-Provence, 212–13, 215, 242

Alamon, Pierre, 39, 41, 56

Albano, Cardinal of (Niccolo Brancaccio), 126, 143, 145, 162, 187, 189, 195, 223

Albany, Regent of Scotland, 259

Albornoz, Gil Alvarez Carillo, Cardinal, 20, 25, 113, 163

Alexander V, Pope (Pietro Filargi), 238–9, 243–4

Alfonso V, King of Aragon, 259, 260, 262, 263, 264

Alfonso, Bishop of Jaën, 50–1, 53–4, 69, 77–8, 84

Aljubarrota, 100

Alpartil, Martin de, 12, 147; eye-witness of siege, 167, 168, 170 177–8, 179, 182, 187, 188; on Lagrange, 189; given leave, 193, 202; at Marseilles, 214; in second siege, 242; writes chronicle, 268

Amiens, Cardinal of, see Lagrange

Ammanati, Bonifacio, Cardinal, 154, 161, 168, 178, 179, 180

Anagni, 10, 18, 75–85, 178

Anglesola, Berengar, Cardinal of Gerona, 154, 161, 166, 180, 233

Anjou, see Louis

Aquila, Bishop of, 107, 109

Aragon, passim; Peter's homeland, 16, 29, 94, 100–1; his mission to, 93–101; supports him, 153–4, 156–7, 164, 171–5, 179, 181, 186, 200, 201, 202, 234; he takes refuge in, 231; his activities in, 240–1, 243, 248–50; deserts him, 255, 256, 258–9, 262–3. See also Alfonso V, Ferdinand I, Martin I, Pedro IV

Aranda, Francisco de, 181, 187, 192, 193, 207, 212, 238, 243, 265, 266

Arles, 154, 174, 180, 181, 186

Armagnac, Count of, 10, 11, 234, 241, 252, 259, 264, 268

Armagnac, Jean d', Cardinal, 233

Auch, see Flandrin

Augustinus Triumphus, 24, 73

Avignon, passim; see especially Chapters 1, 5, 6, 7; Palace, 17–18, 129, 131–2, 163–71, 175, 178, 186, 190; papacy established at, 19; Gregory XI leaves, 37–8; Clement VII returns, 95; Peter returns, 111; his livrées, 15, 116, 143, 257, 270 (n. 19); town, life in, 28–9, 117, 185, 190; Peter's election, 125–9; Dukes' mission, 139–45; first siege, 161–71; relieving expedition from Aragon, 173–5; Peter's escape, 186–8; returns to him, 190; cardinals stay at, 203, 221; second siege, 241–2; Sigismund at, 257

Baldo degli Ubaldi, Pietro, 87

Bar, Louis de, Cardinal, 154

Barcelona, Peter at, 93–4, 101; Climent at, 172, 174, 188; Peter again at, 240–1; confusion in, 258; Climent builds cathedral nave, 263

Basilio of Levanto, 93, 106–9

Beaublé, Pierre, 180, 190–1

Beaufort family, 37, 38

'Benedict XIV' (Bernard Garnier), 267–8

Bernaldez, Captain, 92–3, 95, 106, 201, 244

Berry, John Duke of, 113, 122, 123, 138; character, 140–1; Duke's mission, 139–45; 155, 158, 186; and restoration, 190–2; in power, 223, 257

Blau, Pierre, Cardinal, 147, 154, 155, 161, 189, 226, 248

Boisratier, Guillaume, 145, 269, 271

Bologna and University, 121, 150, 212, 229, 237, 244

Boniface VIII, Pope (Benedetto Caetani), 18, 50, 136, 178

Boniface IX, Pope (Pietro Tomacelli); elected pope, 115; 118, 120, 123, 125; negotiations with, 148; Fernando's mission to, 149–53; Ravat's, 197–9; simony of, 197–8; death, 199

Boucicaut, Geoffrey, besieges Peter, 162–71; 178, 200; penance, 221

Boucicaut, Jean, Marshal, 163, 200, 203, 216, 221, 223, 225–7

Bourbon, Duke of, 113, 122, 130, 155, 202, 204

Boyl, Geoffrey de, Cardinal, 154, 161, 166, 168, 180

Brancaccio, Cavaliere, 149, 152; and see Albano

Braquemont, Chevalier de, 186

Bridget, St. (of Sweden), 21–2, 27–8, 50, 54, 88, 97

Brittany, Cardinal of (Hugh de Monte-lais), 52, 57, 59, 62, 63, 71

Bruni, Leonardo, 211, 222

Brut, tapestry, 113, 249, 261, 268

Bulls, Clement's to Burgundy, 118; Dudum cum filii Belial, 119; Scrutator mentium, 195; Peter's to Charles VI, 224–5; Exsurgat Deus, 240; Acerbis infesta, 263

Burgundy, Philip the Bold Duke of, 113, 118, 122–3, 130, 131; Dukes' mission, 139–45; character, 140; 153, 161, 172, 174, 186; and restoration, 190, 191; 195; death, 205, 238

Burgundy, John the Fearless Duke of, 205, 207, 223, 242

Butillo (Francesco Prignano), 104–8

Caffa, 201, 218

Calatayud, 100–1, 249

Cambrai, 156, 190, 191

Camera Apostolica, 18, 39, 43, 112; and see Camerlengo

Camerlengo, the (I. Pierre de Cros), 68, 69, 73, 85

Camerlengo, the (II. François de Conzié) see Conzié

Canary Islands, 201

Carpentras, 190, 192, 201

Carthusians, 133, 183; and see Aranda and Ferrer (Boniface)

Caspe, Compromise of, 243

Castel Sant'Angelo (Rome), 46, 52; cardinals take refuge in, 63, 68–9; held against Urban, 73–4, 95; 188, 197, 199

Castile, Peter in civil war, 16; his mission to, 96, 98–100; changing attitudes, 146, 153, 183, 234, 241; and Aragon, 243; Climent in, 258

Catalans, Catalonia, in Aragon, 96; language, 94, 172–3, 174; fateful decision at Caspe, 243; seamen and soldiers, 92, 95, 106, 242; Peter in, 231, 240; bishops, 259

Catherine, St. (of Siena), 12; and Gregory XI, 22, 25–6, 30–8, 42, 43, 46, 47; and Peter, 33–7; 79, 97; and Urban, 71, 79, 86, 87; in Rome, 88–9; death, 89; 165, 215, 239; canonised, 257

Catherine, St. (of Sweden), see Karin

Cauchon, Pierre, 206–7, 211, 232

Cedula, the, 125–6, 127, 129, 136–7, 141

Celestine V, Pope (Pietro da Morrone), 136

Cesena, 47

Chalant, Antoine de, Cardinal, 201, 205, 226, 233, 234, 235; deserts to Pisa, 236, 238; in Scotland, 259

Champs, Gilles de, 141, 159, 176

Charles V, King of France, 35, 75, 89, 94, 104

Charles VI, King of France, plans Italian expedition, 113–14; insanity, 114, 122, 131, 153; life saved, 122–3; letter to cardinals, 124–5, 128; summons first synod, 138; accepts way of cession, 139; conflict with Peter, 142 seq.; meets Wenzel, 155–6; summons third synod, 158; withdraws obedience, 160; 174, 180, 185, 189; restores obedience, 191, 194; 200, 205, 216, 217; Peter's bull to, 224–5

Charles of Durazzo, King of Naples, 89, 103–4, 109

Châteauneuf-du-Pape, 39, 221

Château Renard, 188–9, 193, 195, 202

Cherson, Bishop of, 218–19, 220
Cividale, Council of, 239
Civitavecchia, 152, 260
Clemanges, Nicholas de, 12; Rector of University, 120–3; introduces d'Ailly, 129, 134; Peter's librarian, 156; his secretary, 201, 205, 211, 220, 225; persecuted, 226, 240; at Constance, 260
Clement VI, Pope (Pierre Roger de Beaufort), 131, 166
Clement VII, Pope (Robert of Geneva), character, 29, 53, 112–13, 116; as Cardinal of Geneva, 25, 40, 42; Cesena, 47; and conclave in Rome, 52, 53, 54, 64, 269; afterwards, 70, 72, 75, 76, 80, 82; as Pope, 85, 86, 90; returns to Avignon, 95; hopes, 95–6, 112–20 passim; disturbed, 123–4; death, 124; finances, benefices, 132; and Pierre de Luxembourg, 130; d'Ailly, 131; Berry, 141; Castile, 258
Clement VIII, Pope (Gil Sanchez Muñoz), 101, 267, 268
Climent Çapera, Francisco, Peter's secretary, 98, 99, 101; his man in Aragon, 172–3, 174, 181, 188, 231; bishoprics, 193, 241, 255, 263; nuncio, 258; still loyal, 262; builds Barcelona nave, 263
Colette, St., 203
Collioure, 231, 255
Colonna, family, 18, 197, 201
Comtat Venaissin, 154, 163, 190
Constance, Council of, 245–7, 250, 251, 253, 256–62; 'deposes' Peter, 261
Conzié, François de, to Paris, 123, 124; under Peter, 132, 147, 148, 149, 157; deserts, 161; reinstated, 189, 199, 214; serves Pisan popes, 240, 242
Corbie, Arnaud de, 160–1, 162, 190, 192
Corneto (Tarquinia), 43–4, 220
Correr, Antonio and others, 212–13, 215, 217, 219, 225, 239
Corsica, 154, 201
Cossa, see John XXIII
Coste, Jean de la, 159
Councils, General, proposals for, 78, 123, 189, 195, 196, 228; objections to, 82, 95, 120, 139, 151; suddenly popular, 229, 232; repudiated, 267; see Perpignan, Pisa, Cividale, Rome, Constance
Councils of Avignon Obedience, proposed, 183, 184–5; see also Paris Synods

Cramaud, Simon de, Patriarch of Alexandria, at first synod, 138–9; abroad, 146, 153; at third synod, 158–60; rebel, 179, 181–2, 186, 190; at fourth synod, 208, 209; in mission to popes, 211, 214–19, 234; at Livorno, 226; condemned, 233; at Pisa, 238, 239; defends John, 245
Cyprus, 118, 201, 236, 241

Dietrich of Niem (Nieheim), Prignano's assistant, 24, 78; at Naples and Nocera, 103–9; rejoins, 110; under Boniface, 115, 198; under Innocent, 204, 205; under Gregory, 215, 219, 220; writes memoirs, 239; and John, 244, 263
Doizé, Fr, 12, 261
Dominicans, 22, 34, 130, 203, 233; and see Catherine, Raimondo, Vincent
Dukes, French, see Berry, Bourbon, Burgundy, Orleans
Dunkeld, 166

Easton, Adam, Cardinal, 105, 109
Ehrle, Franz, Cardinal, 12, 270, 271
England, 35, 36, 94, 96, 100, 114, 118–20, 124, 146, 153, 159–60, 220, 237, 257
Eymeric, Nicolas, 66–7, 134, 135, 147

Ferdinand I, King of Aragon, Peter's verdict for, 243; at Morella, 249–50; at Perpignan, 252; deserts Peter, 255, 257, 258
Fernando, see Perez
Ferrer, Boniface, 165, 181, 183, 186, 233, 236
Ferrer, see Vincent
Fieschi, Ludovico, Cardinal, deserts to Peter, 200–1; 203, 206, 233; deserts to Pisa, 236, 238
Fillastre, Guillaume, Dean, 208, 211
Finale, 205
Flanders, 94, 114; English 'crusade' in, 118–19, 120, 140
Flandrin, Guigon, 206–7, 225, 232, 264
Flandrin, Jean, Cardinal of Auch, 144, 162, 233
Flandrin, Pierre, Cardinal of St. Eustace, 58
Florence, war with papacy, 25–6, 30–1, 42, 43, 47, 70, 77; negotiations, 72, 79, 89, 90; Peter's intermediary, 148, 199; attempt to win over, 201, 203, 204; and Gregory, 220; John's tomb, 265

Florence, Cardinal of (Pietro Corsini), 52, 58, 59, 66–7, 142
Foix, Count of, 201, 241, 252
Fondi, 84, 89, 91, 93
Fondi, Count of, 52, 72, 75, 80, 84, 148, 149, 152
France, *passim*; and Boniface VIII, 18; and popes at Avignon, 19, 36, 115–16; Peter's early attitude to, 26, 37, 92; and Schism, 75, 87, 94; Italian expeditions, 104, 113–15; Peter's mission to, 120 *seq.*; his relations with, Chapters 6, 7, 8 *passim*; withdraws obedience, 161–2; restores it, 190–1; final breach, 226; civil war in, 242; last contacts with, 234, 248, 264; Sigismund and, 253, 254, 257; Schism prolonged in south, 267–8; *see* Paris
Franciscans, 35, 79, 164, 233
Froissart, 156, 163, 168

Gascony, 94, 164, 207; *and see* Italy (Gascon partisans in)
Gaudelin, Pierre, 73–4
Geneva, Robert Cardinal of, *see* Clement VII
Genoa, 42, 109, 110, 152; Peter enters, 200–1, 202–5; Gregory and, 216; 221, 228
Germany, 36, 94, 140, 146, 182, 206, 220, 237, 245; *and see* Sigismund, Wenzel
Gerona, Cardinal of, *see* Anglesola
Gerson, Jean Charlier de, 47; moderate, 139, 147, 152, 160; to Bruges, 156; pro-Peter, 185, 191–3; pro-Council, 195–6, 208; 209, 211, 215; breach with Peter, 230–1; and Pisa, 237, 238; in danger, 242; and Constance, 247, 256, 257, 261, 263; and Martin V, 264
Gibbon, Edward, 58, 65, 246
Giffone, Leonardo di, Cardinal, 139, 142, 144, 165, 190, 194
Glandève, Cardinal of (Bertrand de Lagery), 13, 49–52, 54, 61, 71, 92, 98
Glendower, Owen, 201
Gloucester, Duke of, 264
Gratian, 74, 229, 254
Gregory X, Pope (Teobaldo Visconti), 137
Gregory XI, Pope (Pierre Roger de Beaufort), and Peter, 25; and Catherine, 22, 25–6, 30–1, 37, 42, 43, 47, 87; moves to Rome, 37–47; death, 47; and Martin de Salva, 90; debts, 183

Gregory XII, Pope (Angelo Correr), reign, 209–27, 232, 234; 'deposed', 238; holds Council at Cividale, 239; abdicates, 246; theological makeweight, 247; nephews, *see* Correr
Guigon, *see* Flandrin

Hawkwood, Sir John, 21, 34, 47
Hayton, John, 144–5, 147
Henry V, King of England, 257
Henry of Trastámara, King of Castile, 16
Hughes, P., 197
Hus, John, 250–1

Ile-St-Honorat, 217
Illueca, 16, 100, 103, 267
Innocent VI, Pope (Etienne Aubert), 137
Innocent VII, Pope (Cosimo de' Migliorati), 199, 204, 205, 209, 217
Isabelle, Queen of France, 114, 207, 232
Italy, *passim*; *see* Rome and other cities by name; opinion in, 30, 36, 47, 50, 86, 197, 205; and Schism, 95; Peter in, Chapters 2 and 3, pp. 93, 200–5, 220–8; French expeditions to, 104, 113–15; Gascon partisans in, 117, 148, 181, 201, 248; Peter's last hopes of, 251–2, 260, 264

Jaën, *see* Alfonso
Jews, 101, 134, 153, 248
Joan of Arc, 114, 207, 268
Joanna I, Queen of Naples, 40, 72, 88, 89, 92, 95, 96, 103–4, 251
Joanna II, Queen of Naples, 251–2, 260
John XXII, Pope (Jacques d'Euse), 135
John XXIII, Pope (Balthazar Cossa), 13, 93, 237, 238; pope, 244–6, 250; tomb, 264–5
John of Gaunt, *see* Lancaster
'Judas' issue, 134–5, 167, 270–1 (n. 23)

Karin (St. Catherine of Sweden), 21, 50, 54, 88

Ladislas, King of Naples, 197, 201, 216, 220, 223, 225, 234, 245, 248, 251
Lagrange, Jean de, Cardinal of Amiens, shipwrecked, 42, 44; and Urban, 72; and Clement, 112; and Peter, 127, 128, 139, 143, 161, 162, 179; death, 189

Lancaster, Duke of (John of Gaunt), 120, 124

Langenstein, Henry of, 121

Lateran, 21, 55, 70–1, 149, 152, 264

Lestrange, Elie de, 139, 159, 181, 206

Leulinghem, 120, 124

Libro de las Consolaciones, 265–6

Limoges, Cardinal of (Jean de Cros), 51, 58, 59, 60, 68, 69, 72, 94

Limousins, 21, 28, 51–2, 74

Livorno, 42, 44, 203, 222, 226

Louis of Anjou, King of Provence (the elder), 35, 95–6, 103, 104, 115

Louis of Anjou, King of Provence (the younger), 116, 183, 188, 202, 205, 248

Lucca, 31, 222, 225

Luna, family, 16, 153, 154; arms, 9

Luna, Antonio, 154

Luna, Celestina, 101

Luna, Pedro, 154, 174

Luna, Rodrigo, 154, 164, 242, 250, 260, 261, 263, 266

Luxembourg, Pierre de, 130


Malesset, Guy de, Cardinal of Poitiers, before conclave, 51, 52; supports Clement, 94, 112; 127, 129; moderate attitude, 143, 162, 179, 184–5; negotiates restoration of obedience, 186, 189, 190; 194, 195; at Livorno, 226; presides over Pisa, 237

Malla, Felipe de, 258

Mandeville, Simon de, 234

Marmoutier, Cardinal of (Géraud de Puy), 63, 70

Marseilles, 41; Peter at, 192, 196, 211; Treaty of, 212; mission to, 214; 231

Marseilles, Bishop of, 56, 61, 62

Martin I, King of Aragon, character, 153; at Avignon, 154; aids Peter, 166, 171–4, 200, 202, 231, 240; death, 242–3

Martin the Younger of Aragon and Sicily, 202, 240

Martin V, Pope (Ottone Colonna), 262–4, 267

Martin de Salva, see Salva

Masconi, Domenico, 147, 149, 152

Medina del Campo, 99–100, 117, 141

Menendo, Bishop, 93, 201

Milan, 116, 141, 201

Milan, Cardinal of (Simone di Bursano), 52, 59, 66–7, 72–3

Milan, Cardinal of (Pietro Filargi), see Alexander V

Montefiascone, 118, 201, 215

Montirac, Pierre de, Cardinal of Pamplona and Vice-Chancellor, character, 21; and Catherine, 22, 26, 30, 31, 33; and Prignano, 23, 74; stays at Avignon 21, 38; accepts Clement, 95; and Pamplona, 90, 102

Montpellier, University, 15, 16, 17, 22, 24, 81, 267

Mont-St-Michel, Abbot of, 159, 176, 208, 211

Morella, 249–50

Muñoz, see Clement VIII


Nájera (Navarete), 16

Naples, and Urban, 23, 72, 103–5, 109; French (Anjou) in, 112, 116, 117, 183; Gregory XII flees to, 239; and see Joanna I, II, Charles of Durazzo, Ladislas

Narbonne, 255, 256, 260

Navarre, 91, 96; Peter's mission to, 102; 183, 233, 252

Neufchâtel, Jean de, Cardinal, 143, 161, 165, 167

Nice, 152, 201, 205, 237

Niem, see Dietrich

Nocera, 105–9, 162

Noëllet, Guillaume de, Cardinal, 57, 58

Normans, 'nation' at Paris University, 156, 159, 160, 176, 186, 188, 190

Norwich, Bishop of, his 'crusade', 118–19


Ogilvy, Henry de, 249

Orleans, Louis Duke of, 114, 116, 122–3; in Dukes' mission, 139 seq.; character, 141; becomes Peter's ally, 144; 153; and Wenzel, 155, 156; 160; Peter's protector, 174, 180, 183, 185, 186; effects restoration of obedience, 190–1; meets Peter at Tarascon, 195; warns him, 207; last help, 211; murdered, 207; see Petit

Orsini, Jacopo, Cardinal, 45, 52, 58, 59, 60, 61, 70, 72, 76

Ostia, 45


Pamplona, 90, 93, 102

Pamplona, Cardinals of, see (I) Montirac, (II) Salva, Martin de, (III) Salva, Miguel de

Papal States, 20, 25, 29, 35, 37, 43, 95, 197, 219

Paris, *passim, see* France

Paris, Synods, first, 138–9; second, 153; third, 158–61; fourth, 208–9; fifth, 232

Paris, University, description of, 121–2; hostile to Clement, 94, 118, 120, 122, 123, 124; opinion-poll, 121, 123; and d'Ailly, 130; and Peter, 132–53 *passim*, 158, 176, 179; disillusioned, 185, 190; reconciled, 192–3, 195; again hostile, 206, 207, 208, 215, 217; condemned, 232; *and see* Normans

Pécs (Fünfkirchen), Cardinal of, 221

Pedro I the Cruel, King of Castile, 16

Pedro IV the Ceremonious, King of Aragon, 94, 96, 98, 101

Peñíscola, 9–11, 249, 255, 256–68 *passim*

Perez de Calvillo, Fernando, Cardinal of Tarazona, Peter's conclavist, 56, 57, 61, 68–9, 74–5, 76, 99; Curial bishop, 138, 144; mission to Rome, 149–53; cardinal, 154; in siege, 161, 166, 167, 180; death, 194

Perpignan, Council of, 228, 231–6, 237, 238, 240, 241

Perpignan, Conference of, 251–5

Petit, Jean, 140, 209, 211; defends Orleans' murder, 223, 242; condemned 233

Petrarch, Francesco, 30

Pileo di Prata, Cardinal, 117–18

Pisa, and Catherine, 22, 31; inclines towards Peter, 201, 203, 204; meeting proposed at, 216, 222; cardinals flee to, 225

Pisa, Council of, proposed, 226, 228, 232, 233, 234; meets, 236–9; 'deposes' Peter, 238; doubtful or repudiated, 241, 246, 247, 253, 261

Plaoul, Pierre, 159, 160, 211, 215, 233

Poitiers, Archpriest of, 237, 246

Poitiers, Cardinal of, *see* Malesset

Portofino, 42, 44, 228

Portovenere, 42, 221–7, 231, 238, 255

Portugal, 96, 100, 119

Port Vendres, 231

Prades, Jaime de, 186–7, 193, 222, 223, 225, 228, 231, 233

Prignano, see Urban VI, Butillo

Provence, restores obedience, 183–4; Peter escapes to, 188; *and see* Louis

Raimondo da Capua, Fra, 31, 32, 34, 35, 36, 88, 89

Ravat, Pierre, Cardinal, works for Peter, 159, 181, 184–5, 193; mission to Rome, 197, 199; in France, 206; at Livorno, 226; cardinal, 233, 234, 258

Reims, royal meeting at, 155

Reims, Archbishop of, 226, 237, 239, 252

Ribalta, Francisco, 187

Richard II, King of England, 109, 114, 197

Richard of the Sewer, 169, 179

Rimini, 239, 246

Rodez, 268

Rodrigo, *see* Luna

Romani, Juan, 187, 204

Rome, *passim;* Urban V's move to, 20–1; Bridget and, 28; Gregory XI's move to, 20, 22, 25–7, 36–8, 39–44; his entry, 45–7; Peter in, 47–55 *passim*; unrest in, 49–54 *passim*; conclave in, 55–64; after, 65–77; Peter leaves, 80; Catherine in, 88–9; state of under Roman popes, 115, 197–9, 204, 215–16; Fernando's mission to, 149–53; Ravat's, 197, 199; French, 215–17; Peter to seize, 223, 225; Ladislas and, 216, 225, 245; Council of, 244–5; Peter's last hopes of, 252, 260, 264; Martin V enters, 264; *and see* Castel Sant'Angelo, Lateran, Santa Maria in Cosmedin, Tor Sanguigna, Vatican

St. Andrews, University, 249, 262, 268

Saint-Denis, Abbot of, 211, 226

Saint-Martial, Hugo de, Cardinal, 162

Salamanca, University, 101, 248–9, 265, 268

Salembier, L., 247, 251

Salutati, Coluccio, 148

Saluzzo, Amadeo di, Cardinal, 125, 126, 186, 189, 190, 242

Salva, Martin de, Cardinal of Pamplona, and Urban, 72; and Peter, 89–93; cardinal, 102; and *cedula*, 125, 136–8; and Dukes, 143–4, 158; in siege, 161, 165, 168–9; released, 178; at Arles, 180; memoranda, 181–2, 184–5; helps Peter escape, 186, 188; death, 193; his white paper, 193–4, 234

Salva, Miguel de, Cardinal of Pamplona, 200, 205

Salvador, Simon, 147, 216–18, 226, 248, 264

Sanchez Muñoz, *see* Clement VIII

Sangro, Cardinal, 104–8

Santa Maria in Cosmedin (Rome), 15, 48-9, 51, 74

Santa Sabina, Prior of (Gonsalvo), 54, 77, 82-4

Saragossa and Archbishop of, 235, 255, 262, 268

Sardinia, 96, 154, 201, 236, 240

Savona, 42, 203, 212, 215-20 passim

Savoy, 94, 201, 228, 234, 236, 241, 252

Scotland, decides for Clement, 94; loyal, 118, 181, 234, 236, 241, 259; accepts Martin V, 262; and see St. Andrews

Seidlmayer, M., 66, 269

Seppelt, F. X., 66, 197

Serra, Pedro, Cardinal of Catania, 154, 161, 204

Serres, Madame de, 248

Sicily, 96, 154, 202, 234, 236, 248

Siena, 32, 46, 87, 220-1

Sigismund, Emperor, 245, 247, 249-55, 257, 261, 262, 263

Spain, passim; see Aragon, Castile, Catalonia, Navarre

Stratton, Robert, 73

Synods, see Paris


Tarascon, 175, 195, 196

Tarazona, see Perez

Tarquinia, see Corneto

Tarragona, Archibishop of, 262

Tebaldeschi, Francesco, Cardinal of St. Peter's, 52, 56, 57, 59, 61-4, 77, 84

Thury, Pierre de, Cardinal, 117, 126; leading rebel, 139, 161, 179, 180, 186, 189, 190; and Treaty of Marseilles, 212; later changes, 223, 226, 242

Tor Sanguigna (Rome), Peter's palazzo at, 48, 50, 53, 68, 74, 153

Tortosa, 201, 243, 248

Toulouse, University, 159, 181, 183, 185, 206

Tours, Archibishop of, 160, 190, 208, 211, 213, 214, 252

Turenne, Alys de, 13, 32-3, 40

Turenne, Raymond de, 40, 46

Urban V, Pope (Guillaume de Grimoard), 20-1, 36, 39, 43

Urban VI, Pope (Bartolommeo Prignano), official at Avignon, 23-4; in Rome, 53-4; election, 58 seq.; problematical, 65-6; accepted, 66-71; strange behaviour, 71 seq.; deserted, 75 seq.; final breach, 84; in Rome, 86 seq.; at Naples, 103-4; at Nocera, 105 seq.; tortures cardinals, 107-9; escapes, 109-10; death, 115


Valencia, 96, 97, 154, 173, 243

Valentinois, Countess of, 32

Valois, N., 12, 66, 156, 161, 176, 191, 269-72

Vatican, appearance, 55; conclave in, 55-64; cardinals fetched back, 68-9; and passim

Venice, 209, 218, 220, 232, 239

Venice, Cardinal of (Giovanni da Piacenza), 108-9

Vergne, Pierre de, Cardinal, 70

Viaour, 268

Vice-Chancellor, see Montirac

Villefranche, 203, 228-9

Villeneuve-lès-Avignon, 19, 29, 140, 142, 161, 169, 183, 189, 241, 242

Vincent Ferrer, St. 12; works with Peter, 97-9, 102; and Jews, 101, 134; Peter saves from Inquisition, 134-5; leaves Avignon, 165; at Genoa, 203; at Caspe, 243; critical, 248, 250, 252; breaks with Peter, 254, 256; death, 257

Visconti, see Milan

Viterbo, 10, 21, 65, 204, 205, 215, 219, 220

Viviers, Cardinal of (I. Pierre de Sortenac), 52, 54, 61

Viviers, Cardinal of (II. Jean de Brogni), 190


Wenzel, Emperor, 155-6, 191, 194, 197

Westminster, Abbot of, 153


Zabarella, Francesco, Cardinal, 230